The Green Depression

The Green Depression

American
Ecoliterature
of the
1930s and 1940s

Matthew M. Lambert

University Press of Mississippi / *Jackson*

The University Press of Mississippi is the scholarly publishing agency of the Mississippi Institutions of Higher Learning: Alcorn State University, Delta State University, Jackson State University, Mississippi State University, Mississippi University for Women, Mississippi Valley State University, University of Mississippi, and University of Southern Mississippi.

www.upress.state.ms.us

The University Press of Mississippi is a member of the Association of University Presses.

Copyright © 2020 by University Press of Mississippi
All rights reserved

First printing 2020
∞

Library of Congress Cataloging-in-Publication Data

Names: Lambert, Matthew M., author.
Title: The green depression : American ecoliterature in the 1930s and 1940s / Matthew M. Lambert.
Description: Jackson : University Press of Mississippi, 2020. | Includes bibliographical references and index.
Identifiers: LCCN 2020022855 (print) | LCCN 2020022856 (ebook) | ISBN 9781496830401 (hardback) | ISBN 9781496830418 (trade paperback) | ISBN 9781496830425 (epub) | ISBN 9781496830432 (epub) | ISBN 9781496830449 (pdf) | ISBN 9781496830456 (pdf)
Subjects: LCSH: Ecocriticism. | Ecocriticism in literature. | Ecology in literature. | Environmental justice in literature. | Nature in literature.
Classification: LCC PN98.E36 L36 2020 (print) | LCC PN98.E36 (ebook) | DDC 810.9/3609043—dc23
LC record available at https://lccn.loc.gov/2020022855
LC ebook record available at https://lccn.loc.gov/2020022856

British Library Cataloging-in-Publication Data available

To my grandparents,
Millard and Mildred Hale
and
Willard and Ruth Lambert,
who came of age during the Great Depression.

Contents

Acknowledgments ix

Introduction 3

CHAPTER 1 *The Last Frontier* 21

CHAPTER 2 *Back to the Land* 59

CHAPTER 3 *The Postpastoral City* 99

CHAPTER 4 *Futuramas and Atom Bombs* 131

Conclusion 167

Notes 173

Bibliography 191

Index 201

Acknowledgments

First and foremost, I'd like to thank my wife, Deanna Burkett, for her love, patience, support, advice, and encouragement over the past six or so years of drafting and revising *The Green Depression*. I am also grateful to David Shumway, Kathy Newman, and Rich Purcell for their mentorship and valuable feedback on the project; the Carnegie Mellon University Department of English faculty and students for their comradery, guidance, and support; Sheila Liming and Dave Haeselin for their friendship, adventurous spirit, and inspiring intellect; the Schaffer family and the CMU English Department for their financial support; Chris Raczkowski for getting me interested in depression-era literature; Katie Keene and the other editorial staff at the University Press of Mississippi for taking a chance on the project; the anonymous readers for their encouraging and helpful feedback on my manuscript; Peter Tonguette for his careful and much-appreciated copyedits; all of the scholars mentioned in the following pages for their important work on environmental and/or depression-era literature and film; any scholar of the period I may have unintentionally omitted; and the Wabash College Department of English faculty for providing me the space and backing to complete revisions over the past few years. Lastly, I would like to thank my parents, Mike and Becky Lambert, and my sister, Brooke Thomas, for their love and support.

The Green Depression

Introduction

On the afternoon of May 11, 1934, the New York socialite, conservationist, and suffragist Rosalie Edge recounted watching dust collect on "the ivory keys of her grand piano, tables, and bookshelves." Going outside of her Fifth Avenue apartment, Edge saw a billowing cloud approaching from the west: the sky darkened, streetlights burned in the middle of the day, and people ran through the streets attempting to escape "the strange, thick air" (Furmansky 165–66). That afternoon, a dust cloud originating in the Great Plains had made its way across the continent to dump land on the nation's largest city for "five hours," leaving it "under the weight of 1,320 tons" of dust (Egan 152–53). The dust from this storm is reported to have even covered ships "three hundred miles off the Atlantic coast" (5).[1]

I begin *The Green Depression* with this episode for a few different reasons. First, as Edge's reaction shows, the "Dust Bowl"—a term used to describe a rash of dust storms hitting the southern plains in the panhandle region of Texas, Oklahoma, and Kansas between 1933 and 1941 (Worster, *Dust Bowl* 15)—helped shift attitudes regarding the effects human practices could have on the natural environment. As Donald Worster argues, the event illustrated "the inevitable outcome of a culture that deliberately, self-consciously, set itself that task of dominating and exploiting the land for all it was worth" (4). By destroying the natural sod of the southern plains, the pioneer farmers who cultivated the land left the dirt vulnerable to the area's dry winds. When drought hit the area in the early 1930s, the farmers' crops were no longer able to protect the dirt from the high winds and the land was taken away by storms (13). The experience struck Rosalie Edge "as perhaps never before that nothing less than the planet itself was at stake in her crusade for nature" (Furmansky 166). Together with the period's other major environmental disasters—including the 1927 Mississippi Flood and the use of atomic bombs on Hiroshima and Nagasaki in 1945—the Dust Bowl would push conservation-minded activists and authors to reevaluate the severity that human activities could have in disrupting the natural world.

I also begin this book with the preceding anecdote to suggest that, as historian William Cronon has argued, "city and country have a common history, so their stories are best told together" (*Nature's* xvi). In the case of *The Green Depression*, residents of both the city and the country share the ecological effects of unsustainable and inequitable use of natural resources. Their environmental struggles ranged from wilderness and rural landscapes to highly developed urban environments. Not only do the following chapters share Cronon's interest in the ecological reclaiming of cities, they also build on recent work by historians that reevaluates the importance of the 1930s and 1940s to the development of environmental thought. Donald Worster, Timothy Egan, Sarah Phillips, Neil Maher, and Douglas Brinkley have all focused on shifts in conservationist thought during the period that served as a bridge to the "environmentalism" of figures like David Brower, Rachel Carson, Stewart Udall, and others in the second half of the twentieth century.[2] If historians have picked up on the importance of environmental issues and thought during the 1930s and '40s, critics of environmental literature and other forms of culture have had less to say about the period. While the occasional ecocritical article or book has focused on individual depression-era authors or regions, no large-scale attempt has been made to identify ways that authors from around the US depicted and responded to environmental issues and ideas.[3]

To fill this gap, *The Green Depression* argues that authors from the 1930s and '40s contributed to the development of modern environmental thought in three distinct ways. First, they recognized, as never before, the apocalyptic effect that humans could have on the environment, particularly in response to the Dust Bowl and the period's other human-made environmental disasters. Next, they depicted the ecological and cultural value of nonhuman animal "predators" and "pests." As Edge and other conservationists like Aldo Leopold realized during the period, animal predators and pests like wolves and hawks that compete with human interests play an important role in maintaining healthy biotic communities.[4] For some authors in the 1930s and '40s, these predators and pests also contribute cultural and political value to human communities. And third, many authors laid the groundwork for what we now refer to as "environmental justice" by directly connecting environmental exploitation with racial, economic, and gender inequality. In response to the stock market crash and ensuing depression, which left almost 25 percent of the population unemployed (McElvaine 75), authors during the 1930s and '40s became highly attuned to intersections between environmental and social forms of exploitation.

To argue that depression-era authors contributed to the development of modern environmental thought does not mean suggesting that these authors understood themselves as "environmentalists" as we understand the term today. According to the Oxford English Dictionary (OED), "environment" meant something different in the first half of the twentieth century, generally referring to an "area surrounding a place or thing." But, starting in the late 1940s, the term did start taking on the meaning we now associate with environmental thought: "The natural world or physical surroundings in general, either as a whole or within a particular geographical area, *esp. as affected by human activity*" (italics mine, OED). In identifying the interrelation of humans and their environments, the authors and filmmakers I will focus on in *The Green Depression* often anticipate the latter meaning, even if they did not use the word.

Furthermore, it's important to clarify the scope of my project. I do not use the term "depression-era" to refer solely to authors writing in the period associated with the Great Depression (roughly lasting with greater or lesser intensity from the 1929 stock market crash to World War II). As Michael Denning argues, "[T]he culture of the

Popular Front, the culture of the 'thirties' lasted well into the postwar era" (25). While not all the authors included in the following chapters were part of the leftist "front" of cultural artists responding to the economic "crisis of hegemony" ushered in by the stock market crash (22)—though many of them were—they all responded to the environmental "crisis of hegemony" bookended by the 1927 Great Mississippi River Flood and the development, use, and threat of nuclear weapons in the mid-to-late 1940s. Because of the Great Depression's tremendous influence on responses to environmental issues during *and* after the 1930s, I use "depression-era" as a frame for considering literature from roughly 1930 to 1950.

In fact, the intersection of the social and environmental in depression-era cultural works echoes a similar shift towards social understandings of environmental issues in conservationist thought occurring during the period. While the conservation of Progressive-era figures like Theodore Roosevelt and Gifford Pinchot stressed the professional and scientific management of natural resources for the sake of efficiency and the public good (Phillips 7), New Deal conservationists focused on the conservation of natural resources in order to alleviate poverty and "raise the living standards of the people" (9), particularly of rural populations whose conditions, the latter believed, contributed to the onset of the Depression (3). New Deal conservation programs like the Civilian Conservation Corps (CCC) helped set the stage for the development of environmentalism in the second half of the twentieth century by extending the conservation theories and practices of a handful of scientists, bureaucrats, landowners, and hunters "to CCC's working-class enrollees, to residents of local communities situated near Corps camps, and . . . to the country as a whole through national media coverage" (Maher 10–11). This isn't to say that the CCC and other conservation programs of the era did not have social and economic limitations. Though African Americans and Native Americans were allowed in the CCC, they were often segregated into separate camps (106). Furthermore, women were limited to a single "CCC-like camp," called Camp Jane Addams, where they learned "domestic skills that could help their families weather the Great Depression" (82). In attempting to alleviate rural poverty, the New Deal ran into other issues. Liberal policy makers during the period often found themselves unable to counter the dominant interests of powerful landowners in the South and West who tended to profit most from rural relief (Phillips 239). The Agricultural Administration Agency (AAA) administered payments to landowners to stop growing certain crops, leading to the mechanization of southern farming and the dismissal of thousands of tenants and sharecroppers (Cowdrey 164–65). According to Robin D. G. Kelley, the AAA payments also helped break the organizing activities of the largely African American Sharecroppers' Union (SCU) in Alabama during the 1930s (53–56).

In addition to social, economic, and political limitations, New Deal programs also had negative environmental effects. Wilderness activists Aldo Leopold and Robert Marshall were particularly critical of the campgrounds, picnic areas, hiking trails, roads for cars, and other modern recreation-based construction projects of the CCC.[5] These types of projects, they argued, would destroy the isolating qualities and ecological health of wilderness areas (9). Leopold objected to CCC attempts to change environments by stocking forests and streams with game and fish as well as using nonindigenous trees and plant life to reforest areas (9). In addition, Rosalie Edge rallied against a proposal by the National Park Service to poison the pelicans at Yellowstone Lake to reduce their ability to compete with anglers for fish (Furmansky 141), a request that echoed the Bureau of Biological Survey's predator eradication program in the first half of the twentieth century (Worster, *Nature's Economy* 260).[6] While these critiques seem to rehash the preservation versus conservation debate best illustrated by the damming of Hetch Hetchy Valley in Yosemite National Park begun in 1914, the adherence of interwar wilderness advocates to a mixture of conservationist and preservationist attitudes troubles making narrow distinctions between the two outlooks. As Paul S. Sutter has argued, many wilderness advocates like Leopold and Marshall were trained foresters who still believed in wise management of natural resources for the public good, even if they rejected the "single-minded commodity focus of utilitarian forestry" (14–15). Furthermore, they tended to reject the idea of "pristine and unworked nature," instead focusing their efforts on "protecting large areas from road building, automobiles, and the various forms of modernization that characterized the interwar years" (196). Marshall was also a progressive social thinker who championed creating wilderness reserves for Native Americans to protect tribal traditions. He also supported providing working-class Americans with more access to wilderness areas, as long as doing so did not include building roads and other modern conveniences within such areas that would impede on their wildness (Sutter 196, Glover 219).

Urban areas also attracted reformers during the 1930s and '40s who attempted to create more open, clean, and livable cities. The Works Progress Administration (WPA) and urban commissioners like Robert Moses created, renovated, and/or maintained thousands of parks and other recreational spaces in urban landscapes, including in or near working-class neighborhoods (Federal Works Administration, Caro 372, 455). Clarence Stein, Henry Wright, Lewis Mumford, and other "regionalist" urban designers and critics proposed more radical versions of urban landscapes that were sustainably integrated into the environment. Using the English designer Ebenezer Howard's "garden city" concept, these figures envisioned and, in some cases, designed cities built into the countryside that would attempt to include many of the modern conveniences and cultural amenities of the traditional city (*The City*).

In addition to focusing on wilderness, rural, and urban landscapes, conservationists and social activists also concentrated on the social and environmental effects of science and technology. During the early years of the Depression, the status of science declined due to its perceived "social irresponsibility" in contributing to "technological unemployment" (Kuznick 351). Capitalizing on the frustrations of scientists, who were often excluded from New Deal job programs, corporations offered them opportunities to conduct research at "corporate laboratories," helping to establish the industrial and military dominance of science in the post-World War II era (351), a collusion that Rachel Carson and other environmentalists would critique in the second half of the twentieth century. In response to the relationship between scientists, corporations, and the military, some scientists began to recognize "the social consequences of their work and assume responsibility for instigating progressive social change" (346). Though perhaps more interested in the social rather than environmental consequences of science at this point, they offered a model for postwar scientists and environmental activists to follow, particularly after the development and use of atomic bombs.

In identifying the broad shifts in conservation, urban design, and science occurring during the 1930s and '40s, I do not mean to suggest that all the authors addressed in the following chapters were aware of these changes, but, to varying degrees, many of them were. Leopold was directly involved in conservation efforts as a forester, professor, and author, and authors like William Faulkner and Ernest Hemingway were aware of conservation ideas through their experiences as hunters (Buell, *Writing* 190; Hemingway 272). While at Barnard College, Zora Neale Hurston took classes in anthropology with Franz Boas, whose ideas concerning cultural relativism would change the way anthropologists understood the value of so-called "primitive" cultures (Hemenway 63). Boas encouraged Hurston to collect black folklore in the South and even wrote the forward to her book *Mules and Men* (1935). James T. Farrell, Nelson Algren, and Richard Wright all studied or came into contact with sociologists like Robert Park, Ernest Burgess, and Louis Wirth, who were part of the Chicago School of Sociology and often adopted methodologies associated with plant ecology (Cappetti 137).[7] Ralph Steiner and Willard Van Dyke's *The City* was scripted by Lewis Mumford and influenced by Clarence Stein and Henry Wright, who produced the documentary film (Gillett 75). Science fiction author Judith Merril corresponded with scientists concerning the effects of nuclear radiation on the human body (Newell and Lamont 34).[8]

Though not necessarily connected to the depression-era changes in conservationism, anthropology, sociology, physics, and biology, the authors written about in the pages that follow all responded to and helped shape prominent cultural ideas concerning the relationship between humanity and the natural world. These ideas are what early American Studies scholars like Henry Nash Smith and Leo Marx call "myths" and "symbols," which circulate through cultures, according to Alan Trachtenberg, like ideology. Trachtenberg writes, "Myths operating as symbols, or symbols embedded in images, function ... as the indispensable forms whereby and in which a society constitutes its agreed-upon collective reality (667). While the methodology and assumptions shared by these critics would come under attack in the 1970s, their focus on ways that cultural texts support and, in some cases, contest ideology still influences literary and cultural studies scholars (671). Many of the ideological "myths" that Smith, Marx, and later American Studies critics have identified as underlying social and cultural beliefs in earlier American historical experience reemerged during the 1930s and '40s in the wake of economic and environmental crises.[9] While some depression-era literary works and films supported these myths, others critiqued and expanded upon them in a more environmentally sustainable and socially egalitarian manner.[10]

Of the critical work conducted by American Studies scholars, Leo Marx's reevaluation of pastoralism in *The Machine and the Garden* (1964) and "Pastoralism in America" (1986) has especially influenced my analysis in *The Green Depression*. For Marx, the pastoral is a cultural mode often used in two distinctive ways. In its simple or "sentimental" usage, the pastoral offers an escape from the city into a more rural or wild landscape (*The Machine* 5). In its more "complex" form, the pastoral seeks to "qualify, call into question, or bring irony to bear against the illusion of peace and harmony" in idyllic nature (*The Machine* 5, 25). While the former type of pastoralism typically supported dominant and residual cultural myths circulating in American society during the nineteenth and early twentieth centuries, the latter type was often used in American literary works to critique these myths and their ideological underpinnings (25). Instead of offering nature as an escape, complex pastoralism "acknowledges the reality of history" by recognizing "the power of a counterforce, a machine or some other symbol of the forces which have stripped the old ideal of most, if not all of its meaning" (363). By identifying ways that pastoralism could be used to critique both unchecked industrial progress and idyllic escapism, Marx helped reclaim the mode for new generations of literary and cultural scholars.

In addition to highlighting a more critical function of pastoralism, Marx also demonstrated ways that the mode is relevant to a broad range of different literary genres. For the critic, a text need not solely focus on the themes, landscapes, and characters associated with the traditional pastoral to engage in complex pastoralism. He writes, "[I]t may be confined to a scene or episode (a 'pastoral interlude') within a poem, drama, or novel which is not, strictly speaking, a pastoral" (*The Machine* 25n). This is important to Marx's argument as only some of the literary texts he addresses in the book—like Thoreau's *Walden* (1854) or Twain's *Adventures of Huckleberry Finn* (1884)—are consistently focused on rural/wilderness characters, landscapes, or themes. Others, like Melville's *Moby-Dick* (1851) or Fitzgerald's *The Great Gatsby* (1925), only contain "pastoral interludes." The latter works of literature, according to Marx, often participate in an inversion of the machine in the garden in which "the industrial landscape [is] pastoralized" (356). Thus, even Fitzgerald in *The Great Gatsby*, with its highly artificial suburban (West Egg), industrial (valley of the ashes), and urban landscapes (Manhattan), participates in complex pastoralism for Marx. Though Marx finishes *The Machine in the Garden* in the 1920s with Fitzgerald, depression-era literature also often contains pastoral interludes that demonstrate an engagement with complex pastoralism during the period. In doing so, it joins a literary tradition of using the pastoral to better understand ways that nature functions in American history and culture. What makes depression-era literature's use of complex pastoralism different from earlier uses of the mode is its more direct depiction of ideas associated with environmental thought as well as its attempt to create "alliances with the hitherto disadvantaged carriers of emergent values" who have traditionally felt "little or no appeal" for values associated with environmental thought (Marx, "Pastoralism" 66).

While *The Green Depression* relies heavily on Marx's understanding of pastoralism, it also recognizes limitations in his use of the term. For one, literary scholars during the 1970s—particularly feminists, post-structuralists, and new historicists—became increasingly suspicious of pastoralism, even in its complex form, seeing it as reinforcing or evading American gender norms and imperial interests (Buell, *The Environmental* 34–35). Though the American pastoral certainly has been used to support cultural myths underlying forms of imperialism, sexism, and racism, these uses are not implicit to its form. As Lawrence Buell points out, the mode has also been used as "a dream hostile to the standing order of civilization" (50), even by women and African Americans.[11] For Buell, American literary texts "that celebrate an ethos of rurality or nature or wilderness over against an ethos of metropolitanism" hold what he refers to as a "pastoral ideology," meaning an "implicit position of dissent from or consent to the prevailing political system" (n449). Forms of pastoral ideology in cultural texts that resist economic, racial, and gender hierarchies, according to Buell, support the mode's "constructive potential rather than its role as a blocking agent or inducer of false consciousness" (33).

Next, Marx primarily seems interested in what he calls our "most respected writers" (*The Machine* 10), who tend to be white, male authors from middle- or upper-class backgrounds.[12] But Marx's complex pastoralism is often appropriated by working-class, female, and nonwhite authors. As Michael Denning has argued, the Great Depression initiated the careers of many writers of different ethnicities, races, genders, and classes (xv). Building on Denning's argument, I will show that depression-era African American, Native American, female, and working-class authors appropriated complex pastoralism in unique ways to call attention to the intersection of social and environmental forms of exploitation in wilderness, rural, and urban landscapes as well as in uses of science and technology during the period. In doing so, these authors often create forms of pastoralism akin to what Terry Gifford calls the "postpastoral."[13] According to Gifford, the "postpastoral" moves beyond more contemporary criticisms of pastoralism, particularly by including an awareness of the "creative-destructive" property of nature as well as ways that environmental exploitation reflects "the same mindset as the exploitation of women and minorities" (153, 165). In appropriating pastoralism, depression-era authors include these criteria by depicting spaces, processes, human groups, and nonhuman species often ignored in traditional uses of the mode. To do so, they often turn to literary naturalism, which, with its interest in biology, natural history, and the marginalized, makes a unique counterpart to pastoralism. While literary critic Alfred Kazin claimed in *On Native Grounds* (1942) that the compulsion "to shock," even in the best literary naturalism during the 1930s and '40s, proved that the genre "was really exhausted and could now thrive only on a mechanical energy bent on forcing itself to the uttermost" (371, 381), later literary critics have seen more value in naturalism during the period. Donald Pizer has argued that American naturalists differ from their European counterparts by relying on a "variable and changing and complex set of assumptions about man and fiction" rather than on a strict adherence to genre rules about biological and environmental determinism (xi). Pizer particularly sees authors of the 1930s as less deterministic than earlier naturalists in that they depict an understanding of the economic forces influencing one's life as "difficult but achievable" (15). Denning calls the coupling of pastoralism and naturalism in 1930s literary works set in urban, working-class neighborhoods the "ghetto pastoral." This body of work, he argues, blends naturalism's "strategy of degradation and debasement" with pastoralism's "strategy of elevating and ennobling the simple" (230, 251).[14] For Denning, the pastoral aspects of the genre have less to do with the presence of rural or wild nature in urban landscapes than in representing simple, shepherd equivalents who represent and speak complex ideas.[15] But urban novels of the period do often include pastoral interludes populated by nonhuman animals and rural/wilderness landscapes. In combining aspects of pastoralism and naturalism in these interludes, many depression-era literary works create more nuanced depictions of ways that the human and nonhuman world intersect.

To show the reach of environmental thinking during the period, the first three chapters in *The Green Depression* focus on wilderness, rural, and urban landscapes. In the first chapter, "The Last Frontier," I argue that depression-era authors respond to the social and environmental legacy of the frontier—including widespread dust storms and flooding, the disappearance of wildlife through overhunting, and the poor social, economic, and environmental conditions for American Indians in the West and African Americans in the South—in an attempt to recover landscapes, human groups, and nonhuman species largely erased by western expansion and economic development in the US. The chapter begins by identifying ways that Walt Disney's animated feature *Bambi* (1942) depicts the value of wilderness by endowing select nonhuman animals with American middle-class values. It then focuses on ways that William Faulkner and Ernest Hemingway move beyond Disney's problematic depiction of wilderness by de-emphasizing anthropomorphic qualities and values in their depictions of wild animals and calling attention to the ecological and cultural value of nonhuman predators. While Faulkner depicts the cultural, economic, and environmental effects of deforestation and predator eradication on white and black southerners in *Go Down, Moses* (1942), Hemingway identifies the exploitive practices of the American frontier in *Green Hills of Africa* (1935) to call attention to similar practices he sees occurring in East Africa during the period. Lastly, the chapter focuses on Salish author D'Arcy McNickle's depiction of Native American frontier experience in his first novel *The Surrounded* (1936). In the novel, McNickle appropriates Frederick Jackson Turner's "palimpsest," a metaphor the historian uses to describe the layers of changes to frontier lands in the wake of western expansion. For McNickle, using the palimpsest helps uncover the social, cultural, and environmental scars that frontier practices and policies have left on indigenous groups and lands in the West.

The second chapter, "Back to the Land," shifts to rural landscapes to identify ways that depression-era authors, particularly African Americans, critique back-to-the-land movements during the period rooted in exploitive agricultural and economic practices. For these authors, monocultures, racial hierarchies, and uncritical forms of anthropocentricism in the American South have negatively affected rural landscapes and their inhabitants, both human and nonhuman. First, the chapter analyzes the nostalgia and forms of violence underlying back-to-the-land visions of apologists for the antebellum South represented by the Southern Agrarians' *I'll Take My Stand* (1930), William Alexander Percy's *Lanterns on the Levee* (1941), and the films *Jezebel* (Wyler, 1938) and *Gone with the Wind* (Fleming, 1939). The chapter then identifies ways that Erskine Caldwell and Richard Wright create what Christopher Reiger calls "antipastorals" to highlight the exploitive and unsustainable forms of violence against land and people underlying plantation nostalgia and myths during the period. In the final section of the chapter, I argue that Zora Neale Hurston uses nonhuman animal stories in black folklore to reevaluate unsustainable forms of environmental, economic, and racial exploitation. I particularly focus on her depictions of nonhuman "beasts" and "pests," which call into question the narrowly anthropocentric and racialized uses of these categories.

While the first two chapters focus on landscapes usually associated with nature writing and environmental thought, the third chapter, "The Postpastoral City," shifts to the urban, which has increasingly become of interest to ecocritics and other environmental humanists. The chapter argues that depression-era novelists examine the social and environmental value and accessibility of "green" spaces and nonhuman forms of nature in urban landscapes, ranging from parks and other recreational spaces to overgrown vacant lots and "commensal" animals that thrive in cities. First, James T. Farrell's *Young Lonigan* (1932) and Nelson Algren's *Never Come Morning*

(1942) depict urban parks and playgrounds as largely disconnected from their characters' experiences. While Bruno and his gang in *Never Come Morning* prefer to spend their time under bridges and in back alleys rather than in the heavily manicured and policed parks of Chicago, Farrell's young protagonist, Studs Lonigan, ultimately rejects the feelings of interconnectedness he experiences in Chicago's Washington Park for the ethos of individualism, toughness, and racial superiority celebrated by his largely white, lower-middle-class South Side neighborhood. If Farrell's and Algren's characters ultimately reject new forms of knowledge they encounter in parks that destabilize the negative forms of place-attachment they use to experience the world, Mike Gold, Tillie Olsen, and Richard Wright focus on the inaccessibility of "green" spaces and/or mobility for their characters. For Gold's young Lower East Side protagonists in *Jews Without Money* (1930), New York's urban parks are largely inaccessible due to physical distance. Instead, they use the neighborhood's vacant lots to find open spaces to play in and experience forms of nature that broaden their understanding of place. Olsen's young Mazie in *Yonnondia: From the Thirties* (1974) experiences an even more severe lack of green and open space in the noxious meatpacking district of Omaha. Her recreational space is mostly limited to a neighborhood dump, where she begins to recognize the toxic effects of what Rob Nixon calls "slow violence" on the working-class children and their families. Finally, Wright's use of rats in *Native Son* (1940) reveals the economic and environmental squalor experienced by the Thomas's and other African American families trapped in Chicago's "Black Belt" *and* symbolizes a sense of mobility and defiance that Bigger comes to admire later in the novel. In endowing rats with virtues not typically associated with the species, Wright joins Hurston in critiquing narrowly anthropocentric *and* racialized uses of categories like "beasts," "predators," and "pests."

The fourth chapter, "Futuramas and Atom Bombs," shifts away from geographical landscapes to focus on debates over technology during the period, first by focusing on "the world of tomorrow" depicted by the 1939–40 New York World's Fair. The fair illustrates a debate over the uncritical celebration of scientific and technological progress—what David Nye calls the "technological sublime"—that attempts to obscure the environmental and social impacts of industrial, commercial, and militaristic uses of science. Science fiction authors of the 1930s and '40s like Ray Bradbury also began identifying the human and non-human costs of technology, particularly after the development and use of atomic bombs to end World War II. In *The Martian Chronicles* (1950), Bradbury envisions the future colonization of Mars through the environmental and social legacy of the American frontier and the apocalyptic potential of atomic war on Earth. In her story "That Only a Mother" (1948) and first novel *Shadow on the Hearth* (1950), Judith Merril also connects the legacy of the frontier to the development and use of atomic bombs, rooting both in a patriarchal response to social and environmental otherness. Merril particularly subverts mid-century gender norms by resituating "hysteria" as a masculine response based on insecurity and fear that has devastating consequences on the human body and natural world. Like Bradbury and Merril, George Schuyler depicts the uses of technology to support dominant power structures in his serialized novel *Black Empire* (1936–38). For Schuyler, technology is an instrument of white supremacy, used by European and American colonial forces to physically and intellectually enslave black people around the world. By depicting black leaders who use technology to intellectually surpass and violently defeat their former white conquerors, Schuyler critiques racist assumptions of white superiority. Though Schuyler is less interested than Merril and Bradbury in depicting the environmental effects of technology on the nonhuman world, his inclusion of solar and hydroponic forms of technology in the novel envisions more socially oriented and environmentally sustainable uses of technology that anticipate current debates over renewable energy. The conclusion reflects on some similarities between the environmental and social issues of the 1930s and '40s, suggesting further work that literary critics can do on depression-era ecoliterature.

In examining the roles of wilderness, nonhuman animals, urban parks, and environmental disasters in depression-era literature, *The Green Depression* seeks to make a few key contributions. First, it argues for the importance of American literary and cultural works of the 1930s and '40s in understanding the development of modern environmentalism in the second half of the twentieth century. In addition to offering my own analysis of the expression of environmental thought in depression-era literature, I also seek to highlight ways that other ecocritics have written about the period. Next, the book contributes to a growing body of scholarship that sees environmental thought as important to the experiences and culture of African Americans. As historian Kimberly Smith argues, "[t]here is a great deal in the black political tradition to explore" regarding African Americans' understanding of their relationship to "the natural environment" and "the norms that ought to govern that relationship" (3–4). These concerns find expression in African American literature, as Paul Outka, Kimberly Ruffin, and other literary critics have pointed out.[16] In what follows, I hope to add to this body of work by describing ways that black authors of the period respond to environmental ideas and issues to depict African American experience. Next, *The Green Depression* offers new ways of reading depression-era or "popular front" literature, building on scholarship that focuses on responses to economic, racial, and gender inequality during the 1930s and '40s.[17] In addition to contributing to understandings of environmental, African American, and popular front literature, *The Green Depression* seeks to help extend ecocritical analysis to literary genres that focus on cities and other highly developed built environments, including urban fiction and sci-fi.[18]

By describing the 1930s and '40s as an economic *and* environmental "crisis of authority," the book also seeks to open a conversation on how experiences and ideas from the period have influenced and can inform responses to the intersections of environmental, social, and economic issues in our own time—particularly in light of contemporary interest in the "Dust Bowl" in Octavia Butler's novels *Parable of the Sower* (1993) and *Parable of the Talents* (1998), Ken Burns's documentary *The Dust Bowl* (2012), and Christopher Nolan's film *Interstellar* (2014). What lessons and ideas do these and other cultural texts recognize in the Dust Bowl experience to help respond to current drought and other global-warming created issues? What other issues in the 1930s and '40s (urban, wilderness, etc.) help inform our responses to current environmental and social forms of exploitation?

Above all, I hope *The Green Depression* will help generate further discussion about the contributions that depression-era literary and cultural works made to the development of environmentalism in the US and elsewhere. While historians have had a lot to say about environmentalist thought during this period, literary and cultural scholars have yet to identify the expression of environmental ideas in depression-era culture in a sustained way. What follows is not meant to be exhaustive. By providing ecocritical readings of literary works and films from the period, the following chapters seek to initiate a conversation—one that I hope will continue long after the publication of this book.

Chapter 1

The Last Frontier

Of the different geographical environments discussed in *The Green Depression*, perhaps none is as fraught with different meanings as wilderness. While the Wilderness Act of 1964 would define the term as "an area where the earth and its community of life are untrammeled by man, where man himself is a visitor who does not remain," debates over the function of such spaces became particularly contentious during the 1930s and '40s. Some wilderness enthusiasts of the period pointed towards the importance of such areas to American economic, aesthetic, and recreational interests, a view perhaps best illustrated by the Civilian Conservationist Corps (CCC). Franklin Roosevelt's extremely popular New Deal program employed over three million American young men for almost a decade "planting 2 billion trees... and developing 800 new state parks" (Maher 4). The latter included building "campgrounds, picnic areas, hiking trails, and... motor roads" to expand recreational access to wilderness (or wilderness-like) areas to more Americans (8). According to historian Neil Maher, the CCC not only "transformed conservation during the Great Depression in ways that helped environmentalism to blossom after World War II," particularly by expanding conservation from an "efficient use of natural resources" to include "concern for human health through outdoor recreation, for wilderness preservation, and for ecological balance" (10), it also introduced the importance of conservation to working-class Americans, who often had little access to wilderness areas or conservation ideas (11). More radical social thinkers like Robert Marshall saw the subsistence-based lifestyle required by living in harsh, undeveloped, and sparsely populated environments as offering an alternative to the economic depravity and racial intolerance he associates with American capitalism. In *Arctic Village* (1933), Marshall describes his fifteen-month-long experience living among "the happiest folk I had ever encountered" in and around the towns of Wiseman and Needles, located in the Upper Koyukuk region of Alaska (3).

On the other hand, Marshall, Leopold, and others warned against the effects that a larger human presence in wilderness areas would have and rallied against roads and other development projects that would modernize these regions and make them more accessible (9). This isn't to say that Marshall and Leopold, as well as other wilderness enthusiasts associated with the Wilderness Society, co-created by Marshall in 1935, believed that humans should avoid wilderness spaces altogether. Instead, they argued that "wildness," rather than modern human convenience, should dominate these spaces (Sutter 14).[1] Closely related to debates over wilderness, the legacy of the frontier still loomed large in the cultural imagination of Americans, even as its devastating social and environmental effects became better understood. Frontier practices and policies, including the unregulated expansion and agricultural development of land opened by western expansion, led to the onset of severe drought and dust storms in the Great Plains. As Worster argues, the Dust Bowl was a product of frontier settlement that began in the last two decades of the nineteenth century (4, 82–84).

In the following chapter, I argue that depression-era authors and (to some degree) filmmakers contributed to transformations in conservationist thought during the period by emphasizing the importance of protecting wilderness spaces, wildlife, and the rights and autonomy of indigenous human populations in maintaining healthy human and nonhuman communities. In the first section of the chapter, I examine the effect of Walt Disney's animated feature

Bambi (1942) on attitudes towards wilderness and hunting after its release. In creating characters that combine anthropomorphic characterizations with realistic physical detail, the film uses the animated film medium to encourage filmgoers to identify with the nonhuman species it depicts. Despite its effectiveness in creating non-anthropocentric forms of identification, the film's reliance on normative middle-class values and cute nonhuman animal characters leads it to omit species that may threaten human physical safety and economic interests but play important roles in maintaining ecosystems. In the second section of the chapter, I argue that authors William Faulkner, Ernest Hemingway, and Aldo Leopold depict hunting in ways that attempt to highlight the ecological *and* cultural importance of animal predators often ignored in idyllic depictions of wilderness like *Bambi*. I particularly focus the chapter on Hemingway's *Green Hills of Africa* (1935), arguing that his depiction of hunting in East Africa during the 1930s restages the legacy of the American frontier experience to critique overhunting, predator eradication, and, to some extent, imperial practices towards indigenous populations. While Hemingway's critique of Western imperialism is perhaps less pronounced than his concern for overhunting, Salish author D'Arcy McNickle creates a more indigenous-informed understanding of the frontier's environmental and social legacy in his first novel *The Surrounded* (1936). In the third section of the chapter, I argue that McNickle appropriates Frederick Jackson Turner's "palimpsest" in the novel to uncover the social, cultural, and environmental scars that frontier practices and policies have left on indigenous groups and lands in the West. The understanding of Native American experiences he works out in *The Surrounded* would also inform his position as a writer and field agent for the Bureau of Indian Affairs (BIA) during the agency's brief attempts under the Indian Reorganization Act (1934) to reverse a half-century of federal assimilation policies.

Together, the authors discussed in this chapter helped set the stage for the kind of environmental thinking that would develop in the second half of the twentieth century. In arguing for the non-anthropocentric value of wilderness areas, resources, and nonhuman inhabitants, they contributed to the expansion of conservationism beyond its earlier more utilitarian focus. Their depictions of animal predators as ecologically and culturally important to the American landscape also challenged dominant assumptions concerning these species that fueled environmentally devastating predator eradication programs in the early twentieth century. Furthermore, they contributed to a growing awareness of ways in which the destruction of wilderness spaces affects human populations, particularly by depicting the physical and economic danger of human-influenced flooding and dust storms. And their more inclusive depictions of indigenous populations offered a critical alternative to the dominant racial discourses of the period, particularly by identifying the environmental and social effects of expansionist and colonial practices.

Walt Disney's Middle-Class Wilderness

Disney's 1941 animated feature, *Bambi*, depicts a forest where wild animals live in harmony in a kingdom ruled by a benevolent stag (Bambi's father). The primary danger to this animal utopia is man, whose hunting activities and carelessness with fire threatens the lives of the animals and the health of the forest. Based on Felix Salten's 1924 Austrian novel, *Bambi: A Life in the Forest*, Disney's film became a highly influential critique of hunting and model for later nature films (Cartmill 185).[2] Though the film has been critiqued for its simplistic depiction of hunters as well as for "its pervasive and repellant cuteness" (178), its depictions of animals in wilderness spaces introduced ensuing generations to the value of nonhuman life beyond human consumption and use. While its pungent if often exaggerated critique of human hunters certainly played a part in creating forms of identification and empathy with forest animals, other factors also helped create these responses in audiences. The film combines realistic anatomical detail with familial, middle-class values to illustrate the innate value of forest animals. But in projecting normative values onto select animals, *Bambi* contributes as much to segregating nonhuman animal species as to protecting them. If the largely sanitized, cute, and noble animals depicted in the film are worth saving, what about the less cuddly species that roam the forest? In a period in which conservationists like Aldo Leopold and Rosalie Edge were arguing against entrenched attitudes towards animal predators like wolves, coyotes, and hawks in conservationist thought, *Bambi* ends up supporting environmentally destructive predator-prey binaries that distinguish between killable and non-killable animals. By the same token, the normative, middle-class values expressed in the film code the absent species as social and, to some degree, racial others. While other animal-focused Disney films of and after the period often directly depicted animals in racialized ways, using stereotypical speech and mannerisms in crows, apes, hyenas, and other less admired animals, *Bambi*'s omission of such species obscures their place altogether.

In terms of its legacy, *Bambi* is best remembered for its anti-hunting sentiments. Walt Disney was an animal lover and anti-hunter advocate, particularly after witnessing his older brother shoot a male rabbit mating on his family's farm in Missouri. As Matt Cartmill describes the experience, "Walt dissolved in tears when Roy [his brother] broke the thrashing rabbit's neck, and he refused to touch the rabbit stew their mother served that evening" (166–67). The film would emphasize the cruelty Disney saw hunters inflicting on animal populations by portraying sportsmen as faceless killers, indiscriminately shooting animals of all species, ages, and genders. Furthermore, the hunters in the film are either careless or malicious with their use of fire, causing severe damage to the forest and its inhabitants. In the final hunting sequence in the film, the human characters use fire to chase animals from their hiding spots. In response to its portrayal of hunting, the film came under attack by sportsman clubs and magazines, which called it everything from an unfair caricature of modern hunters to an example of left-wing, Marxist propaganda. Early critiques of the film by sportsmen organizations focused on its depictions of practices they argued were not used by most hunters, including shooting doe, hunting in the spring, and using dogs and fire to force animals out into the open (179).³

But the film's real power occurs in its novel depiction of forest animals. Its first and most important innovation lies in the animation techniques used to more realistically capture the physical detail and body language of nonhuman animals. Earlier animated films and shorts relied on animal characters drawn with "rounded outlines, rubbery consistency, and quasi-human form" to make them easier to animate, more humorous, and anthropomorphically identifiable. But as Cartmill points out, the subject matter of Salten's narrative "could not be put in the mouth of a cartoon deer that looked like Clarabelle Cow with antlers" (168–69). While Disney allowed animators to express the characters' emotions through human facial expressions, he forbid the use of "human body language" (169). Instead, he had his animators spend months studying and sketching live and filmed deer (169). The final product, according to Cartmill, gives the animals and forest a presence and "unique beauty" missing in the "staccato rhythm" of previous animated films.⁴

If the animation techniques used for the film helped create more anatomically accurate and aesthetically pleasing forest animals, the inclusion of the period's dominant American values in their characterizations helped make them highly identifiable, particularly for "white middle-class audiences" (Thomas 43). As Brennan M. Thomas notes, "The creatures of Bambi's world . . . are governed by a complex social order which promotes civility and amiability and recognizes species, gender, and familial bonds as linked substructures of that order" (44). This includes socializing young animals like Bambi and Thumper, the fawn's young rabbit friend, into the social roles they will play in the residing hierarchical structure. The film particularly uses Thumper, Thomas points out, to model the transition from "a four-legged embodiment of an American child's underdeveloped sense of etiquette," where "immediate gratification supersedes politeness," to a functioning member of forest society (44). The socialization aspect of the film includes supporting dominant gender roles in which female animals are the primary caretakers of the young and males are typically absent or protect the family from a distance (48). Bambi's father only shows up in the film during times when the young buck is in trouble—as when hunters shoot and kill his mother or, later, when they shoot Bambi while he tries to flee from the fire. For Thomas, the film "naturalizes" the above-mentioned middle-class values and social roles "by superimposing them upon humanized depictions of nature" (48). But the film also naturalizes the forest animals it depicts by endowing them with these valued behaviors and roles. In doing so, it helped support distinctions between acceptable and nonacceptable wilderness animals. The latter are depicted in later Disney films as outcasts, schemers, and bullies and often racialized by using darker colors and stereotypical mannerisms and speech patterns.[5] *Bambi* largely omits such animals, with the exception of Friend Owl, whose predatory instincts are not acknowledged, and the hunters' dogs, whose ferocity seems a product of human influence and training. The hunters' influence on the dogs is one of the primary remaining direct influences of Salten's source novel on the film. As Cartmill notes, "[T]he dogs and other . . . domesticated animals [in the novel] . . . pass their lives in a psychopathic tumult of worshipful adoration, hatred, and fear of man and detestation of themselves" (165). Other than the dogs, the film leaves out the animal predators present in Salten's novel.[6]

One reason Disney may have omitted animal predators from the film was that their presence undermines his critique of human hunters. If violence is already a daily part of the natural world, then why critique humans for participating in that violence? As addressed in the next section, hunters like Hemingway even saw themselves as offering their prey a less painful and prolonged death than animal predators. Disney may have also left out animal predators in the film in order to highlight the more devastating effects humans have on wilderness forests and their inhabitants. His inclusion of fire in the final hunting sequence lends support for this concern in the film. For Thomas, this use of fire alludes "to the devastating impact technologies can have when perverted into weapons" (56). Though it's unclear whether the fire is set deliberately or accidently, it becomes a tool for hunters to drive game out into the open more easily. In its uncontrollability and destructiveness, the fire gives the final hunting sequence in the film a nightmarish and apocalyptic tone, creating dark shadows and hues that distort the wounded Bambi, his father, and the other animals as they flee the burning forest. While they eventually find safety on a small river island, the apocalyptic danger lingers on as they watch the forest burn around them. This all-engulfing aspect of the fire distinguishes it from earlier dangers faced by the animals, whether from human bullets or spring storms. The lightning and thunder of a spring storm at the beginning of the film, interrupting the forest idyll with a similar sense of danger, is portrayed as a brief and necessary disturbance accompanying the life-giving rains brought by the arrival of spring.

But in omitting predators from its forests, the film ends up defining wilderness spaces by the non-predators that appear to live in harmony with each other. In doing so, the film supports a view of predators coming under question by conservationists, including hunters, during the period. These proto-environmentalists began critiquing early twentieth-century federal programs in the US that targeted species like coyotes and wolves known for feeding on livestock. As environmental historian Donald Worster describes it, the "utilitarian conservationism" of the Bureau of the Biological Survey (BBS) in the Department of Agriculture led to the extermination of "two million coyote" between 1915 and 1957 (260).[7] For ranchers, foresters, and government officials, Worster continues, coyotes and other predators represented "an outrageous defiance of man's righteous empire over nature" (260).[8] But if *Bambi* misses an opportunity to use aspects of animation to depict predator animals in unique and innovative ways, authors William Faulkner, Aldo Leopold, and Ernest Hemingway move beyond the film in their depictions of these species.⁹ Each of these authors depict animal predators in ways that highlight a growing understanding of these species' importance to wilderness and human landscapes.

Hunting with Leopold, Faulkner, and Hemingway

While *Bambi* ignores the role hunters played in the development of conservationist and environmental thinking, Leopold, Faulkner, and Hemingway use hunting encounters with nonhuman predators to emphasize the latter's ecological and cultural value.¹⁰ In "Thinking Like a Mountain," Aldo Leopold describes one such encounter that eventually led to his break with predator eradication programs. After shooting at a wolf and her pups, Leopold recounts gazing into the dying mother's eyes and realizing the mistaken thinking behind such programs. He writes, "[T]here was something new to me in those eye—something known only to her and to the mountain . . . I thought that because fewer wolves meant more deer, that no wolves would mean hunters' paradise. But after seeing the green fire die, I sensed that neither the wolf nor the mountain agreed with such a view" (130). As Leopold comes to realize, predators like wolves play an integral part in limiting the effects of deer on the mountain range. In removing the predator's role, humankind upsets a balance necessary for both predator and prey to survive. Not only was Leopold able to recognize the ecological effects that overhunting animal predators caused, he also recognized its effects on human populations.¹¹ For Leopold, violently contorting nature to human uses results in "dustbowls, and rivers washing the future into the sea" (132).

Like Leopold, William Faulkner also embodies early forms of environmentalist thought centered around the importance of nonhuman predators.¹² In the hunting stories of *Go Down, Moses* (1942)—particularly "The Bear" and "Delta Autumn"—Faulkner depicts the timber industry's destruction of the primeval Mississippi forests and floodplains and its subsequent effect on human well-being. For Susan

Scott Parrish, these stories provide a back story for understanding the causes of the Great Mississippi Flood of 1927 (35). At the end of "Delta Autumn," Ike McCaslin concludes that a *"land which man has deswamped and denuded and derivered in two generations"* to create the wealth and prejudices produced by cotton in the South will use "[t]he people who have destroyed it . . . [to] accomplish its revenge" (italics in original, 347). As Parrish points out, Ike is referring to "a complex set of anthropogenic changes such as wetlands drainage, cotton monoculture, massive deforestation by the timber industry, and the building of ever-higher levees to manage the Mississippi and its tributaries by straightening and containing the sources" (34). These changes to the land, she continues, would help turn the 1927 flooding of the Mississippi River into a massive environmental disaster (40). Like the severe dust storms in the following decade, the Mississippi Flood of 1927 and other flooding across the US during the period was a consequence of human industry. In disrupting the ability of bottomland forests and floodplains to slow down and absorb running water during hard rains and relying on a "levees-only" solution to flooding, southerners created the conditions for the retribution that Ike alludes to in his lament for the wilderness (Barry 91, Saikku 36). By the end of the flooding, "water covered 27,000 square miles, land in seven states where almost a million people lived; 13 major crevasses occurred; roughly 637,000 people became homeless; 154 refugee camps were run by the Red Cross, where a mostly African-American population lived for months . . . [and an] estimated . . . 1,000 were killed in the Delta region alone; 50% of all animals in the flooded areas drowned. And financially, there were at least one billion dollars in losses" (Parrish 40).[13]

Published fifteen years after the flood and describing events well before it, *Go Down, Moses* ascribes the disappearance of Mississippi forests to shifting ways of understanding wilderness. As the primeval forest and its inhabitants lose their mythic quality for the characters in the stories, the land becomes *"deswamped and denuded and derivered"* at an ever-greater pace, helping to create the conditions that would influence the severity of the Great Mississippi Flood. For the sportsmen of Jefferson, the wilderness serves as an escape from the demands of civilized life into an "Arcadian" space that fosters a return to "a simple life and humble submission to natural laws" (Pitavy 93). The hunters' experience in the uncultivated forests includes glimpses of a vulnerability they share with other nonhuman animals to the physical conditions of nature, an experience akin to what Anat Pick calls "creaturely poetics" (3). As a primeval place "bigger and older than any recorded document" (Faulkner 183), the wilderness allows them to recognize their "own fragility and impotence against the timeless woods, yet without doubt or dread" (192). Instead of doubt and fear, they rekindle attributes they ascribe to the natural world, including the "will and hardihood to endure and the humility and skill to survive" (184). As in Leopold's encounter with the wolf in "Thinking Like a Mountain," the hunters' experience of the wilderness revolves around their relationship to an animal predator: a bear referred to as Old Ben. Each year, the hunters "rendezvous with the bear" and return to Jefferson after a couple of weeks "with no trophy, no skin" (186). Because of Old Ben's strength and cunning, the men endow it with human and, occasionally, mythic qualities. Not only has he "earned a name such as a human man could have worn and not been sorry" (221), Old Ben appears to blend into the woods, acting as a ghostly embodiment of the wilderness's transcendental properties. Ike McCaslin's first glimpses of the bear suggest this bond: "It didn't walk into the woods. It faded, sank back into the wilderness without motion as he had watched a fish . . . sink back into the dark depths of its pool and vanish without even any movement of its fin" (201).

Though Old Ben and the forest create for the hunters a "creaturely" experience that begins breaking down barriers between species, Ike recognizes that both the bear and the wilderness are becoming "an anachronism indomitable and invincible out of an old dead time, phantom, epitome and apotheosis of the old wild life which the puny humans swarmed and hacked at in a fury of abhorrence and fear" (185). The beginning of the end for Old Ben and the forest occurs after the bear transgresses his status by appearing to kill one of Major de Spain's colts. As de Spain tells the other hunters after finding the colt missing, "I'm disappointed in him. He has broken the rules. I didn't think he would have done that. He has killed mine and McCaslin's dogs, but that was alright. We gambled the dogs against him; we gave each other warning. But now he has come into my house and destroyed my property, out of season" (205). Like Leopold's wolf, Old Ben's ignores human property rights, an act that changes the hunters' perception of him. For Christina M. Colvin, de Spain's frustration with Old Ben results in a form of "speciesism" that judges him as an "animal . . . available for killing or harm" (97). The new status of the bear is heightened after they find the corpse of the colt near camp with "its throat torn out and the entrails and one ham partly eaten" (Faulkner 205). Even though the hunters are never certain that Old Ben killed the colt—as there is evidence that Lion, the wild dog Sam traps with the colt's corpse, might have done it—they use it as an excuse to finally kill the bear. The decision illustrates "a complicated ethical dilemma" between "environmentalist propensities" and "tribal or selfish values" that Lawrence Buell refers to as "environmental doublethink" (*Writing* 190). While Buell ascribes this dilemma to Major de Spain's decision to sell the hunting camp to the timber industry, it perhaps best fits the hunters' decision to try to kill Old Ben, since the act helps initiate their changing attitudes toward the wilderness that leads de Spain to sell the property. They are caught between their respect for the intelligence and mythic quality of the bear and its possible transgressions against human property rights. In the end, their choice to kill Old Ben reduces the bear to a mere "animal," supporting ontological differences between humans and nonhumans that legitimize the latter for "killing or for harm" (Culvin 97). Lion, with his "yellow eyes" that stare with "a cold and almost impersonal malignance like some natural force" (Faulkner 209), also falls squarely in the nonhuman category, leaving him killable for the sake of trapping Old Ben.[14]

In addition to Old Ben's transgression against the men's property, the timber industry's looming threat and eventual destruction of the

South's remaining wilderness also transforms the hunters' "grand narratives" about the forest and its animals (Culvin 104), particularly as the industry gradually encroaches on de Spain's hunting camp and the men's hunting grounds. The killing of Old Ben destroys much of the last vestiges of wilderness as a space through which to experience the Arcadian timelessness of nature, leading de Spain to eventually sell the camp to the industry. When Ike subsequently returns to the camp, he finds the area developed with a "new planning-mill already half completed which would cover two or three acres and what looked like miles and miles of stacked steel rails red with light bright rust of newness and of piled crossties sharp with creosote, and wire corrals and feeding-troughs for two hundred mules at least and the tents for the men who drove them" (304). Towards the end of his life, Ike must drive "two hundred miles" to find "wilderness to hunt in" (324). Additionally, he finds that the new generation of his kinsmen is even further disconnected from the remaining forest and its wildlife as they fail to follow traditional forms of conservation by shooting a doe (348).

As François Pitavy argues, Faulkner uses the destruction of the wilderness to depict the Arcadian impulse as "the impossible dream of man's desire to inhabit an eternity which his temporal condition, his heritage, precludes" (103). For Thomas L. McHaney, Ike's inability to reconcile his family's heritage with his affinity for the wilderness leaves him unable "to live with responsibility in either of [the] . . . realms" (108, 115). Both critics ultimately see Ike as an impotent figure who misses an opportunity to model ecological forms of living by renouncing his inheritance and withdrawing from the world. But Ike's recognition that the destruction of wilderness affects the ecological stability of the region and the human and nonhuman inhabitants who depend on it make him an environmental Cassandra unable to find an audience who takes his warning seriously. Like Leopold, Ike believes that the "abuse" of the "land" stems from seeing it "as a commodity belonging to us" rather than a "community to which we belong" (Leopold viii). As he explains to his cousin McCaslin

Edmunds, "[God] created man to be His overseer on the earth and to hold suzerainty over the earth and the animals on it in His name, not to hold for himself and his descendants inviolable title forever, generation after generation, to the oblongs and squares of the earth, but to hold the earth mutual and intact in the communal anonymity of brotherhood" (246). Instead, the southerner's attempt to profit from the land is "founded upon injustice and erected by ruthless rapacity and carried on ... with at times downright savagery not only to the human beings but the valuable animals too" (285), a savagery that, through devastating hunting and land cultivation practices, would reduce a healthy and widespread black bear population in Mississippi to less than "12 individuals" by 1932 (Simek et al. 159). Though Ike does not explicitly foresee flooding as revenge for treating the land and its inhabitants as a commodity, his unheeded warning anticipates and alludes to the great human-made environmental catastrophes from the late 1920s to the postwar era, including the Great Mississippi Flood, the Dust Bowl, and the threat of nuclear fallout. Similar to the conversion experienced by Leopold in the years following his encounter with the dying wolf, Ike sees human-induced ecological disasters as a glimpse of what Kate Soper calls "realist' nature." For Soper, Leopold, and McCaslin, this is an understanding that nature "is indifferent to our choices, will persist in the midst of environmental destruction, and will outlast the death of all planetary life" (159–60). Such an awareness can remind humanity of the hubris involved in environmental exploitation, the danger of which affects the existence of both nonhumans *and* humans.

Leopold and Faulkner were not the only authors to use hunting to explore conceptual shifts in the importance and function of wilderness and its nonhuman inhabitants during the period. While often considered one of the major "American macho imitators" of Victorian "imperial hunting" (Buell, *Writing* 185), Hemingway is sometimes skeptical of the Victorian hunting values and practices he inherits from figures like Theodore Roosevelt. Examining Roosevelt's influence on the author, Suzanne Clark calls it "one of emulation but also of disillusionment" (64). In *Green Hills of Africa*, his account of a 1933 hunting trip in East Africa with his second wife, Pauline Marie Pfeiffer, Hemingway occasionally depicts humanity's responsibility towards wild spaces, nonhuman predators, and indigenous populations in ways that move beyond traditional conservationist thought of the early twentieth century.[15] While Faulkner turns to the past to lament the environmental practices leading to the destruction of wilderness spaces in the South, Hemingway turns to Africa, where he attempts to experience frontier conditions no longer available in the United States. In doing so, he highlights the Western imperialist practices that have destroyed wilderness spaces and inhabitants in the US and are destroying them in Africa. Like Leopold and Faulkner, he also attributes environmental disasters like dust storms and floods to wilderness destruction and sees nature as indifferent to human interests.

Throughout the book, Hemingway often practices traditional forms of conservation followed by other hunters of the late nineteenth and early twentieth centuries. These include closely following game limits, not shooting animals from vehicles, showing good sportsmanship with other hunters, and making clean kills.[16] He writes, "I did not mind killing anything, any animal, if I killed it cleanly, they all had to die and my interference with the nightly and the seasonal killing that went on all the time was very minute and I had no guilty feeling at all" (272). But Hemingway's occasional failures to adhere to the sportsman code force him into new ethical engagements with the land and its inhabitants. As Ryan Hediger claims, Hemingway often faces ethical choices that do not neatly conform to the code, and these choices force him to "constantly revisit the principles with which he confronts animals and place" ("Hunting, Fishing" 42). While Hediger sees Hemingway as practicing a more active form of ethical engagement in his later life and works, including his second trip to East Africa from 1953 to 1954 (recounted in his posthumously published book *Under Kilimanjaro* [2007]), the critic recognizes moments of this engagement in *Green Hills of Africa*. At times in the latter book, hunting becomes less a pursuit of animal trophies than an attempt to experience and depict Africa and its human and nonhuman inhabitants on their own terms (39–41).

Hemingway particularly expresses this form of ethical engagement when he reflects on the agonizing deaths of a group of hyenas that he fails to cleanly shoot. While his African gun bearer, M'Cola, teases him about the poor shots, the author uses rhetorical flourishes to mimic bouts of anxiety over the suffering he causes the animals. This anxiety is particularly of interest as the nonhuman species under question is often reviled for its perceived behavior towards humans and other animals. As biologist Stephen E. Glickman notes, both African and European cultures have ascribed various myths and stereotypes to hyenas that portray them as "hermaphrodites, scavengers, singers of sad songs, smelly, ugly, and, ultimately, comical in their failure to comprehend the 'realities' of our perception" (506, 527). While not hunted to near extinction like wolves in the US, the hyena's public image has often left environmentalists less interested in focusing on the "preservation of hyena habitats and the long-term prospects for these species" (503). But the tone and excess of Hemingway's prose in the above-mentioned scene works to undermine stereotypes associated with hyenas that lead M'Cola to laugh at their suffering. In doing so, his depiction of the species moves beyond the narrow anthropocentric meanings and value ascribed to it and creates forms of identity and empathy with a typically despised animal "predator" and "pest." As in his depictions of other animals throughout his work, Hemingway shows a great deal of "sympathy" and respect for the hyenas that he encounters in *Green Hills of Africa* (Murphy 167, Hediger "Pity and the Beasts," 141).[17]

Hemingway's description of the dying animals begins with a sarcastic rejoinder to M'Cola's response. He writes,

> Highly humorous was the hyena obscenely loping, full belly dragging, at daylight on the plain, who, shot from the stern, skittered on into speed to tumble end over end. Mirth provoking was the hyena that

stopped out of range by an alkali lake to look back and, hit in the chest, went over on his back, his four feet and his full belly in the air. Nothing could be more jolly than the hyena coming suddenly wedge-headed and stinking out of high grass by a donga, hit at ten yards, who raced his tail in three narrowing, scampering circles until he died. (37)

The sarcasm and anger bubbling beneath his descriptions of the hyenas continues. In what he calls "the great joke of all" and "the pinnacle of hyenic humor" (37), he describes a hyena eating its own intestines after being shot: "[T]he hyena . . . that hit too far back while running, would circle madly, snapping and tearing at himself until he pulled his own intestines out, and then stood there, jerking them out and eating them with relish" (37–38). His bursts of frantic and stream-like prose continue in the following paragraph as he goes into a metonymic list of descriptors attached to the hyena: the "hermaphroditic, self-eating devourer of the dead, trailer of calving cows, ham-stringer, potential biter-off of your face at night while you slept, sad yowler, camp-follower, stinking, foul, with jaws that crack the bones the lion leaves, belly dragging, loping away on the brown plain, looking back, mongrel dog-smart in the face" (38).

Literary critics and others often view Hemingway's descriptions of the dying hyenas as contributing to negative stereotypes associated with the species. For Glickman, Hemingway's depictions of them echo both Western accounts of hyenas as ugly and cowardly, perhaps best represented by Theodore Roosevelt's depiction during his African safari in 1909, and African understandings of them as embodying "greed, gluttony, stupidity, and comical foolishness" (506–507, 527).[18] According to Jeremiah M. Kitunda, Hemingway deliberately distorts M'Cola's reaction "to amuse his audience" (134). As Kitunda explains, the Kamba (M'Cola's tribe) considered hyenas a "ritual animal" whose killing was "practically taboo." If killing hyenas was granted due to their excessive "predatory activities," it had to be conducted using special techniques as the species "represented a bad omen" and was seen by the tribe "as harbingers of death." A "careless" killing of a hyena "was tantamount to inviting bad luck" (133). As even Kitunda recognizes, however, M'Cola's response may have been conditioned to ignore tribal beliefs and customs through colonial influences (134). Hemingway is certainly aware of this conditioning and spends much time throughout the book criticizing European colonialism for turning indigenous populations into imitators of European tastes and values by removing them from their cultural and ecological ties to the land. Though his interpretation of African "authenticity" is layered with condescension and ignorance regarding the conditions of African populations during colonial occupation, his concern for veracity suggests his unwillingness to fabricate events to provide his reader a cheap laugh.

Instead of viewing these passages as contributing to the myths and stereotypes projected onto hyenas or as merely critiquing indigenous Africans like M'Cola from a white Euro-American imperialistic position, they become moments when Hemingway identifies with the self-eating hyena and other "animals turned inside out" (Strychacz 31). Having just recovered from amoebic dysentery after arriving in Africa, Hemingway may have been more inclined to identify with the hyenas' suffering due to his debilitating bout with the illness. He writes, "[I] experienced the necessity of washing a three-inch bit of . . . large intestine with soap and water and tucking it back where it belonged an unnumbered amount of times a day" (Hemingway 283). Thomas Strychacz argues that the experience leads Hemingway to use "metaphors of food and corresponding processes of digestion and excretion" to express anxieties over the reduction of animal bodies from "food" to "trophy heads" (25). These anxieties are particularly apparent in the text, the critic continues, during passages in which "exuberant rhetorical excess" expresses his problematic "consumption of Africa" (26). The anxiety Hemingway experiences over consuming East Africa appears in the rhetorical flourishes describing the death of the hyenas. In combination with the haphazard way in which he shoots the hyenas, these flourishes suggest that Hemingway kills the nonhuman animal species due to their poor reputation. As such, they take on similar qualities as Leopold's wolf and Faulkner's bear as well as the other predator "vermin" systematically hunted close to extinction during the late nineteenth and early twentieth centuries. While Leopold more pointedly articulates his understanding of the role animal predators play in the biotic community, Hemingway suggests the beginnings of a similar identification with an often-hated nonhuman animal through the excretive rhetorical flourishes used to describe their deaths. Both authors (as well as Faulkner) point toward a growing anxiety over the right of hunters to shoot predators thought to play a negative role in human and nonhuman communities.

Hemingway also shares Leopold and Faulkner's awareness of the devastating effects that overhunting and human development have on the natural world (Murphy 165).[19] For the author, parts of Africa during the 1930s still embodied the frontier vitality and ecological health that America once held. In the book, he believes that the largely virgin country he hunts in the final section of the book is a contemporary version of the frontier during his grandfather's time: "Our people went to America because that was the place to go then. It had been a good country and we had made a bloody mess of it and I would go, now, somewhere else as we had always had the right to go somewhere else and as we had always gone" (285). But, Hemingway continues, this land is continually threatened by the arrival of white civilization, which in overdeveloping nature for economic ends, destroys its vitality and lure. He writes, "The natives live in harmony with it. But the foreigner destroys, cuts down trees, drains the water, so that the water supply is altered and in a short time the soil, once the sod is turned under, is cropped out and, next, it starts to blow away as it has blown away in every old country" (284). Hemingway's attribution of the blowing away of soil to the removal of sod alludes to the Dust Bowl and puts him in line with Leopold and Faulkner in recognizing the self-destructive effects that human practices ignoring regional ecologies can have on environments. He also shares their view of nature as ultimately indifferent to human concerns.[20]

Furthermore, Hemingway's use of "foreigner" to refer to white Euro-American explorers and settlers on the North American continent inverts typical understandings of Western expansion and white superiority. Instead of seeing the latter as a noble spread of ideas and opportunities, he depicts them as causing a parasitic exploitation of a land once kept healthy by indigenous populations (Hediger 40). Hemingway's critique of Eurocentrism offers an appreciation of indigenous populations that avoids at least some of the primitivism in depictions of such groups by Euro-Americans up to this time. Taking a dialectical view of primitivism, Suzanne del Gizzo sees it as embodying more than just Western attitudes of cultural superiority in Hemingway's work, including his writings about Africa. He also uses it to critique aspects of Western culture and create potential sites for cultural exchange between Westerners and indigenous populations (498–99). While Africa, she argues, allows the younger Hemingway "a space of recreation that could help him discover or recover aspects of himself" (505), it also offers him opportunities for "cross-cultural interaction and cross-racial identification" that questioned both "the cultural norms and restrictions of society" and "the public persona he had created" (519). Del Gizzo views the safari recounted in *Green Hills of Africa* as primarily a trophy hunt "that participated in an imperialistic and disrespectful relation to the African land and peoples" (505), but there are moments when he attempts to drop his imperialistic condescension in the book, particularly towards tribes he sees as not yet disturbed by Western influence. The "very handsome and extremely jolly" Masai he meets towards the end of the expedition are one such example (218, 219). In their playfulness and generosity, they represent for the author "the first truly light-hearted people I had seen in Africa" (219). While Hemingway romanticizes the Masai to a large degree, viewing them as a disappearing remnant of authenticity on the African continent, he does describe them as holding an "attitude" he associates with "the best of the English, the best of the Hungarians and the best of the very best of the Spaniards." This attitude is one of "unexpressed but instant and complete acceptance that you must be

Masai wherever it is you come from." For Hemingway, such acceptance represents "the most clear distinction of nobility when there was nobility." He concludes, "It is an ignorant attitude and the people who have it do not survive, but very few pleasanter things ever happen to you than the encountering of it" (221). Hemingway's reflections on the Masai suggest an understanding of nobility as a cross-cultural and cross-racial state of mind and action rather than one based on Western culture and heredity. In transgressing racial boundaries, this form of nobility undermined the dominant colonial discourse that viewed Africans as less civilized than Europeans.[21] For Hemingway, the Masai are like-minded stewards of a fertile land that has not yet been over-hunted and developed. Unfortunately, the author is unable or unwilling to see many of the differences between his position and that of the Masai as well as his role in damaging the landscape. By finding this "un-hunted pocket in the million miles of bloody Africa" (218), Hemingway opens the door for other hunters to exhaust it.

Despite moments of ignorance regarding African landscape and cultures, Hemingway echoes the shifts in conservationist thought during the period that were laying the groundwork for later environmentalists as well as his own changing attitudes towards the continent in the second half of the twentieth century. Like Leopold and Faulkner, Hemingway shows an awareness of the devastating effects that narrow forms of anthropocentrism often have on human *and* nonhuman interests. Instead of viewing wilderness as something people should develop for economic interests or leave unspoiled by human presence, these authors saw it as a space through which humans could come to identify with other animals, particularly species that are feared or hated due to their perceived transgressions against human physical safety and economic interests. In the case of Faulkner and Hemingway, the new forms of ethical engagement also occasionally led to critiques of imperialism and/or racism. Similarly, D'Arcy McNickle would call attention to connections between forms of environmental and social exploitation in frontier landscapes, though from a position more firmly rooted in the perspective of the colonized subject. In

The Surrounded (1936), McNickle uses his experiences growing up on the Flathead Reservation in western Montana to call attention to the deep scars left on indigenous groups and land in the former frontier of the American West.

The Indigenous Palimpsest

If, as Hemingway recognizes in *Green Hills of Africa*, the frontier conditions that captured the imagination of Americans and spurred rapid economic growth in the US no longer existed in the first third of the twentieth century, the cultural, historical, and environmental legacy of the frontier lived on during the Great Depression. For liberal New Dealers, such as Secretary of Agriculture Henry Wallace, the frontier had moved beyond landscape to become a social and economic quest to "invent, build and put to work new social machinery" (11). Supporters of traditional forms of American individualism and exceptionalism reinvigorated the individualism proposed by the traditional frontier myth—particularly through Western novels and films—and made stars like John Wayne the embodiment of its renewed energy (Wills 311). There are even progressive forms of the traditional frontier myth, as in Robert Marshall's *Arctic Village*. In the 1933 book, Marshall, a forester and wilderness activist, describes his year-and-a-half-long experience among the 127 white, Eskimo, and Indian residents living in the 15,000 square miles of the remote Alaskan upper Koyukuk, calling them "on the whole the happiest folk I had ever encountered" (3). While Marshall depicts a more racially inclusive version of frontier experience by creating more rounded and sympathetic depictions of indigenous populations, he often joins the other politicians and authors mentioned above in appealing to what William Cronon calls the more "dubious arguments about democracy" associated with Frederick Jackson Turner's "frontier thesis" (171).[22] In doing so, Marshall and company tend to ignore the devastating effects that frontier practices had on indigenous groups and lands of the American West.

Perhaps no novel of the period more vividly describes these effects than D'Arcy McNickle's *The Surrounded*. In depicting the legacy of the frontier from a perspective rooted in the Native American experience, McNickle qualifies some of the more romantic ideas associated with frontier experience. As the half-Salish author informed John Collier, Franklin Roosevelt's head of the Bureau of Indian Affairs and primary architect of the Indian Reorganization Act of 1934: "I am interested in writing about the West, not in the romantic vein in which it has been dealt with in the past but with the object of revealing, in fiction, as it had been revealed by historical writers of the past generation, the character which was formed by the impact of the Frontier upon the lives of the people who settled it" (qtd. in Parker 35). In divesting the frontier of its more romantic and mystical notions, he uncovers the social and environmental effects of frontier policies like assimilation and allotment. Not only did the Dawes Act of 1887 begin a process that would dispossess Native Americans of two-thirds of their land, it also functioned to strip tribes of their cultural heritage by outlawing tribal customs and ceremonies (Glover 160, Hine and Faragher 465). The effects of these practices created "landless Indians living in incredible poverty, an infant mortality rate more than twice that of the white population, widespread alcoholism and crime" (Taylor 9). The agricultural practices associated with white American settlement and Native American allotments in the West also contributed to the severity of drought and erosion during the 1930s (Hine and Faragher 508).

For McNickle, the social and environmental effects of federal, cultural, and economic policies associated with the frontier are intricately linked. In *The Surrounded*, the author engages in what we now refer to as "environmental justice" by depicting the environmental and social effects of colonial policies towards indigenous groups and their lands. To do so, McNickle adopts a method of literary excavation akin to Frederick Jackson Turner's "palimpsest," a metaphor the historian uses to describe the layers of geographical development on frontier landscapes. While Turner uses the palimpsest to describe the development of former frontier lands in eastern states that had already transitioned from cattle ranging to farming to manufacturing (11), the metaphor became an appropriate image to describe the West in the 1930s, by which time a half-century of white settlement and economic development had left major changes on the land and its inhabitants. Like Turner's palimpsest, McNickle's novel calls attention to these changes to describe the general process of frontier settlement. But in focusing on the palimpsest-like landscape, McNickle also uncovers ways of life buried under layers of exploitive assimilation and land practices. Since the attempted erasures on palimpsests are never fully invisible, the metaphor became particularly appropriate for McNickle in depicting the layers of influence and development on Salish land, identity, and culture.

Attempting to peel away the layers and recover the attempted erasures of frontier history often proves difficult for the characters in *The Surrounded*, particularly due to the dislocations and misunderstandings that continually influence the characters' experiences. The novel follows Archilde, the half-Salish protagonist of the novel who returns to the Flathead Reservation in western Montana after years away at an Oregon Indian boarding school. Torn between his white father's agricultural capitalism and his Salish mother's renewed interest in tribal traditions, Archilde eventually ends up in jail, suspected of murdering a game warden while hunting with his mother in the mountains. Partially based on McNickle's own experience growing up the child of a white father and Métis mother on the Flathead Reservation in St. Ignatius, Montana, *The Surrounded* became an attempt to convey, according to Dorothy R. Parker, "a deeply moving tragedy" of being "surrounded, by the mountains, by the old traditions, and by the white people's culture and institutions" (47). On a personal level, the novel became a way of reconciling his own personal history, including his relationship with his parents and his Native American identity. As Parker notes, the major revisions made in the novel between its initial and later drafts reflect McNickle's own growing concern over of his cultural heritage and Native American experience, land usage, and self-determination. While earlier drafts of the novel are set in the same location and involve the murder of the game warden, the final draft shifts to a more informed exploration of the historical conditions and experiences of the Salish tribe as well as McNickle's own precarious connections to both Salish and white American culture (40–42). Combining research on early Western frontier conducted at Columbia University, correspondence with the Flathead Agency, and his own experiences growing up on the Flathead Reservation (43), McNickle attempted to recover a history buried by decades of federal economic and cultural policies.

Appearing on the heels of the Indian Reorganization Act, the novel opens a space in which to examine the social and environmental effects of Manifest Destiny obscured by romanticized incantations of the frontier. For the Salish in the novel, the appearance of white settlers near the hunting grounds of the Salish begins a trajectory of development and changes that soon make clear to them that, as Modeste tells Archilde and others, "the people had lost their power" (McNickle 73). According to the Salish elder, the arrival of guns, followed by Christianity, leads to the dissolution of tribal traditions, and the lines indicating Salish cultural identity begin to grow fainter for each new generation. The brutal and vengeful conflict between tribes intensified by the introduction of guns causes the younger generation to believe "the world had always been bitter" (72). Similarly, the arrival of the mission and government boarding school leaves Archilde's generation disillusioned and apathetic regarding their tribal identity. As Archilde tells the group of tribal elders after recently returning to the reservation from Oregon, "If I had been born in the old days . . . then I would not be as I am now. You people talk about the old days as if they were here. But they're gone, dead" (63). Modeste agrees with him, telling the group, "[W]hat our children are like they cannot help. It began before their time'" (63). But if Archilde initially feels dislocated from Salish traditions while listening to Modeste's narrative, he also begins to experience a renewed interest in Salish experiences and culture that lessens his resistance to this part of his identity: "[He] felt something die within him. Some stiffness, some pride, went weak before the old man's bitter simple words" (McNickle 74). He continues, "He had heard the story many times, but he had not listened. It had tired him. Now he saw that it had happened and it left him feeling weak. It destroyed his stiffness toward the old people. He sat and thought about it and the flames shot upward and made light on the circle of black pines" (74). The effect of the firelight on the surrounding pines serves a dual purpose. On the one hand, it represents the illumination of a past from which Archilde feels estranged and cannot escape. But the lighted trees also allude to the containment of Salish culture and foreshadows Archilde's imprisonment at the end of the novel.

The mountains outside of town also create a similar ambivalent effect for Archilde. Joining his mother for a hunting excursion in the mountains before winter sets in, he begins to reconnect to traditional Salish attitudes towards the land. But he also experiences deeply set forms of control that infiltrate the undeveloped and isolated landscape. As they progress higher into the mountains, their movement is described as an attempt "to go backward in time rather than onward in mountain fastness" (116). In some ways, they succeed in recovering a sense of cultural heritage with their ancestors who had crossed "the mountains to hunt buffalo" (116). Archilde describes how his ancestors would have similarly experienced the "sway of the horse," the "warmth" of the "sun," and "the same aspect of tree and rock and mountain" (116). Later, when lying beneath the night sky, Archilde echoes the nascent connection he feels to earlier Salish hunters due to the shared generational experience offered by the wilderness landscape: "The sky was overladen with stars. If you looked closely there were stars in the grass as well—dew turned to ice on the tips of glass blades. . . . He heard the horses breathing and moaning in their sleep. They had lain down in a close group. Owl called to each other. This was as it would have been. Certainly the night had not changed with the years" (120).

But as Archilde continually discovers, the mountains' role in the experiences of the Salish have significantly changed. First, he notices that the mountains themselves are "empty of life," alluding to over-hunting in the area: "Games was scarce. After two days of riding they had not seen so much as a deer track. The mountains indeed were empty. If any creatures existed there they had gone into the blackest bowels of the mountain" (116). This change particularly affects Archilde when he comes across a full-grown buck and his family and finds that he cannot shoot them. The narrator informs us that Archilde doesn't shoot because of the lack of excitement and necessity that shooting a deer now invoked: "The excitement was in matching one's wits against animal cunning. The excitement was increased when a man kept himself from starving by his hunting skill. But lying in wait and killing, when no one's living depended on it, there was no excitement in that" (121). Archilde's refusal to shoot also suggests that he recognizes the harmful effects of current hunting practices, used by white hunters and the younger Salish. The narrative later emphasizes this latter reason after they encounter his brother, Louis. Bragging about shooting a "yearly doe" (124), Louis's actions point towards a growing unawareness of and/or disregard for the natural cycles that allow wild animals to propagate in wilderness areas.

The second change occurs in Archilde himself. His experiences in the mountains often echo the cultural disconnection he describes to Modeste. While reflecting on the night sky's significance in connecting him to his ancestors, Archilde's mind suddenly shifts to the city: "He saw the gleaming lights of a city, any city, with people moving, in the street, in large rooms—light and sound and smell of a different world. As soon as he thought of that he cared not what the mountains were like, either now or long ago. It came over him in a surge. This, his home, was a strange country" (120). Archilde's experiences of city life in Portland, Oregon, where he lived before returning to Montana, compel him to see the world much differently than his elders and ancestors. As McNickle understood, the effects of assimilation and urbanization in the West needed to be accounted for in attempts to understand the experiences and conditions of American Indians. This isn't to say that McNickle discounts the power of wilderness to rekindle a sense of Salish identity and connection to the land. Instead, he suggests that this must always be understood in relation to the changes and conditions initiated by the arrival of white settlers.

If white influence is felt in the emptiness of the mountains, changing attitudes towards game, and the allure of the city, it is also more directly felt in the physical presence of representatives of the white law. In the mountains, they encounter two figures that represent the reach and severity of this law. First, they meet Sheriff Quigley, who is looking for horse thieves like Louis hiding in the mountains. Though Quigley lets the mother and son pass after briefly questioning them, Archilde continues to feel his "sinister" presence throughout the hunting trip, especially after they later do encounter Louis. The second "arm of the law" is the game warden (124), who appears after Louis shoots the doe and tries to arrest them. Archilde protests that they are exempt from "all game laws by special treaty" (125), but the warden ignores him and tells them that they are under arrest. That Archilde protests the game law "though he really knew nothing about it" further attests to his disconnection from tribal history and politics, while the absence of "leniency in the voice" and actions of the game warden suggest the unbending power white institutions show towards indigenous populations (125). The situation further escalates when Louis argues in Salish with his mother about fleeing into the forest. The incident that follows results from miscommunication, which McNickle saw as informing many of the injustices experienced by American Indians. The narrator informs us, "He [the warden] didn't know that Louis was frightened and wanted to dash for the woods, and that the old lady was calling him a fool. 'Wipe your nose and get ready,' she was saying. To the game officer it sounded menacing and he watched them closely" (126). Though Louis plans to give up, the warden interprets his demeanor as menacing and shoots him when he grabs his rifle to pack it up. The warden's misreading of the situation leads to his own death, as Archilde's mother kills him with a hatchet blow to the head. It also leads to Archilde's eventual capture and prison sentence as the warden's suspected murderer. McNickle's use of the game warden not only represents white law but also suggests the role conservationist thought can play in discriminating against native populations. His refusal to consider the possible exemption the Salish have concerning game laws points towards the precariousness of Native American rights, including a right to work out their own fragile relationship to the wilderness and their past.

Because of the constraining and seemingly fatalistic forces alluded to by the firelight on the trees and depicted in the chain of events related to the game warden's death, critics have noted elements of literary naturalism in the novel. For Louis Owens, the naturalism of the novel is expressed through Archilde's inability to "understand much less order and control the world he inhabits" (247). But like other naturalist works of the 1930s, *The Surrounded* may not be as deterministic as Owens claims. While there appears to be little hope or promise in the deterministic political and cultural environment of Archilde and the other Salish characters in *The Surrounded*, the novel identifies a key problem McNickle sees underlying relationships in post frontier America: miscommunication. The lack of open, tolerant lines of communication between American Indians and white American settlers and government officials, exacerbated by waves of economic and cultural changes to Western landscapes and their inhabitants, helped lead to continual misunderstandings and conflict. As Parker notes, McNickle consistently returns to this question in each of his novels: "How do people communicate (or fail to do so) across cultural barriers when language itself, the basic tool of communication, derives from radically different modes of perception?" (225). This includes communication between whites and Native Americans as well as among Native Americans themselves, something McNickle would experience as an agent for the Bureau of Indian Affairs (BIA).

The social and environmental effects of miscommunication and cultural intolerance are further developed in a scene where Archilde encounters an emaciated mare and her colt while riding through a "wild and barren" fenceless area near St. Xavier referred to by residents as the "Badlands" (McNickle 236). Not only does the scene allude to the long history of miscommunication between white settlers and American Indians in the West, it also offers an interesting inversion of the relationship between whites and the Salish by putting Archilde in the shoes of his people's oppressors. The "grotesque" mare—"unbelievably thin and gaunt . . . [with] [e]very vertebrae . . . visible, even to the point where the rib was attached . . . [her] tangled mass of hair and mud which hung all the way to the ground . . . far too heavy for her to lift" (238)—fills Archilde with pity. But when he tries to capture and help her, he is surprised to find that she resists: "She would allow him to come within a few yards, nosing him all the time, then she would whirl awkwardly on her shaking legs and trot off. She stumbled frequently, tripping on her outgrowing hoofs, which were like shovels on her feet" (239). Archilde finally decides to chase her down and rope her but is again surprised by the mare's speed and determination to escape him. Resolute in his decision to capture her even though he knows she may die from the chase, Archilde's pity begins to take on a perverse logic: "Her dejection was his reward, she would not let him forget it" (240). He eventually ropes her, and the two create a grotesque image as he leads her away: "The sun had set and in the evening light a rider on a strong white horse led an unprotesting skeleton on a rope" (241). The mare soon falls over in exhaustion, and Archilde ends up shooting her "in a rage that was partly resentful at the unfairness of the whole episode and partly interrupted sleep" (242). He spends the rest of the night guarding "her worthless carcass" from coyotes (242).

Archilde's reaction to the mare acts as a counterpoint to the paternalistic Indian agent, Mr. Parker, who describes his job as "like moving into a ready-furnished house . . . overrun by domesticated animals which had to be fed and nursed, and you had no time for it if you were expected to keep the house from falling in on you" (McNickle 151). Both misrecognize themselves as protectors of nonhuman animals who they deem unable to look after themselves. Similarly, both Mr. Parker's reflections on his job and Archilde's experience of the mare call attention to a mortal stubbornness in the subjects they perceive themselves as helping. As the Indian agent continues, "[N]ot a few of the pets had died before your time and others threatened to die" (151–52). But for Mr. Parker, the Salish are domesticated and primarily a nuisance rather than any threat to white civilization. His use of the term "pets" particularly positions the Salish as unruly dogs and cats that stubbornly refuse their masters' commands, stripping them of human agency and value. For Archilde, on the other hand, the mare represents a wildness missing from Mr. Parker's domesticating vision. While Archilde's blindness in his encounter with the mare leads him to momentarily identify with the assumptions and aims of white civilization in their contact with American Indians on the frontier, it also highlights a wildness that moves beyond bestiality or primitiveness, instead illustrating traces of the autonomy and defiance the Salish are attempting to rekindle through a return to cultural traditions. As Archilde's mother, the first of the Salish to convert to Christianity, begins to realize, "She had lost something. She was pagan again. She who had once been called Faithful Catharine and who had feared hell for her sons and for herself—her belief and her fear alike had died in her" (173). She later subjects herself to a Salish whipping ceremony, outlawed by white settlers "as being too barbarous" (206), in order to relinquish Christianity and return to the old ways.

In addition to uncovering a sense of power that resists the domesticating forces of white civilization, the "Badlands" scene also unearths the environmental legacy and consequences of exploitive forms of frontier agriculture and the practice of allotment. The environmental changes caused by frontier agricultural practices, including dividing land not suitable for small scale farming into Native American allotments (Taylor 4), threaten the health of the land in McNickle's western Montana. While the worst of the storms associated with the Dust Bowl hit the lower plains in the Oklahoma-Texas-Kansas-Colorado panhandle region, much damage also occurred in the upper plains region in Montana and the Dakotas, leaving them "almost as arid as the Sonoran Desert" (Worster 11). McNickle's depiction of drought in St. Xavier suggests a similar situation: "Pastures were burned to a dull brown, hayfields yielded poorly, springs that had always been dependable dried up; not a drop of rain fell after the middle of May. The climax to the summer of misfortunes came, for one rancher at least, in the middle of the night toward the end of August, when ten stacks of wheat, waiting to be threshed, caught fire and burned to the last straw" (231). Overhearing the white ranchers discuss the situation, Archilde feels little sympathy for them. He reflects, "If they would walk through Indian town . . . they would see that one summer was like another. In years of abundance no less than in lean years, the Indians sat in their dark doorways with no expectations, looking out upon a world of meaningless coming and going" (232). As Timothy Egan notes, American Indians viewed drought during the period as punishment for white settlers' abuse to Native Americans and the land. He recounts a short anecdote about One Bull, nephew of Sitting Bull, offering to reverse the drought by lifting the curse of his uncle who believed that the land would avenge the mistreatment of his people by white settlers (123).[23] Archilde's response likewise suggests his understanding of drought as a consequence of the rancher's poor treatment of the Salish and their land.

If McNickle uses fiction to unearth traditional Salish attitudes towards land and culture and to help illustrate the need for more open lines of communication in the post-frontier West, he would also bring these understandings to his fieldwork and writing as an agent for the Bureau of Indian Affairs (BIA). McNickle joined the BIA after the passage of the Indian Reorganization Act in 1934, which marked a major transition for the agency as well as for federal policies towards American Indians. Under the direction of John Collier, the bureau attempted to create recognized forms of tribal autonomy and authority, particularly for tribes not formerly recognized by the US government. It also began increasing the amount of land owned by indigenous tribes by halting the government's practice, according to the dictates of the Dawes Act, of selling unallotted "surplus" land to whites (Parker 70). Hired by the agency in the hope that his Salish background might make him a more effective communicator with Native American tribes, McNickle worked with Métis living along the Canadian border in Montana and North Dakota, who due to their mixed racial and national heritage were not tribally recognized by the US federal government (68, 71). One particularly important contribution McNickle made in his work with the BIA was recognizing and advocating for the importance of training field agents in anthropology, which would provide them tools to better understand and help communicate with different Native Americans tribes (73–74).

This isn't to say that the New Deal-era BIA did not rely on and help circulate romantic understandings of tribal and frontier life. Unlike Collier, who envisioned the bureau establishing, according to Parker, "an ideal human community grounded on nonmaterial values that would somehow emerge from within the community itself" (Parker 75), McNickle recognized the improbability of this romantic and somewhat mystical vision. While he tended to support Collier's reforms as "moving in the right direction" (76), he was ultimately skeptical of the top-down policies originating from paternalistic, white New Dealers.[24] Recognizing the historical development of former frontier land and experiences of indigenous groups, as well as the fact that many of the latter weren't interested in returning to the tradition of their ancestors due to their assimilation into American life, McNickle believed in a more nuanced form of Native American self-autonomy. As his biographer, Dorothy Parker, explains, "If Indian people chose to maintain tribal identity and tradition, he would fight to help them keep their land and culture. If they chose to assimilate into white society, he would assist them in achieving that goal as well. The obligation was to ensure freedom of choice, not the forced continuance of some mystical 'community' as the ultimate hope of Western people" (76). Graham Taylor also notes McNickle's difference from other BIA agents in recognizing the importance of giving tribes a dominant role in solving the major issues facing

Native Americans during the period (116). For McNickle, returning a sense of self-determination to indigenous groups would create more democratic forms of community—messier yet more realistic than the communities Turner roots in American frontier experience.

Not only did the New Deal attempt to reverse decades of federal policy towards American Indians to help restore a greater sense of self-determination and autonomy, it also attempted to provide them greater access and control of former frontier lands in the West. If drought and dust storms left white farmers in a precarious economic situation, it ended up benefitting some tribes who were given land bought by the US government in the Land Utilization Project. Created to restore unprofitable or poorly treated agricultural lands across the US to combat soil erosion, the Project led to the government acquiring 11.3 million acres, most of them in the plains. Some of this land was given to Native American tribes who, uninterested in farming, would restore the grass to the land and eventually use the land for grazing livestock (Worster 190–91, Egan 256).

Robert Marshall, the socialist reformer and wilderness activist mentioned at the beginning of this section, also worked for Collier at the BIA. His job encompassed three interrelated areas of the new BIA policy on land redistribution, first by helping tribes gain back lands with timber resources that could be used to create Native American-owned logging ventures. He also worked with American Indians to help curb overgrazing on their lands and to restore wildlife in areas on or near reservations that they had traditionally relied on to survive (Glover 161). Though Marshall was sometimes overconfident in the tribal compromises he helped broker (171), he tended to encourage tribes to work out their own solutions and listen to concerns they had with the proposals he made (169–70, 204–205). That said, his attempts to secure large wilderness preservation areas in and around reservations, often without tribal input, became one of his more controversial moves as part of the BIA. For Marshall, preserving wilderness on reservations would help Native Americans protect cultural values and traditions by allowing them *some* venue of escape from the influence and containment practices of white developers (Catton 59–60). While his actions sought to safeguard Native American cultural heritage and land use, his oversight in not confiding his plans to members of the tribe placed him more in line with the liberal paternalism of Collier than the grassroots approach of McNickle (Sutter 228–29). If McNickle sees wilderness as an often-fraught space for Native Americans to reestablish a sense of identity and place at odds with the modern world, he would probably agree with Marshall that wilderness protection could and should play a large role in creating, rediscovering, and maintaining a closer relationship to the land and its inhabitants. Archilde does find value and a sense of identity during his time in the mountains, even if these aspects are quickly threatened by the presence of Sheriff Quigley and the game warden. But McNickle also suggests the importance of understanding the influence of other landscapes on his character, including the agricultural landscape of Archilde's father and the urban landscape of Archilde's recent past.

Despite the "Indian New Deal's" attempt to help American Indians regain control over decisions related to cultural identity and land use, its efforts were short-lived. By the mid-to-late 1940s, land reclamations projects by the US government slowed down, leading only to the acquisition of 11.3 million acres of the originally proposed 75 million (Worster 190). The new direction of Collier's Bureau of Indian Affairs also soon ended as it continuously came under attack by groups like the American Indian Federation (AIF), an organization begun in 1934 made up of economically prosperous, assimilated Indians, conservative Protestant Christianized Indians, and more radical proponents of self-autonomy extremely suspicious of the BIA. The AIF saw in the bureau "an atheist-communist international conspiracy" (77), especially coming down hard on McNickle for a favorable review he published in the bureau's journal *Indians at Work* on Oliver La Farge's *The Enemy Gods*, a novel they viewed as un-Christian (Parker 76–80). The BIA's New Deal phase began to fizzle out towards the end of the decade, and Collier officially resigned in January of 1945. McNickle stayed on at the bureau until 1952, trying to curb its decline but was unsuccessful due to a declining budget and general congressional lack of interest (110). As McNickle and other Native American activists of the period would learn, the romantic strain of the frontier held a powerful sway over the American imagination. Attempts to critique or reinterpret this strain by pointing towards the scars that frontier practices and policies left on people and land led to a cultural and political backlash further fueled by the communist "witch hunts" of congressmen like Martin Dies and Joseph McCarthy in 1930s, '40s, and '50s. *The Surrounded* would also fail to garner much in terms of sales and exposure. Though critics generally enjoyed the novel, considering it a more accurate portrayal of Native American experience than most books on the subject, the novel sold poorly in the precarious economic climate of the era and quickly went out of print (Parker 56). Despite its lack of financial success and limited availability, the novel too became a smudge on the palimpsest of frontier history. The University of New Mexico Press would republish *The Surrounded* in 1978, introducing the novel to a new generation of American Indian writers and activists interested in building upon its revision of frontier history (56). McNickle, too, would go on to serve as program director and help develop the Center for American Indian and Indigenous Studies at the Newberry Library in Chicago from 1971 until his death in 1977 (239–40). The center, now bearing McNickle's name, was created as a resource for Native Americans to recover and tell their own history (241).

While forms of economic development and cultural hegemony often work to erase alternative forms of social and environmental interactions, they are never fully successful in doing so. As in Turner's "palimpsest," traces of early experiences, traditions, and land use are always present, even if only faintly visible. For McNickle, frontier relations and landscapes offered an archive through which to uncover the history of the American West from history and perspectives of American Indians. In both *The Surrounded* and his work with the BIA, McNickle used this act of recovery to help American Indians regain power and autonomy. Though the novel failed to attract public attention and the new direction of the BIA was short-lived, McNickle continued chipping away at the romantic narrative of the frontier through fiction, research, and activism. His efforts would influence later generations of Native American authors and activists to reinterpret the social, cultural, and environmental effects of frontier practices and offer an alternative history of the American West.

Conclusion

The conservation of wilderness spaces played an important role in literary works and films during the 1930s and '40s. Unlike earlier conservationists, Disney, Leopold, Faulkner, Hemingway, and McNickle attempted to create new forms of identification with wilderness spaces and their inhabitants that moved beyond seeing them in terms of economic or recreational value. Instead, these authors and filmmakers highlighted ways that wilderness could establish potential sites where the relationships between humans and the larger biotic community could be strengthened. In many cases, they created social forms of conservationist thought that also took into account the effects of wilderness destruction on human groups, including racialized "others" that depended on these spaces both for physical and cultural survival. But as McNickle and others recognized, the burgeoning environmental ideas forming out of conservationist thought during the period were not just confined to wilderness areas. As the remaining chapters argue, they also appear in depression-era depictions of, and debates over, rural and urban landscapes as well as the role of technology in American society.

Chapter 2

Back to the Land

By the mid-1930s, the rural-to-urban migration patterns of the previous decade stalled as more Americans stayed on or returned to farms (Worster 48). From the New Deal's agricultural and homestead programs to the Southern Agrarians' critique of encroaching industrialism in the South, there was a resurgence of interest in the rural as a solution to the economic woes of the Great Depression. This resurgence appealed to a residual Jeffersonian pastoralism, a myth articulated in the nineteenth century as the "garden of the world." According to Henry Nash Smith, the "garden" as a "master symbol" that conveyed "fecundity, growth, increase, and blissful labor in the earth, all centering about the heroic figure of the idealized frontier farmer" captured the "assumptions and aspirations" of a rapidly developing and expanding American society (123–24). Likewise, the rural myth promised depression-era unemployed workers disenchanted with a stalling industrial and urban-focused economic system an alternative future of abundance, self-reliance, and community.[1]

But the period's residual pastoralism also led to an awareness of major tensions obscured by agricultural work. Not only did conservationists, political leaders, and authors begin to recognize the garden myth's culpability in creating the conditions that lead to widespread flooding and dust storms in the 1920s and '30s,[2] they also highlighted the harsh life often associated with agriculture as well as the racial and economic hierarchies underlying many rural communities. Nowhere were the difficulties and inequities of rural life more apparent during the period than in the American South. Decades of primitive farming and hunting practices in the region led to severe soil erosion, wild animal depletions, and the development of soil toxins and parasites, while the use of slavery and sharecropping exacerbated economic and racial inequalities.[3]

In this chapter, I argue that authors of the 1930s and '40s responded to the period's residual pastoralism in ways that exposed important tensions in rural agriculture and social life. They also, in some cases, envisioned alternative environmental and social relationships rooted in different understandings of the land and its inhabitants—both human and nonhuman. In doing so, this chapter covers similar ground as Christopher Rieger's important work in *Clear-Cutting Eden: Ecology and the Pastoral in Southern Literature*. As Rieger argues, some depression-era southern writers "reject the static, passive conception of nature implied in the traditional pastoral garden, where humans are above nature, controlling and shaping it at will." Instead, they develop what he calls "ecopastorals" that position "people and their environments in reciprocal relationships" and "more consciously intertwine representations of nature with issues of class, race, and gender" (7). Like Rieger, I see southern authors during the period depicting, critiquing, and/or envisioning new forms of the pastoral mode. What follows reiterates *and* extends Rieger's analysis to describe the unsustainable violence underlying traditional uses of pastoralism, while also identifying forms of ecology and environmental justice underlying alternative uses of the mode.

In the first section of the chapter, I focus on the appropriation of the garden myth in literature and film of the period about the American South. For authors John Crowe Ransom and William Alexander Percy and filmmakers William Wyler and Victor Fleming, the plantation system of the "old" South created a sacred bond between humans and the land. The second section of the chapter identifies ways that other depression-era southern authors expose the economic, racial, and/or anthropocentric violence underlying the forms of agriculture championed by Ransom and others. For Erskine Caldwell and Richard Wright, the myths surrounding antebellum southern life ignore major forms of environmental, economic, and racial violence perpetuated by sharecropping. While Caldwell and Wright create "antipastorals" that critique the pastoral myths associated with agrarian thought in the South, Zora Neale Hurston envisions alternative relationships between humans and landscapes in rural areas. In the third section of the chapter, I identify ways that Hurston's depictions of black folklore model more inclusive and sustainable social and environmental forms of rural life.

Like the wilderness, rural landscapes are often thought to inherently support closer relationships between the human and nonhuman world, particularly as opposed to cities or other built environments. This noncritical form of pastoralism ignores the negative effects that modern farming can have on rural ecologies and social structures. As Raymond Williams observes in *The Country and the City*, "It is important to remember how much damage to the environment was and is being done by the capitalist mode of progressive agriculture; this is not a crisis of manufacturing industry alone" (301). But Williams also sees "some rural writers" as informing our understanding of "the complexity of the living natural environment" (300). This chapter seeks a similar dialectical view of pastoralism: to contribute to the critique of simplistic understandings of rural life while highlighting residual and emerging environmentalist values at work in rural cultures during the 1930s and '40s.[4] African American authors during the period particularly recognized the destructive and creative capabilities of pastoralism in the American South.[5] In describing ways that depression-era black authors critiqued reactionary forms of human-nature relationships while envisioning new forms of these relationships, *The Green Depression* contributes to recent scholarship that sees African American literary works as directly engaged with environmental ideas.

Plantation Pastoralism

While southern plantation owners in the mid-nineteenth century tended to consider the "garden myth" as naïve, arguing that working the land did not bring one closer to the soil or produce more free-minded citizens (Smith 143–44), the garden became a popular pastoral symbol of the American South during the 1930s as a response to economic crisis, encroaching industrialism, and the rise of southern progressive thought. The Southern Agrarians' 1930 collection of essays, *I'll Take My Stand*, set the tone for the decade's use of the garden myth to valorize southern agricultural life and propone it as an alternative to the economic and environmental precariousness of the industrial North. In their opening "Statement of Principles," the Agrarians collectively support agrarianism as an alternative social and economic system: "The theory of agrarianism is that the culture of the soil is the best and most sensitive of vocations, and that therefore it should have the economic preference and enlist the maximum number of workers" (xlvii). In the collection's first essay, "Reconstructed but Unregenerate," John Crowe Ransom develops the theory's potential to create more spiritual and sustainable relationships to the land in ways that often appeal to the garden myth. He writes, "[The agrarian] identifies himself with a spot of ground, and this ground carries a good deal of meaning; it defines itself for him as nature. He would till it not too hurriedly and not too mechanically to observe in it the contingency and the infinitude of nature; and so his life acquires its philosophical and even its cosmic consciousness" (19–20). In contrast to the spiritual values he associates with southern agriculture, Ransom identifies what he refers to as northern "science" and "progress," leading to "an unrelenting war" on nature (7). The result, he goes on to say, is that "[n]ature wears out man before man can wear out nature" (9).

Other authors and filmmakers from the period also appeal to the garden myth to venerate the agrarian values they associate with the South. In his popular 1941 autobiography *Lanterns on the Levee*, Mississippi planter and poet William Alexander Percy uses similar rhetoric and imagery to describe sharecropping "as humane, just, self-respecting, and cheerful a method of earning a living as human beings are likely to devise" (280). Pitying "the telephone girls, the clerks in chain stores, the office help, the unskilled laborers everywhere . . . for their poor and fixed wages . . . their slave routine, their joyless habits of work, and their insecurity," he exalts "the limber-jointed, oily-black, well-fed, decently clothed peasants on [his family's plantation] Trail Lake" (280).[6] Even depression-era Hollywood films set in the antebellum and/or early postbellum South appeal to similar pastoral imagery in order to venerate the agrarian legacy of the "old" South. As Edward D. C. Campbell Jr. argues, the popularity of cultural works depicting nostalgic views of rural life in the South lay in their ability to offer depression-era audiences a "sense of wealth and ease which was vicariously experienced and eagerly accepted as proof that the nation had its moments of prosperity" (74). He writes, "That the image was historically untrue or that the contemporary agricultural South suffered miserably throughout the Depression could be momentarily forgotten amid the splendor of *Gone with the Wind's* counterargument . . . that the ruination of the old way constituted the destruction of much that was good" (76). Victor Fleming's 1939 film version of Margaret Mitchell popular novel *Gone with the Wind* depicts an idyllic southern landscape from the moment the film begins. The opening credits roll over a series of pastoral postcard-like shots of life and land in the antebellum South—including rustic fence posts and magnolia trees drenched in the light of dusk, listless clouds floating across a technicolor blue sky, a pasture where horses lazily eat and wander about, a river steadily rolling in the moonlight, trees of countless pink and white flowers, and an old water mill. We also see shots of African American slaves contentedly hoeing, picking crops, and laboring at other daily tasks while white southerners leisurely row on a pond. The series of postcards ends with a painted backdrop of Tara, the O'Hara family's house and land, which will serve as a symbol for the beauty and glory of the antebellum South throughout the film. Soon after the credits end, Gerald O'Hara tells his daughter

Scarlett, "Do you mean to tell me, Katie Scarlett O'Hara, that Tara, that land doesn't mean anything to you? Why, land is the only thing in the world worth working for, worth fighting for, worth dying for, because it's the only thing that lasts." In arguing for the endurance, beauty, and deliberateness of southern land, the Agrarians and others reimagined it as a garden that needed protection and/or renewal in the face of an encroaching modernity. In laying bare the precariousness and destruction of the industrial and financial system, the Great Depression offered agrarians and rural enthusiasts an ideal moment to critique northern "science" and "progress."

But the nostalgic depictions of the "old" South by depression-era southern apologists overlooks the real conditions of agricultural workers and land in the region. As Reiger argues, their "theoretical model for relating to the natural world" is often marred by an "overt romanticizing of the past and propagandizing for racial hierarchy" (5). First, these authors indiscriminately slip between the garden myth and what Henry Nash Smith calls the "plantation" myth. For Smith, antebellum southern planters used the plantation myth to create a "pastoral tradition and feudal romance" that stressed "the beauty of harmonious social relations in an orderly feudal society" (151). To create this more leisurely experience, planters distanced themselves from agricultural labor by situating themselves at the top of a feudalistic social order. As mentioned above, antebellum plantation owners often criticized early proponents of the Homestead Act because they considered the latter's conception of agricultural labor naïve (Smith 143–44). While extolling the virtues of working on the land in "Reconstructed but Unregenerate," Ransom often slips into an appeal for the plantation, as when eulogizing the feudal "squirearchy" of the pre-Civil War plantation where "relations were personal and friendly" and "people were for the most part in their right places" (14). His defense of slavery, a system he calls "monstrous enough in theory but, more often than not, humane in practice" (14), further contradicts the value he places on working the land by positioning the plantation owner far away from direct contact with the soil.

Though purporting to use the garden myth to support a leisurely graciousness towards the land and its inhabitants, the Agrarians and Percy primarily use these myths in a power struggle against encroaching political, cultural, and economic interests in the South. John Fekete has argued, the Agrarians' "deep mystification of the Southern past" relied on a "*culture of control* involving the social, political, and ideological aspects necessary for dominating black slaves and keeping non-slave-owning whites in line" (58, 59). Michael Kreyling agrees: "[T]he Agrarians produced the South in the same way that all historically indigenous social elites produce ideological realities: out of strategies for seizing and retaining power (cultural, political, sexual, economic, and so on) that are then reproduced as 'natural'" (6). As both Fekete and Kreyling suggest, the Agrarians' arguments were less about protecting the environment than in protecting the planter's top position in the hierarchy of the South. To position themselves as an alternative to industrialism and an emergent political progressiveness in southern intellectual thought, the Agrarians fashioned a conception of the southern social and environmental relations based upon a "natural" order beyond human control.[7] They based this order, as Kreyling notes, on a metaphysical binary separation of the divine and natural from the human and artificial (Kreyling 10–11). In fashioning a divinely given South, the Agrarians turned southern history, culture, race relations, agricultural practices, and economics into "natural" products. Since these products were "natural," according to the Agrarians, then they must be "good" or "right" and should be protected from human meddling, particularly those seeking to bring science and industry as well as economic and racial equality to the South.

But in using the garden and plantation "myths" to give "historical intention a natural justification" and make "contingency appear eternal" (Barthes 142), the Agrarians and other "old" South apologists supported an unsustainable system of land cultivation. Their mythic view of the southerner's relationship to the land showed little understanding of the environmental consequences of the antebellum period's agricultural practices. Relying on monocultures of cotton and corn row crops, continuously clearing new lands and abandoning the old, allowing livestock to graze on fallow land, and overhunting wild areas to supply the region's bulk of food led to severe ecological effects (Cowdrey 76–80). If the Agrarians ignored or were unaware of the ecological consequences of southern agriculture, they certainly accepted and valued the social and environmental violence underlying its practices. For them, violence becomes the means through which to protect the southerner's relationship to nature and the social hierarchy necessary to sustain this relationship. In "Remarks on the Southern Religion," Allen Tate argues that southern tradition is a "fact that must be constantly defended" through the "violence" of reactionary politics (163, 174–75). For Tate, "radical" conservative politics is a violent act used in "cutting away the outgrowth and getting back to the roots" (175). Conservative southerners must hack away at the outgrowth they deem excessive to create a cultural, political, and physical landscape that protects the southern values and hierarchies the Agrarians associate with the antebellum South.

In the work of the depression-era's plantation tradition, the "violence" applauded by Tate underlies two major tropes. In the first trope, a precarious southern landscape must be conquered and maintained by violent force. In *Lanterns on the Levee*, Percy depicts uncultivated nature as a vicious struggle for physical nourishment and survival. Viewing the southern garden as a "fight for sunlight waged by those unhappy things rooted against their will in the shade," he goes on to describe the consequences of letting plants battle without intervention: "They thrust emaciated feelers, gangling and scant of leaf, toward a spot of light. To escape the deeper shadow they twist themselves into ungainliness. Branches die so that the remnant whole may survive. They are bleached as by a sickroom. They seem to have lost not only their beauty but their dignity in straining for the golden warmth that is the source of their life" (334). The comparison between the southern garden and southern society becomes more explicit as he goes on to compare the battle-scarred plants to the southerners he sees in town: "the passers-by, sickly, out of shape, ugly with strain, who still search for the sunlight vital to their needs and never found, or found and lost" (334). Though he applauds the harsh struggle that makes southerners stronger and "so glad of life" (334), the paternalism and disdain he shows to black and poor white southerners alike illustrates the planter class's role in shaping the growth of life in the South.

The importance of controlling a precarious and violent nature is also alluded to in the title of Percy's autobiography, which refers to a practice associated with levee security on the Mississippi River. Of the Mississippi, he writes, "Every few years it rises like a monster from its bed and pushes over its banks to vex and sweeten the land it has made" (3). For Percy, the river both threatens and replenishes the land southerners depend on. A representative of "savage nature and austere beauty" (13), the river constantly refutes human attempts to understand and control it:

> Man draws near to it, fights it, uses it, curses it, loves it, but it remains remote, unaffected. Between the fairy willows of the banks or the green slopes of the levees it moves unhurried and unpausing; building islands one year to eat them the next; gnawing the bank on one shore till the levee caves in and another must be built farther back, then veering wantonly and attacking with equal savagery the opposite bank. (13–14)

Lanterns on the Levy specifically refers to the practice of patrolling the levees to discover "boils," described by Percy as "small geyser[s] at the base or on the berm of the levee, on the land side" created "by the river's pressure fingering out some soft stratum in the soil of the levee or by a crawfish hole" (246). If not spotted, boils grow larger, eventually leading to breaks in the levee.

For Percy, the failure of levees during floods, particularly the Great Mississippi Flood of 1927, creates a state of emergency and chaos that reinforces a second major trope in the work of southern apologists during the period. This trope involves the use or threat of violence against southern African Americans to maintain racial and economic hierarchies in the South. This violence is justified through social and cultural practices that dehumanize African Americans by depicting them as childlike beasts of burden and/or violent predators. These exploitive uses of violence are depicted in Zora Neale Hurston's *Their Eyes Were Watching God* and Richard Wright's "Down by the Riverside" when powerful storms threaten the precarious environmental and social order created by southern whites, and African Americans are conscripted into levee protection, rescue, and cleanup (Green 112–13). In doing so, the latter bear the brunt of a regime made even more savage and authoritarian by the breakdown of the white southern planter's sense of control. Janie Crawford, the protagonist of Hurston's most famous novel, warns her husband Tea Cake, "Dey's [white people] grabbin' all de menfolks dey kin git dey hands on and makin' 'em help bury de dead" (Hurston 169). Tea Cake ignores her warning and ends up conscripted into a work gang of blacks and poor whites, forced at gunpoint to separate and bury the white and black dead bodies. After Mann, Richard Wright's protagonist in "Down by the Riverside," gets his family to the hospital by rowboat during a severe flood, soldiers immediately order him to help at the levees. When Mann protests from extreme exhaustion and grief (his wife dies on the journey), a soldier replies, "Aw, c mon, nigger! What in hells wrong with you? All the rest of the niggers are out there, how come you don't want to go?" (301). Even Percy describes the police ransacking the African American section of town to find workers to unload a ship with Red Cross provisions and shooting an African American resident for refusing to comply.

To justify their violent treatment of African Americans in the South, white southerners ascribe them with bestial characteristics kept in check by slavery and sharecropping. As Paul Outka argues, "the figure of the beast" became the most commonly used trope in the postbellum period "to negate the manifest humanity of 'black people and to 'purify' whiteness/humanity of any identity with blackness/nature" (136). Faulkner recognizes and depicts the deluded perception supported by the trope at the end of *Go Down, Moses*'s "Pantaloon in Black." In the story, a deputy justifies the lynching of Rider, a black sawmill worker accused of killing a white man named Birdsong, by describing African Americans as "devoid of normal human feelings and sentiments . . . [as] a damn herd of wild buffaloes" (Faulkner 147). For Christina Culvin, the deputy's conception of Rider as less-than-human leaves him unable to recognize that "grief, confusion, and outrage over his wife's death" help lead Rider to kill Birdsong (97)—not to mention the latter's long history of cheating black workers at dice. While Faulkner depicts the delusional nature of the trope, Percy shows little hesitation in using the trope to defend traditional hierarchies in the South. He sees environmental states of emergency, racial hatred by poor whites, and northern progressive thought as all threatening to keep southern blacks from exhibiting "the most beautiful manners in the world" and revert them into a savageness he sees as the race's natural state (286). He writes,

> Apparently there is something peculiarly Negroid in the Negro's attitude toward, and aptitude for, crimes of violence. He seems to have resisted, except on the surface, ethics and to have rejected our standards. Murder, thieving, lying, violence—I sometimes suspect the Negro doesn't regard these as crimes or sins, or even as regrettable occurrences. He commits them casually, with no apparent feeling of guilt. White men similarly delinquent become soiled or embittered or brutalized. Negroes are as charming after as before a crime. Committing criminal acts, they seem never to be criminals. (299)

Though Percy attributes "the disgraceful riots and lynchings gloated over and exaggerated by Negrophiles the world over" to poor whites in the South, his omission of "man" and "human" to refer to African Americans in this passage also enacts forms of violence against southern blacks by caricaturing them as wild animals to be broken and tamed into servile and more profitable workers. In his use of the reversion metaphor, Percy also appeals to a common white response to black empowerment in the aftermath of the Civil War: that black self-autonomy would result in the race's de-evolution into "a supposedly original primitive state" (Outka 137). The use of caricature, for Percy and other planters, sought to protect "the production of wealth" in the South by reducing racial violence and, in turn, the outward migration of black sharecroppers to northern cities (Wise 118).

Like the Southern Agrarians and Percy, Hollywood films of the 1930s also depict the vulnerability of southern landscapes directly before, during, and after the Civil War. As *Gone with the Wind*'s Scarlett O'Hara begins to understand the importance of the land and the power it gives her, she promises to protect it through violence. In one of the most seminal scenes of the film, Scarlett returns to Tara to find her mother dead, her father insane, and her crops and livestock either stolen or burned. While the scene ascribes violence against the landscape to northern aggression, her response begins to resituate violence as a southern response to the precariousness and chaos of the unkempt landscape. Digging what appears to be a carrot out of the scorched ground, she vows, "As God is my witness, as God is my witness, they're not going to lick me. I'm going to live through this and when it's all over, I'll never be hungry again. No, nor any of my folks. If I have to lie, steal, cheat or kill. As God as my witness, I'll never be hungry again." That this scene concludes the first half of the film by directly preceding the intermission makes it an important counterpart to the pastoral postcard-like images in the opening credits. The scorched land of Tara obscures the real violence perpetrated on southern soil and residents, particularly African Americans, by antebellum practices that would continue as white southerners regained power after Reconstruction.

The film also adds another problematic layer of symbolization in southern uses of the garden and plantation myths by gendering land. The use of the southern genteel female body to symbolize land in the South appeals to what Annette Kolodny calls one of "America's oldest and most cherished fantasy." For Kolodny, the "land-as-woman symbolization" obscures the physical violence behind the domestication of wilderness land by envisioning the latter as a "realm of nurture, abundance, and unalienated labor within which all men are truly brothers" (4). In *Gone with the Wind*, the symbolization is often illustrated through attacks on Scarlett's body. Like the carefully cultivated southern landscape represented by Tara, Scarlett's body is first depicted as a landscape of beauty and abundance vulnerable to violent attack. Her body comes under attack three times during the film. Shortly after the intermission ends, Scarlett encounters one of the Union soldiers who presumably helped destroy Tara. When he attempts to rob and rape her, she shoots him, steals his gold, and (together with Melanie) buries the body. Next, her body comes under attack by lower-class whites. After rebuilding her fortune by investing in a sawmill, another industry that would decimate the southern landscape, she is almost raped again while passing a shantytown in her carriage. Big Frank, a former black slave at Tara, saves Scarlett from the two unidentified lower-class men, and Ashley and Scarlett's first husband, Frank Kennedy, raid the shantytown in revenge. While the first two threats to her body come from outsiders, the last one comes from her husband, Rhett Butler. Here, the symbolic representation of Scarlett's body shifts from cultivated land to unruly wilderness. Unlike previous attempts, Rhett succeeds in raping Scarlett, and, in a moment of unmistakable misogyny, the film supports his "right" to do so. In the film's logic, Scarlett's wildness and defiance pose a problem for the southern man. Like the wilderness that southern planters must tame and cultivate, women also serve as a landscape to dominate and domesticate.

William Wyler's contemporaneous film *Jezebel* (1938) also uses the southern aristocratic female to symbolize the southern land in similar ways. Though much of the film takes place in New Orleans and the scenes that do take place in the country often take place in or around the plantation house, the film's use of the female body exhibits attitudes toward the land and the Southern values and manners it represents. In the film, southern belle Julie Marsden (Bette Davis) continually attempts to provoke and upstage her New Orleans banker fiancé, Preston "Pres" Dillard (Henry Fonda), to get him to discipline her. Pres is often chided by others for not physically disciplining Julie. Even Julie seems disappointed when, in response to one of her provocations, he brings a cane to her room and doesn't use it. Her actions eventually lead Pres to end the engagement, and he soon leaves New Orleans to conduct business in the North. After marrying a northern woman, Pres returns to New Orleans and visits Julie's family at their plantation outside of the city. During his stay, Julie tries to make him jealous by overly flirting with Buck Cantrell, a friend of the family who is a staunch defender of southern manners and an avid duelist. Julie makes one final pass at Pres but is rejected. In revenge, she falsely tells Buck that Pres made a pass at her. To defend her honor—and the honor of the "old" South from the encroaching industrialism represented by Pres (who wants to build a railroad through the South)—Buck challenges Pres's younger brother, Ted, to a duel, Pres having gone back to New Orleans on business. After Ted unexpectedly kills Buck in the duel, the family learns that Pres has yellow fever, which has overtaken the city. To make amends for her actions, Julie decides to accompany Pres to an island being used to quarantine the sick.

Despite the misogynistic overtones it shares with *Gone with the Wind*, *Jezebel* is somewhat more critical in its representation of the "old" South. While depictions of Scarlett and Julie shift between wild and cultivated female bodies that southern men are expected to domesticate and/or protect, *Jezebel* is more critical of the southern manners and customs Julie represents by somewhat siding with the more progressive views of Pres. Pres is attempting to modernize the South through the railroad and foresees the end of slavery. When dining with Julie and her family after his return, he warns them against war with the North. In response, Julie deliberately tries to start an argument between him and Buck over the future of the South. Contrasting Pres's levelheadedness and progressive ideas with Julie's vindictive jealousy and Buck's simpleminded southern patriotism, the film seems to critique aspects of the "old" South that *Gone with the Wind* idealizes. *Jezebel* also takes a slightly more nuanced view on slavery. While the film relies on the same stereotypes of master-slave relations as many other cultural depictions of the antebellum South, particularly in its portrayal of happy slaves singing for the entertainment of their white owners, its depictions of the effects of yellow fever show the equal vulnerability of white and black southerners to disease and death. Towards the end of the film, we see wagons carrying both white and black victims of the fever to burial and quarantine sites—though we are left to wonder whether the bodies will be segregated during burial, as in the case of Tea Cake's experience in *Their Eyes Were Watching God*.

While the shots of white and black victims of yellow fever being carted off together at the end of *Jezebel* perhaps begin to question ways that depression-era southern pastoralists dehumanize racial others in their use of the garden myth, other authors of the period more explicitly critiqued simplistic depictions of agricultural life in the South. If Ransom, Percy, and other authors and filmmakers depict the environmental, cultural, and spiritual connections fostered by plantation forms of southern agriculture, Erskine Caldwell and Richard Wright invert these pastoral myths to uncover the environmental, economic, and/or racial violence supporting them. Zora Neale Hurston also critiques Ransom and company's use of the garden myth while envisioning new forms of southern ecological and social relationships that include human groups and animal species typically left out of idyllic visions of rural life.

The Southern "Antipastoral"

While Ransom and Percy depict southern agriculture as a pursuit of gracious and paternalistic stewardship, other descriptions of depression-era agriculture reveal a less idyllic picture. As Benjamin Wise notes in response to Percy's valorization of sharecropping: "Although the average Delta plantation in 1934 earned over $8,000 a year, the average tenant farmer's net cash income was just over $100. Delta tenant farmers, 90 percent of whom were African American, were on the whole malnourished, unsatisfied, desperately poor producers of a fickle crop that brought wealth to some and poverty to most involved with it" (256). According to Robin D. G. Kelley, the landscape of rural Alabama black sharecroppers "made the poverty-stricken streets of Birmingham look like a paradise" (34). Black sharecroppers faced continual debt and impoverished living conditions. Kelley writes, "Landowners furnished entire families with poorly constructed one- or two-room shacks, usually without running water or adequate sanitary facilities. Living day-to-day on a diet of 'fat back,' beans, molasses, and cornbread, most southern tenants suffered from nutritional deficiencies—pellagra and rickets were common diseases in the black belt" (35). Overlooking the squalid conditions of the black men, women, and children scratching out a living on white-owned land further allowed Percy and others to project a subhuman status upon African Americans.[8]

Not only did southern sharecropping after the Civil War lead to poor economic conditions for African American tenants, it also heavily contributed to the environmental degradation of soils due to planters and bankers only allowing tenants to plant "cash crop" monocultures like cotton. Postbellum systems of agriculture like sharecropping led to the full ascendency of cotton monoculture in the South. While there were examples of diversification and advances in fertilizers to treat exhausted soil, only the most prosperous landowners could afford them (Cowdrey 107, Smith 71). Besides the economic inaccessibility of more sustainable forms of agriculture, there was little incentive for non-landowning tenants to use these more difficult and time-consuming practices. While African American leaders like Booker T. Washington and W. E. B. Du Bois recognized that sharecropping allowed African Americans more autonomy than slavery, they realized that the system did not provide black sharecroppers with the means or power to practice more "responsible, careful farming" (K. Smith 82). Instead of adopting advances in agricultural and conservationist thought, many farmers continued using the methods and crops handed down to them by tradition and/or economic necessity.

Perhaps no novel of the 1930s depicts the mistreatment of land as a product of inherited agricultural practices and economic disparity more explicitly than Erskine Caldwell's *Tobacco Road* (1932). For Christopher Reiger, Caldwell's novel develops an "antipastoral" depiction of southern agriculture that "dismantles the pastoral convention of an independent yeoman farmer working in harmony with the land" (23). In the novel, Jeeter Lester, a Georgia sharecropper, refuses to leave his Georgia farm for the more prosperous cotton mills in Augusta: "The restless movement of the other tenant farmers to the mills had never had any effect on Jeeter. Working in cotton mills might be alright for some people, he said, but as for him, he would rather die of starvation than leave the land" (62). Suggesting Jeeter's stubbornness is the result of "an inherited love of the land" (62), the novel places the blame for the inability of Georgian farmers to raise profitable crops on the continual passing down and use of unsustainable methods of farming. According to the novel's narrator, "The soil had become depleted by the constant raising of cotton year after year, and it was impossible to secure a yield of more than a quarter of a bale to the acre. More and more guano was poured into the fields, and faster and faster was it washed away through the loose sandy soil before the cotton plants were able to reach it" (59).[9] Jeeter even destroys his only other means to make money, selling timber for lumber and firewood, by following the tradition of burning his field every spring to kill boll weevils. The narrator informs us,

> That was the reason they gave for burning the woods and fields, whenever anybody asked why they did not stop burning pine seedlings and standing timber. But the real reason was because everybody had always burned the woods and fields each spring, and they saw no cause for abandoning life-long habits ... If the wood that was burned had been sawn into lumber or cut into firewood, instead of burning to ashes on the ground, there would have been something for them to sell.

Boll-weevils were never killed in any great numbers by the fire; the cotton plant had to be sprayed with poison in the summer, anyway. (114)

Because of this practice, Jeeter is left with only broom-sedge and blackjack, neither of which will burn: "the hottest fire could not hurt those tough scrub oaks" (114). Year after year, he unsuccessfully attempts to sell the unburnable firewood in nearby Augusta, his deep-seated habits and unreflective love of the land leaving him unable to recognize why no one will buy it. For Jeeter and other older farmers, according to Caldwell's novel, harmful habits die hard in a quickly transitioning world. Like "the scrub-oak trees standing blackened and charred," the novel bleakly suggests, these habits "would not die" (165).[10] In addition to death and abandoning the farm for the mills in Augusta, the only other solution in the short novel involves a drastic change in agricultural methods unavailable to the Lesters and other families living in poverty. As the narrator of *Tobacco Road* informs us, "An intelligent employment of his land, stocks, and implements would have enabled Jeeter, and scores of others who had become dependent upon Captain John, to raise crops for food and profit. Co-operative and corporate farming would have saved them all" (62–63). For Reiger, the narrator's alternative is ambiguous and problematic (38–39). Jeeter's unbending stubbornness—captured powerfully by the "scrub-oak trees" comparison—certainly lends support to Reiger's assessment and suggests that *Tobacco Road* is most effective in its antipastoral critique of the sharecropping system that entraps the Lester family.

Like *Tobacco Road*, Richard Wright's collection of sharecropping stories included in *Uncle Tom's Children* (1938) holds ecocritical value in its antipastoral critique of southern agricultural and nostalgia. While Wright is part of "a main current within African American culture [that] has ... expressed a profound antipathy toward ... pastoral space and wilderness" (Bennett 208), his work calls attention to the "ecological burden" often faced by African Americans that causes them to "suffer economically and environmentally because of their degraded status" (Ruffin 3). Wright would quickly come to lament the reception of *Uncle Tom's Children* as a book that "bankers' daughters could read and weep over and feel good about" ("How Bigger" 531). But the power of the stories, as B. Eugene McCarthy argues, are in their ability to create an alternative version of black "history" that "had been destroyed, distorted, or denied" by the region's dominant interests (730). Wright uses the stories to reposition violence in the South as a product of white terrorism, meant to physically and psychologically subjugate southern blacks. To do so, he identifies the racial and environmental exploitation and violence underlying traditional pastoral understandings of southern agriculture. In "Long Black Song," Wright depicts the inevitable racial conflict between southern whites and African Americans trying to economically prosper in ways Percy sees sharecropping as supporting. Silas, a black tenant farmer who is saving to buy the land on which he works, ends up dying in a hail of gunfire as his house burns down around him for shooting the white man who raped his wife, Sarah. As he tells Sarah, "They don have no mercy on no black folks; wes just like dirt under their feet! Fer ten years Ah slaves lika dog t git mah farm free, givin ever penny Ah kin t em, n then Ah comes n fins they been in mah house . . .'" (143). In "Fire and Cloud" and "Bright and Morning Star," Wright depicts the vicious forms of violence and intimidation used against southern African Americans when they organize to protest their conditions. These stories also allude to the dangers faced by sympathetic whites. In providing food, supplies, and shelter to union members and organizers, white supporters imperiled themselves to the threat of being beaten, kidnapped, and lynched (Kelley 38–39, 47–48).

While "Long Black Song," "Fire and Cloud," and "Bright and Morning Star" counter the pastoral myth by highlighting the arbitrary and violent conditions faced by black sharecroppers in the South, two of Wright's other stories in *Uncle Tom's Children* use antipastoral depictions of southern landscapes and race relations to explicitly call attention to the environmental inequities and dangers experienced by black southerners. The first of these stories, "Big Boy Leaves Home," depicts ways that racism establishes unequal access to environmental resources—or, as Carolyn Finney puts it: "[W]ho actually participates in environment-related activities and who does not" (3). In the story, four young black boys skip school to take advantage of a nearby swimming hole on the land of "old man Harvey," who is notorious for his hostility towards African Americans. According to one of the boys, "[J]ust last year he [Harvey] took a shot at Bob fer swimming in here" (25). The boys soon find themselves in a similar situation when mistaken for potential rapists by a young white woman after she discovers them swimming without their clothes. The woman then interprets the boys' attempts to grab their clothes as an attack, and her hysterical screams alert her nearby fiancé, Harvey's son, who immediately begins shooting at the boys. After the son kills two of the friends, Big Boy kills him in self-defense, and the two remaining young boys flee the lynch mob they know will seek retribution.

In the first half of the story, Wright calls readers' attention to the mortal dangers southern African Americans face when attempting to use and enjoy environmental resources. While young white children might receive a slap on the wrist for trespassing on white-owned private property, the four young black boys are viciously attacked for being perceived as black rapists. The boys' nakedness, understood as perfectly normal and innocent for white children, becomes a terrifying sight for the white characters. That these boys have probably not yet experienced (or are in the beginning stages of) puberty underscores the absurdity of the reaction. For young Harvey and his fiancé, the boys' black skin short-circuits any rational response to the situation. Furthermore, the encounter works to shift the attribution of violence from black to white southerners. In the scene, it's the white characters who exhibit extreme forms of violence towards African Americans. When Big Boy kills young Harvey, it is out of self-defense rather than any innate tendencies towards violence. As in "Long Black Song," "Big Boy Leaves Home" depicts black violence as a defensive response rather than as a preemptive attack.

The second half of "Big Boy Leaves Home" further inverts the black beast stereotype through graphic depictions of the sadistic forms of violence that white southerners casually inflict on African Americans. After fleeing Harvey's land and making arrangements through his parents to leave the area, Big Boy hides in a hole in the ground while waiting for a relative to pick him up. From his hiding place, Big Boy watches a group of white men, women, and children torture and eventually kill his young friend Bobo. Big Boy hears the white group brag about the body parts they've taken as souvenirs. They then tar and feather Bobo and set him on fire with gasoline:

> Big Boy trembled and looked. The mob was running down the slopes, leaving the fire clear. Then he saw a writhing white mass cradled in yellow flame, and heard screams, one on top of the other, each shriller and shorter than the last. The mob was quiet now, standing still, looking up the slope at the writhing mass gradually growing black in a cradle of yellow flame.
> "PO ON MO GAS!"
> "Gimmee a lif, will yuh!"
> Two men were struggling, carrying between them a heavy can. They set it down, tilted it, leaving it so that the gas would trickle down to the hollowed earth around the fire. (272)

The white southerners' reaction to violence oscillates between lustful frenzy and religious awe as they mutilate and burn young Bobo. In depicting the methodical, ritualistic, and sadistic white-on-black violence, the scene works to further invert stereotypical representations of African American bestiality and violence. As in the first half of the story, the violence perpetrated by Big Boy as he hides from the lynch mob is primarily defensive. In this case, Big Boy defends himself from nonhuman species. First, he battles a snake for "the safest pit on the hillside" (263). Cast into the wild's primal struggle for survival by the dehumanizing white world, Big Boy overcomes his fear and hesitation by hardening himself against any moral consideration of the snake's claim to the pit: "He stopped, teeth clenched. He had to kill this snake. Jus had t kill im!" (263). In attacking the snake with a stick, he momentarily becomes almost animalistic: "Then Big Boy was upon him, pounding home, one on top of the other. He fought viciously, his eyes red, his teeth bared in a snarl. He beat till the snake lay still; then he stomped it with his heel, grinding its head into the dirt" (263–64). Soon after, Big Boy battles another nonhuman animal species, this one trained by humans to seek him out: "He felt the dog's body heave, felt dognails digging into his loins. With strength flowing from fear, he closed his fingers, pushing his full weight on the dog's throat. The dog heaved again, and lay still . . ." (273). Interestingly, the boy continues to embrace the dog, "long after the last footstep had died out, long after the rain had stopped" (273). While the continued embrace perhaps illustrates Big Boy's fear of moving as other dogs and white southerners search the area, he may also be searching for comfort and safety in the wet, cold, and dangerous situation in which he finds himself. In the dead dog's now-docile and still-warm body, the boy seems to momentarily experience the nonhuman animal as a child might experience a relationship to a pet. Like the snake, Harvey's son, and the lynch mob, the dog provokes Big Boy into attacking, a defensive response made vicious by the racial violence continually faced by southern African Americans.[11]

Likewise, southern African Americans find themselves the primary victims of violence in Wright's "Down by the Riverside" due to the intersection of environmental and racial inequalities. While "Big Boy Leaves Home" focuses on inequitable access to environmental resources and forms of enjoyment, the latter story describes the dangers African Americans face during environmental disasters, including human-created disasters like the Great Mississippi Flood. As both Tara T. Green and Anissa Janine Wardi argue, the flood depicted in the story likely draws heavily from the 1927 flooding that wreaked havoc on the state where Wright was born (Green 118, Wardi 119). Not only were southern blacks in Mississippi exposed to threats of white violence used to keep social and racial order in the face of flooding, they often faced the most danger from flood waters that threatened their homes and lives (Green 111). For Wright, the flood becomes a powerful antipastoral force that temporarily disrupts the social and environmental order created and defended by southern whites. In doing so, it models forms of activity, mobility, and defiance often denied to southern African Americans while still calling attention to the unique dangers they face due to racial and environmental forms of exploitation.

From the very beginning of the story, Wright focuses on the power and danger unleashed by the rising waters. Mann, the story's protagonist, nervously walks around his house while waiting for his cousin Bo to return with a boat so that his family can escape the rising waters: "Each step he took made the old house creek as though the earth beneath the foundation were soggy. He wondered how long the logs which supported the house could stand against the water. But what really worried him were the steps; they might wash away at any moment, and then they would be trapped" (277). To complicate things, Mann's wife, Lulu, has been "sick with a child she could not deliver" over the past "four days" (278), and Bo returns with a stolen rowboat since he only receives fifteen dollars for the mule they intended to sell to buy a boat (281). The stolen rowboat belongs to Henry Heartfield, the local Postmaster known for his hatred of African Americans, and is easily identifiable due to its "white" color (282). Mann and his family set out in the boat for the Red Cross Hospital, which is being used to treat residents and relocate them to higher ground.

The journey to the hospital illustrates the power of the water and its threat to human life and the normally dry land. The churning water that "rustled, gurgled, droned, glistening blackly like an ocean of bubbling oil" calls to mind the monster metaphor used by Percy to describe the 1927 flooding in Greenville (287). Mann constantly "feel[s] the force of the current tugging at his left" (287), and the "walls of solid darkness" and "ghostily" trees further give the landscape a sense of danger and disorder (287). But the flood also provides opportunities for Mann to express his unique capabilities. To safely navigate through the waters, Mann uses his strength and knowledge of the landscape. A submerged yet familiar "oak tree" causes him to imaginatively reconstruct "a quick image of cornfield in sunshine." The image allows him to steer the boat in the right direction at an important "fork of a road" (287). He continually checks his progress along the way by identifying important features of the landscape, as when the "tall, black stack-pipes" of a local factory confirm that he is heading in the right direction (288). Like the oak tree, other objects and features provoke his imagination to recreate the nonflooded version of the landscape. After grabbing "something round, cold, smooth, [and] wet" in the water, his mind begins to reconstruct the scene: "A series of pictures flashed through his mind, but none fitted. He groped higher, thinking with his fingers. Then suddenly he saw the whole street: sunshine, wagons and buggies tied to a water trough. This is old man Toms sto. And these were the railings that went around the front porch he was holding in his hands" (288–89). Scenes like these not only demonstrate Mann's physical, intellectual, and imaginative capabilities, they also work to expose the disorder and chaos underlying pastoral depictions of the sunny South. By juxtaposing bucolic depictions of southern rural life with the dark and menacing flood waters, these scenes hint at the precariousness of and the violence used to create such landscapes. This connection is further stressed through the comparison of the water to oil, the latter invoking images of a wounded and bleeding earth.

If the initial part of the journey to the hospital demonstrates Mann's strength, courage, and knowledge of the land, the second part highlights ways that whites use racism to thwart these physical and mental powers by exploiting them to contain the instability created by the flooding. But it also introduces ways that the river's defiance informs Mann's response to racist-informed violence. The family's progress is immediately checked as they near the Heartfield's place, as the Postmaster immediately recognizes the boat and demands that Mann return it. Before Mann can respond, Heartfield begins shooting. Mann returns fire, killing Heartfield: "The white man fell backwards on the steps and slipped with an abrupt splash into the water. The flash-light went with him, its one eye swooping downward, leaving a sudden darkness. There was a scream" (292). For Green, Mann's reaction is "an expression of humanity" that "asserts his right to save his life and those of his family members" (122). This act, Green argues, is part of Mann's "conversion," a term she uses to describe ways that African Americans "resist death—both social and physical" (121). In other words, Mann asserts his humanity by resisting the Postmaster's attempts to dehumanize him through violence. Mann's own use of violence, mirroring the defiant and chaotic violence of the river, becomes the only response left to him to counter white terrorism in the Jim Crow South—as in the case of Silas, Big Boy, and the other black characters of Wright's stories.

Other white characters in the story attempt to reassert the status quo over the unravelling social order. Though initially marveling at Mann's ability to navigate a rowboat in such treacherous waters, the white soldiers he eventually finds in town continually make disparaging remarks about him and his family, calling him "boy," his wife "bitch," and his unborn baby "picaninny" (296). They take the family the rest of the way to the hospital by motorboat, where Mann discovers that his wife and unborn child have died on the journey. Mann is then separated from the rest of his family and, like other black men, is forced to help shore up the levee and rescue residents still trapped by the flood waters. When he gets to the levee, Mann "see[s] long, black lines of men weaving snake-fashion" on "a ridge of dry land between two stretches of black water" (305). The danger of the job becomes immediately apparent as he witnesses the sudden collapse of a levee section: "Suddenly a wild commotion broke out. A siren screamed. On the levee-top the long lines of men merged into one whirling mass. Shouts rose in a mighty roar. There came a vague, sonorous drone, like the far away buzzing in a sea-shell. Each section it grew louder. Lawd! Thought Mann. The levees gone!" (305). After the levee breaks, the soldiers give Mann and Brinkley, another conscripted black resident, a boat and order them to rescue people trapped by the flood. Their first job is to help the soldiers evacuate the hospital, which is now under threat by the rising waters. Mann doesn't even recognize it at first: "He had been watching for the steps up which he had carried Lulu. But the water had already covered the steps and was making for the first floor" (307). As Green notes, Mann's experience at the hospital illustrates an ambivalent sense of power given to the two black men, who are temporarily allowed to transgress racial taboos in order to save the people trapped at the hospital. Though again commended for his strength and ability, Mann knows that his life is considered less valuable than the white men and women he saves and that under any other circumstance he would not be allowed in such close proximity to them, especially the women (Green 123). What could have become another opportunity for white southerners and soldiers to recognize the vulnerability and humanity they share with African Americans is ignored and racial hierarchies are quickly reestablished.

After rescuing the people trapped at the hospital, Mann and Brinkley are ordered to rescue a white family that has reported being trapped in their house. Unfortunately for Mann, the family is the Heartfields. As they travel to the house by boat, Mann considers telling Brinkley about his earlier confrontation with the family in the hope that Brinkley will turn the boat around and/or help him escape. As Mann decides, debris in the water causes the boat to jerk, and he determines that the moment has passed: "Mann swallowed; then he felt that there would not be any use in his telling; he had waited too long" (313). The combined consequence of waiting too long and the interrupting force of the flood occurs again when Mann considers killing the Heartfields after they recognize him in the house. While standing above the huddled family with an "axe . . . over his head," he is "lifted violently up and swung around" as the water causes the house to tilt (316–17). By the time that he realizes what has happened, he sees Brinkley in the window, asking about the family. Having waited too long once again, Mann realizes, "He could not kill now; he could not kill if someone were looking" (317). For Green, Mann's hesitations attest to the power of Jim Crow, particularly in Mann's uncertainty that Brinkley will help him (124). But the river's interruption in both cases also functions in two other ways. On the one hand, the intervention functions to dissociate the flood with some form of benevolent power. Unlike Faulkner's Isaac McCaslin, Wright does not see the flood as a punishment sent to penalize white southerners for their treatment of the land and African Americans. He seems as skeptical of the river as a space of healing, retribution, or escape as he does Mann's pleas to God to save him from the Heartfields and soldiers (Wardi 122).

On the other hand, the flood destabilizes contingent understandings of what constitutes humanity. Mann's hesitation when threatening the family with the axe undermines how white southerners like the Heartfields perceive African Americans. Mann is not the unwavering beast that the Heartfield's believe him to be. To approach the kind of violence they attribute to him, he must momentarily step outside of himself: "[H]e would swing that axe and they would never tell and he had his gun and if Brinkley found out he would point the gun at Brinkley's head; he saw himself pointing the gun at Brinkley's head; he saw himself in the boat going away; he saw himself in the boat, alone, going away" (316). Brinkley's gaze then calls attention to the dilemma Wright sees African Americans as facing in the absurd racial hierarchy of the South. If he acts on his desire to kill the unarmed white family, he potentially supports the black beast stereotype circulated by southern whites. But if he rejects this desire, he seals his own fate. Though the tilting of the house ultimately chooses for him, his hesitation is an act of choice that ultimately rejects both the black beast stereotype as well as the well-mannered, black protector stereotype, the latter illustrated by Big Sam in *Gone with the Wind*.[12] But the hesitation results in another form of white violence perpetrated on black southerners that the flood cannot wash away. Mann is compared to a "sleepwalker" as he helps the Heartfields out of the house and into the boat (317). Later, he sees a similar passive state in the black people he passes after he is capture: "For a split second he was there among those blunt and hazy faces looking silently and fearfully at the white folks take some poor black man away. Why don they help me? Yet he knew that they would not and could not help him, even as he in times past had not helped other black men being taken by the white folks to their death" (321). For Wright, this sleeplike state illustrates the reach of racial forms of containment that survive and, in some ways, thrive in the chaos of environmental disasters.

The flooding also illustrates an ambivalent presence after Mann and Brinkley take the Heartfields to higher ground. Captured and tried by the soldiers, Mann makes one last defiant attempt to escape his fate: "He would die before he would let them kill him. Ahll die fo they kill me! Ahll die . . . He ran straight to the right, through the trees, in the direction of the water" (326). But the river offers Mann little chance for escape due to the difficulty he finds in running "over the wet ground" and the presence of "shouting white boats" that await him in the water (326). The soldiers quickly shoot and kill Mann, leaving his body at the "water's edge . . . [with] one black palm sprawled limply outward and upward, trailing in the brown current" (327). For Green, Mann achieves conversion through death by the riverside (125), while Anissa Janine Wardi views Mann's inability to find safety in the river as implying that "the only option for the black community . . . is to fight in self-defense" (122). But the presence of the river at the end of the story reiterates the ambivalent depiction of the flood. While the unconstrained river becomes a symbol for defiance and power that recognizes no boundaries between land and water or between white and black southerners, it also helps reinforce white power structures by foreclosing on the possibilities of escape and self-defense. In this sense, Wright refuses to replace the white pastoral fantasy he associates with southern forms of agriculture and rural life with another pastoral vision rooted in some form of benevolent nature.[13]

As in Caldwell's *Tobacco Road*, Wright's use of the antipastoral in *Uncle Tom's Children* provide a powerful critique of southern pastoralism while offering few alternatives—beyond death and defensive violence—to the dominant social and environmental relationships organizing southern society during the period.[14] Unlike Caldwell's characters, Wright's characters also face racial prejudice and violence. If the Lesters' racial position allows them mobility and opportunity, even if they decide not to act on these affordances, the only responses left for Wright's characters to the daily forms of violence inflicted upon them are retaliation, escape, fear, and death. In being denied access to environmental resources and bearing the brunt of environmental disasters, Wright's characters face an "ecological burden" that causes them to "suffer economically and environmentally because of their degraded status" (Ruffin 3). But as Kimberly Ruffin points out, this is only half of the "ecological burden-and-beauty paradox" faced and depicted by African Americans. For Ruffin, a concurrent "experience of ecological beauty results from individual and collective attitudes towards nature that undercut the experience of racism and its related evils" (2–3). If Wright dissects southern pastoralism to highlight the violence and racial inequality that sustains it, Zora Neale Hurston creates alternative forms of social and environmental engagement from African American experiences in the South. Hurston particularly focuses on ways that animals in southern black folklore often function to highlight and envision alternatives to environmental and racial forms of exploitation.

Predator and Pests in Black Folklore

In her fiction and nonfiction, Zora Neale Hurston acknowledges the deep environmental connections that southern African Americans have to rural landscapes.[15] For Hurston, these connections are particularly rooted in her understanding of and relationship to nonhuman animals. In her autobiography *Dust Tracks on a Road* (1942), she reflects on the influence that animal folk tales had on her as a child in Eatonville, Florida: "It did not surprise me at all to hear that the animals talked. I had suspected it all along. Or let us say, that I wanted to suspect it. Life took on a bigger perimeter by expanding on these things. I picked up glints and gleams out of what I heard and stored it away to turn it to my own uses" (605). Animal stories in black folklore became a means for Hurston to reevaluate the connections between the human and natural world, often in ways that call attention to arbitrary ways of ordering landscapes and human relations. As Scott Hicks argues, Hurston uses her childhood memories and experiences of flora and fauna in the Florida landscape as well as her training in anthropology and folklore to stage "anew the ecological problems of her era and place" and use them to critique "ideologies of race, gender, class, and nature" (114). To do this, Hurston promotes a form of conservation that "naturalizes the human" by depicting him/her as part of the natural landscape (116, 120).

According to Reiger, Hurston creates a "personal" version of the ecopastoral "in which the pastoral ideal of harmonic balance is sought as much internally (in the person) as it is externally (in the landscape)" (92–93). Reiger goes on to identify ways that Hurston appeals to aspects of "Afro-Caribbean Vodou" in order to create an "animistic vision of nature" that reflects her characters' inner development (93). While Hurston does employ a conception of nature rooted in hoodoo folk beliefs that sees it "as living, dynamic, and sacred" (93), Hurston's work on black folklore engages environmental thought on the level of culture and community in ways that expand its use beyond the personal. For Hurston, black folklore becomes a means to better understand humanity's connections to the natural world and African American experience in the South. She writes in "Go Gator and Muddy the Water," a chapter on black folklore and music included in the WPA's *The Florida Negro*, that "folklore is the first thing that man makes out of the natural laws that he finds around him—beyond the necessity of making a living" (70). As black slaves were brought to the New World, they built upon residual cultural forms to create new ways of understanding the natural and social world around them (69). Unlike the residual forms of pastoralism supported by the Agrarians and other white proponents of southern agriculture, black folklore does not attempt to erase or subjugate the "other" human groups and animal species that populate the southern landscapes. Neither does black folklore offer a nostalgic or primitivistic rejection of modernity. As David G. Nicholls has argued, black folk culture represents an alternative route to "political modernity and economic autonomy" (10), an understanding at the heart of Hurston anthropological work in the South. In her depictions of black folklore, Hurston emphasizes residual attitudes towards land and other species that can be transformed into emergent forms of environmental and social consciousness. These attitudes are embodied in ways that African Americans have negotiated the color line in the South and made sense of their relationship to the land and the other species that inhabit it. While folk heroes like Big John de Conqueror become the human tricksters through which African Americans outsmart Massa (Master), their animal equivalent is Brer Rabbit (Hurston, "Go Gator" 79). According to historian Lawrence W. Levine, the primary difference between human and animal folk heroes in southern African American folk culture lay in the animal's ability to not only to outsmart his master but also to replace him. But in taking his place, Levine continues, trickster animals like Brer Rabbit often become "as ruthless, as unmerciful, [and] as corrupt as those who sought to control him" (132). In this sense, the trickster animal develops into an active yet ambiguous force on the South's racial hierarchy, exhibiting a powerful sense of autonomy while (at times) appropriating many of the same violent and deceitful means used by white southerners to subjugate African Americans.

While the autonomy that the trickster animal attempts to create and retain is certainly an important part of a political critique exhibited in black folklore, it is also important to note the role that non-trickster animal characters play in black folklore, particularly those animals feared and hated as "beasts" or "pests," such as the alligator, snake, mosquito, and boll weevil. These animals most closely represent the bestial, primitive, and parasitic qualities often projected upon black southerners. In parts of *Mules and Men* (1935), Hurston's collection of folklore writings based upon her excursions into black communities in Florida and Louisiana, Hurston attempts to recover the value and place of so-called animal "beasts" and "pests" in the southern landscape by recounting stories that convey alternative ways of understanding these nonhuman species. In doing, she joins Aldo Leopold and others in critiquing the categories used to relegate these species to a subordinate status in the biotic community. Unlike Leopold, she also uses these species to call attention to the falsity of stereotypes used to dehumanize African Americans.

One story, told by a Polk County black laborer, recounts how the alligator got his fearful and ugly appearance by attributing it to a trick played by the dog. In the tale, God makes Brer Dog and Brer 'Gator without a mouth. In order "to git theirselves a mouth like de other varmints" (105), the two animals agree to cut one for each other. Brer 'Gator carves Brer Dog a mouth first, stopping when the latter tells him to. But when Brer Dog cuts Brer 'Gator a mouth, he refuses to stop, disfiguring the alligator's appearance: "Brer Dog kept right on cuttin' till he ruint Brer 'Gator's face. Brer 'Gator was a very handsome gent'-man befo' Brer Dog done him that a way, and everytime he look in de lookin' glass he cry like a baby over de disfiggerment of his face'" (106). By attributing the alligator's appearance to the cruel joke of another animal, the story de-emphasizes the bestial aspects of the nonhuman animal and depicts it as exhibiting loyalty and vulnerability, traits that encourage admiration and identification rather than fear and revulsion. In another story about the alligator, Brer 'Gator is portrayed as a loving father who cannot join the other animals to provide music for an interspecies community dance because he is taking care of his sick wife and children. When Brer Dog comes to see him about playing in the band, Brer 'Gator lets the dog borrow his tongue to provide drum music for the dance. But the animals wear out the tongue, and rather than tell Brer 'Gator about it, Brer Dog hides from him: "Course de 'gator don't like it 'bout his tongue so he's de sworn enemy of de dog" (107).[16] The alligator's loyalty to his family and generosity to the community again counters typical attributes projected upon such species.

In a final tale about the alligator, another Polk County worker recounts to Hurston a story explaining how the animal gets its red eyes and dark color, this time through a trick played on him by Brer Rabbit. In the story, the alligator is "a pretty white varmint wid coal black eyes" (107), until an incident with Brer Rabbit. While sleeping in the grass, Brer 'Gator feels the rabbit jumping all over him, leaving mud on his white skin. When Gator asks Brer Rabbit what he is doing, the latter tells him, "Ah ain't got time to see what Ah'm runnin' over nor under. Ah got trouble behind me" (108). In response to Brer 'Gator asking him what "trouble" is, Brer Rabbit takes a pine plank, lights it, and sets the grass around Brer 'Gator on fire:

> All around Brer 'Gator de fire was burnin' in flames of fire. De 'gator woke up and pitched out to run, but every which a way he run de fire met him.
>
> He seen Brer Rabbit sittin' up on de high ground jus' killin' hisself laughin.' So he hollered and ast him:
>
> "Brer Rabbit, whut's all dis goin' on?"
>
> "Dat's trouble, Brer 'Gator, dat's trouble youse in." (108)

While the alligator escapes the fire, "he had done got smoked all up befo' he got to the water, and his eyes is all red from de smoke" (108). Not only does the story build upon the other stories' alternative depictions of alligators and illustrate Brer Rabbit's ambiguous role in black folklore, it also calls attention to the arbitrariness of skin pigment.

As in its depictions of alligators, Hurston's recounted folklore also works to recover the value and place of the rattlesnake in the southern landscape. On how the snake got its rattle, a Polk County resident tells Hurston that the snake climbed a ladder up to God to complain that its generations have been killed off because the species is too vulnerable down on its "belly in de dust" (98). In response, God decides to give the snake poison to protect itself and sends him/her back to earth. Soon after, the other animals arrive in heaven to complain to God that the snake has become too dangerous: "He' layin' in de bushes there wid poisin in his mouf and he's strikin' everything dat shakes de bush. He's killin' up our generations. Wese skeered to walk de earth" (98). God calls the snake back up and admonishes him/her for using the poison so freely when it was given only for protection. In response, the snake tells God, "Lawd, you know Ah'm down here in de dust. Ah ain't got no claws to fight wid, and Ah ain't got no feets to git me out de way. All Ah kin see is feets comin' to trample me. Ah can't tell who the enemy is and who is my friend. You gimme dis protection in my mouf and Ah uses it" (99). Moved by the snake's response but concerned about his/her effect on the other animals, God decides to give the snake a "bell" (rattle) for its tail: "When you hear feets comin' you ring yo' bell and if it's yo' friend, he'll be keerful. If it's yo' enemy, it's you and him" (99). Elsewhere in *Mules and Men*, Hurston further demonstrates ways that she values and respects snakes. While staying in a Polk County Saw-Mill Camp, she finds a rattlesnake coiled up in her laundry after an afternoon heavy rain. While the men want to kill it, Hurston convinces them not to hurt her "lowly brother" (150). After everyone quiets down, the snake eventually relaxes and slowly escapes through a hole in the wall. Finally, after leaving Polk County to study "hoodoo" in New Orleans, she describes the snake's value to hoodoo traditions: "Snakes guard . . . herbs and roots and must not be killed" (209).

Not only do feared nonhuman animals like alligators and snakes get more sympathetic portrayals in Hurston's collection and depiction of black folklore, "pests" like mosquitos and boll weevils are also portrayed in humorous and empathic ways that help reimagine their place in the southern landscape. These species are shown to exhibit traits relevant to African Americans attempting to survive the harsh social and environmental conditions of the South, including cooperation, cunning, and persistence. In Polk County, one laborer recounts seeing "a chigger over in de fence corner wid a splinter in his foot and a seed tick . . . pickin' it out wid a fence rail and de chigger is hollerin', 'Lawd, have mercy'" (100). Other laborers trade stories about the persistence and cunning of mosquitos. Whether hiding from mosquitos under an "iron washpot" or "four blankets" (101), they are still bitten. While the first mosquitos "bored right thru dat iron pot," the others "just screwed off dem short bills, reached back in they hip-pocket and took out they long bills and screwed 'em on and come right on through dem blankets and got us" (101). Another laborer tells a story about a mosquito that "bored right thru" a tree to bite his father on the other side of it (101). Finally, stories about the boll weevil, the dreaded beetle that devastated cotton crops in Texas, Mississippi, Alabama, and Georgia in the late nineteenth and early twentieth centuries, also highlight the species' persistence and freedom of movement. One story concerns a boll weevil who lands on "de steerin' wheel of a white man's car" and asks the man if he can drive it. When the man tells the boll weevil that he can't drive a car, the boll weevil replies, "Oh yeah, Ah kin. Ah drove in five thousand cars last year and Ah'm going to drive in ten thousand dis year" (100). While the story emphasizes the boll weevil's persistence, ability to move great distances, and defiant tone in response to the white driver, another boll weevil story highlights the ambivalence of African American attitudes towards the species. When hearing a loud commotion in the field, a black field hand goes to investigate its source: "It was Ole Man Boll-Weevil whippin' li' Willie Boll-Weevil 'cause he couldn't carry two rows at a time" (100).

The boll weevil stories are particularly interesting nonhuman animal subjects of black folklore for the species' infamous reputations in the South as crop destroyers. While the second story portrays them as both master and slave, the first story highlights their mobility and defiance. The latter become the defining features of the animal, particularly in the boll weevil songs of the first half of the twentieth century. According to James C. Giesen, the boll weevil songs "could be heard in the repertoire of dozens of prominent blues and folk singers" (165). Black tenants, Giesen continues, particularly identified with the weevil's continual "searchin' for a home," a reoccurring refrain throughout the verses. In the last verse of Charley Patton's popular 1929 recording "Mississippi Boweavil Blues," the beetle tells the tenant farmer's wife that he might "go north," a line that Giesen sees as an allusion "to a long history of movement of laborers into, within, and from the Delta as well as to an oppressive and violent tradition of landowners attempting to restrict that movement" (97). Huddie "Lead Belly" Ledbetter's version of the song, "The Boll Weevil," recorded in the early 1930s by Alan Lomax when the musician was on death row in Angola, also makes use of the migration theme. Of the last verse of Lead Belly's version, Giesen writes, "Like the boll weevil, ever moving in search of more cotton, laborers migrated from one landlord arrangement to another, in search of a place with economic opportunity and social independence" (42). For Giesen, Lead Belly also makes use of another common theme in the song: "the pest as a kind of trickster" (41). For late nineteenth- and early twentieth-century black tenant farmers in Texas witnessing the effects of the boll weevil on cotton, the pest is constantly able to survive "poisoning, drowning, and burning" (41). In Lead Belly's version, the tenant follows the boll weevil's example by refusing to give his landowner the last bale of cotton left by the weevil. In addition to identifying the beetle's symbolic function in the songs, Giesen also argues that the recording of Lead Belly, Patton, and others informed people across the country about "the day-to-day lives for Mississippi's black sharecroppers" as well as "the ways in which ideas about the boll weevil were inherited, digested, and retold" (100). Ultimately, Giesen's analysis shows the importance of the "pest" to the experience and culture of southern blacks trying to create a sense of place and call attention to the precarious environmental landscapes and racial hierarchies of the South.

If Hurston uses folklore to depict the cultural value of nonhuman "beasts" and "pests" to black experience and identity in the South, she furthers that connection by depicting the shared vulnerability of humans and nonhumans to flooding exacerbated by human changes to the landscape. Hurston's first novel, *Jonah's Gourd Vine* (1934), highlights the effects of the timber industry in the state on flooding (Hicks 119), while her most famous novel, *Their Eyes Were Watching*

God (1937), depicts the overflowing of Lake Okeechobee during a 1928 hurricane in Florida. The high winds of the hurricane caused the rising lake to breech the fifty-seven-mile dike built in the early to mid-1920s to hold back floods and open land for farming (Mykle 68–69). Flooding during the hurricane resulted in the deaths of an estimated 3,000 residents and migrant workers in the area, which accounted for about half of the population (213). In the novel, Janie Crawford and her third husband, Tea Cake, initially ignore the danger of the approaching hurricane, predicted by the migrating Seminoles and wild animals. Because the white people in the area are staying, they feel safe to remain in their shack on the Muck. As Tea Cake informs a fellow worker, "De white folks ain't gone nowhere. Dey oughta know if it's dangerous" (156). The narrator reiterates this response after the winds begin: "The people felt uncomfortable but safe because there were the seawalls to chain the senseless monster in his bed. The folks let the people do the thinking. If the castles thought themselves secure, the cabins needn't worry" (158). The juxtaposition of "cabins" with "castles" draws attention to the precarious structures of the workers, a fragility further emphasized by the limited preparations and defenses available to those who stay: "Chink up your cracks, shiver in your wet beds and wait on the mercy of the Lord" (158). When the fury of the hurricane and subsequent flooding of Lake Okeechobee prove them wrong, they frantically search for higher ground. As they flee, Hurston describes the landscape in much the same way as Wright in "Down by the Riverside": "[T]he wind and water had given life to lots of things that folks think of as dead and given death to so much that had been living things. Water everywhere. Stray fish swimming in the yard" (160). Both authors' descriptions of southern landscapes during environmental disasters focus on ways that objects break free from their human impediments to rearrange the scene in uncanny and grotesque ways. They both also depict ways that such disasters reinforce racial segregation in the face of shared dangers. When Janie and Tea Cake reach Six-Mile Bridge, a "high and safe" place, they find that it is full of white people: "White people had preempted that point of elevation and there was no more room" (164). Instead, they join the African Americans and wild animals looking for higher ground. Unlike the crowded Six-Mile Bridge, Janie and Tea Cake find little competition or danger from the nonhuman animals when they temporarily find safety from the flooding: "Common danger made common friends. Nothing sought a conquest over the other" (164).[17] But human segregation between African and white Americans continues even in the aftermath of the flood. When Tea Cake is conscripted by the white residents to find and bury the victims, he is instructed to examine each body to separate whites from blacks. As a white guardsman tells him, "Got orders from headquarters. They makin' coffins fuh all de white folks. 'Tain't nothin' but cheap pine, but dat's better'n nothin'. Don't dump no white folks in de hole jus' so." When asked about coffins for black victims, the guardsman replies that there are not enough coffins for everyone: "Jus' sprinkle plenty quick-lime over 'em and cover 'em up" (171). The black bodies are tossed into ditches, while the white bodies are kept for coffins.

In looking to nature to envision alternative rural landscapes that are more inclusive of people and nonhuman animals, Hurston builds upon Wright's and Caldwell's critiques of the ecological, racial, and economic forms of exploitation supported by plantation agriculture in the South. Like Leopold, Faulkner, and Hemingway, her empathetic depictions of nonhuman animal "predators" and "pests" challenge commonly accepted understandings of these species. Instead of focusing on their threat to human economic and physical well-being, Hurston emphasizes their cultural importance to African Americans in the South. She further draws connections between black southerners and nonhuman animal species by highlighting their shared vulnerability to natural disasters made more severe by human attempts to control and exploit natural resources. In defining humanity as a part of and reliant on the natural world, she illustrates ways that culture and nature are often interconnected. While culture can violently shape nature into a landscape that supports dominant economic interests and social or racial hierarchies, a process often leading to severe environmental consequences, culture can (and should) also be used to create and support more environmentally sustainable and racially egalitarian ways of interacting with the land and its other inhabitants.

Conclusion

From plantation pastoralism to folk environmentalism, the rural became a space during the 1930s and '40s through which to argue for different social and environmental values. While some writers and filmmakers divested or celebrated the exploitive legacies of slavery and sharecropping in their depictions of southern agriculture, others emphasized the environmental and racial violence underlying such depictions. Some envisioned emergent versions of human and environmental relationships rooted in residual forms of folk culture. Like depression-era authors focusing on wilderness landscapes, the latter two groups of authors echoed shifts in conservationist thought that would inform the development of modern environmentalism in the second half of the twentieth century. Both landscapes became spaces through which to examine the ecological effects of resource exploitation, predator eradication, and racial inequality. But rural and wilderness landscapes were not the only spaces that authors used to explore the intersections between environmental and social issues during the period. Many depression-era authors recognized their intersections in cities across the US, particularly in relation to urban parks, slums, dumps, and "pests."

Chapter 3

The Postpastoral City

According to the *Final Report on the WPA Program, 1935–43*, the Works Progress Administration (WPA) helped develop and renovate over 8,000 urban parks and 12,800 playgrounds as well as "nearly 3,300 stadiums, grandstands, and bleachers, about 5,000 athletic fields, and thousands of handball, horseshoe, and tennis courts" (50). In New York City alone, under the supervision of Robert Moses, the New Deal's Civil Works Administration (CWA) renovated existing parks by repairing trails, sidewalks, playground equipment, and benches, and by planting 11,000 trees (Caro 372). Moses also supervised the development of new playgrounds in the city, opening "60 in 1934, 71 in 1935, 72 in 1936, [and] 52 in 1937" (455). The use of parks, playgrounds, and other "green" recreational spaces to help alleviate major social and environmental issues in the city during the 1930s appeals to the symbolization in American urban history and literature that James Machor calls the "pastoral city." For Machor, the pastoral city, or urban pastoralism, is more than just a version of traditional pastoralism since "city and country are [treated as] equally valuable components in an evolving landscape best served when those components operate in harmony" (14). While the urban pastoral can range "from a preservation of open green spaces in the urban topography to an 'organic' relationship among the inhabitants," at its base "lies an impulse to provide the urban dweller with some means to renew continually his elemental connection to his spontaneous, natural self while remaining a member of society, of the city, in a word, civilization" (14). According to Machor, early American literature often examines the potential of pastoral landscapes in cities to create this connection (203).[1] Though he claims that serious and un-cynical treatment of the urban pastoralism in literature died out after the end of the nineteenth century (215), writers of the 1930s and '40s offered their own versions of the mode in order to consider its continued relevance in creating forms of place, social awareness, and early environmental consciousness in a growingly diverse urban American landscape.

Because depression-era urban pastoralism's focuses more explicitly on the intersection of social and environmental issues than traditional forms of the mode, it often exhibits attributes of what Terry Gifford calls the "postpastoral." Gifford's postpastoral is particularly useful in its attempts to place pastoralism in line with contemporary discourse regarding social justice and environmentalism. According to Gifford, literary uses of the postpastoral move beyond the idyllic and escapist qualities ascribed to pastoralism by exhibiting an awareness of the "creative-destructive" property of nature as well as ways in which discourses celebrating human mastery over nature have often been used to support the subjugation of different genders or races thought naturally inferior (153, 165). In their urban pastoral landscapes, many of the authors I include in the following chapters focus on objects, groups, and species often ignored by traditional uses of the urban pastoral mode. To do so, they often turn to literary naturalism. In bringing together the biological, environmental, and social, literary naturalists during the period created forms of pastoralism that moved beyond the idyllic into more complex social and ecological terrain.[2] The novels addressed in the following chapter combine literary naturalism and the postpastoral to examine the urban pastoral's relevance in creating forms of place, social awareness, and environmental consciousness in working-class urban neighborhoods. Though differing in their perceptions of the form and function of urban pastoralism, these novels invert the mode by including human groups, urban spaces, animal species, and environmental issues often omitted from urban pastoral visions of American cities. James T. Farrell and Nelson Algren see urban parks as valuable yet ineffective in countering forms of gender, racial, and class violence underpinning their lower- and middle-class characters' neighborhoods, while Mike Gold and Tillie Olsen depict ways that working-class children create their own urban pastoral spaces due to the lack of parks and playgrounds in their neighborhoods. Richard Wright, on the other hand, creates his own urban postpastoral vision through his use of rats in *Native Son*. In the novel, rats function to critique urban racial attitudes and containment practices in the Chicago black belt by undermining conceptions of what constitutes human and animal "pests."

The urban naturalist authors discussed in this chapter anticipate the importance that urban landscapes and other highly developed built environments have begun to play in environmentalist thought. In examining pastoralism in urban design, they offer insight into different forms and functions of urban development projects in cities across the country. They help us better understand the persistence of pollution, overcrowding, and racial, gender, and economic inequality in today's rapidly expanding urbanized environments. Finally, in depicting ways that urban residents have interacted and come to identify with animals, including species often detested by human beings, they envision opportunities to create new forms of environmental consciousness through human and nonhuman animal relationships.

Urban Parks, Playgrounds, and Vacant Lots

In *The Cultural Front*, Michael Denning refers to the coupling of pastoralism and naturalism in 1930s literary works set in urban, working-class neighborhoods as the "ghetto pastoral." As mentioned before, these plebian accounts of growing up in urban working-class neighborhoods are less concerned with using direct pastoral imagery than in blending naturalism's "strategy of degradation and debasement" with pastoralism's "strategy of elevating and ennobling the simple" (230, 251). But urban novels of the period often include pastoral depictions that are informed by naturalist tropes of the period, particularly the "grotesque" and what critic Joseph Entin calls "aesthetics of astonishment."[3] In combining pastoralism and naturalism, postpastoral urban novels of the period often call attention to the value *and* limitations of parks and other green spaces in introducing working-class urban residents to more egalitarian and ecologically informed understandings of "place."

"Place" has become an important *and* fraught concept for ecocritics trying to understand ways that humans interact with and connect to the environments and communities that surround them. Defined by Lawrence Buell as "perceived or felt space, space humanized, rather than the material world taken on its own terms" (*The Environmental* 253), place can become a way through which urban characters find new experiences of and connections to the world around them. But holding too strong a place-sense can also eclipse "critical apprehension" of the social norms shared in a particular area or region (253). This is especially the case for characters in the urban novels of James T. Farrell, Nelson Algren, Richard Wright, who often illustrate a negative sense of place by accepting and participating in destructive behaviors like rape, murder, theft, and alcoholism. According to Timothy Morton, one way to effectively counter this narrow sense of place involves thinking "spacious, not place-ist; global, not local (if not universal); not embodied but displaced, spaced, outer spaced" (28). In thinking big, Morton concludes, we find that "there is less of everything" and that "things are less complete . . . [and] independent, than we believed" (33, 36). While Buell and Morton both recognize the limitations of place, Buell doesn't see the need to completely drop the term, especially when it is used in a way that is "mindful of its limitations and respectful that place molds us as well as vice versa" (*The Environmental* 253). Combining the insights of both Morton and Buell, place can be somewhere to return to and expand upon after thinking beyond one's immediate surroundings, relationships, and experiences. Many of the authors addressed below depict place in ways that show its potential in creating "spacious" and "global" forms of consciousness to counter and replace a narrow place-attachment.

Parks, playgrounds, and other green spaces in the ghetto pastorals of the 1930s and '40s offer characters the potential to experience the kind of "spacious" and "mindful" sense of place that Buell and Morton describe. Parks and other green spaces particularly create this kind of experience in James T. Farrell's *Young Lonigan* (1932), his first novel in the Studs Lonigan trilogy (1932–35), which follows the title character, a lower-middle-class, Irish American young man growing up in Chicago's South Side. Studs and his friends tend to establish their sense of place in the streets, alleyways, and pool halls used for fighting, drinking, picking on Jewish and African Americans boys in the neighborhood, and sexual encounters. But urban pastoral spaces in and around the South Side offer Studs an alternative sense of place that pushes against the tough, masculine street ethos by which he lives. Even looking out of his bedroom window at a nearby field of grass works to produce this alternative sense of place: "There was something about the things he watched that seemed to enter Studs as the sun entered a field of grass; and as he watched, he felt that the things he saw were part of himself, and he felt as good as if he were warm sunlight" (53). Likewise, later in the first novel, when he goes swimming in the lake with a friend, he reflects, "Only the lake was ahead of them, vast and blue-gray and nice with the sun on it; and it gave them feelings they couldn't describe" (112). He then proceeds to compare himself to "a cloud that didn't have any bothers and just sailed across the sky.... He floated, and suddenly he liked himself a lot" (112). Both experiences at least partially counter the hyper-masculine world that Studs ascribes to by offering him a glimpse of new forms of connectedness with his surroundings and its other inhabitants.

Perhaps the most developed sense of these alternative feelings and ideas occurs when Studs visits South Side's Washington Park with Lucy. While walking through the park, the narrator uses free indirect discourse to describe Studs's experience of the pastoral setting: "Everything was sun-colored, and people walked around as if they had nothing to do . . . with the sky so blue and the clouds all puffed and white, and floating as if they were icebergs in a sea that didn't have any waves" (86). Initially, the images he sees spur him into envisioning a fantasy world of ease and luxury: "[I]t would be fine if he and Lucy could have wings and fly away past the sky . . . right through clouds . . . past the other side of the sky, where there was nothing . . . until they came to some kind of a place with a palace, and servants, and everything they wanted to make them happy" (86). But the images soon lead him to recognize the fecundity of the landscape surrounding him and his connection to it. He feels that the lagoon is "alive, like it was dancing with the sun" and the sounds he hears are "all, somehow, part of himself" (88).

Despite feeling connected to the objects in the park, Studs soon finds himself skeptical and dismissive of the experience. According to the narrator, "Studs felt goofy and fruity about having it, and felt that he hadn't better let anyone know he had thoughts like that" (88). The narrator later adds, "He usually thought it was sissified to listen or pay attention to such things as birds singing; it was crazy, like being a guy who studied music, or read too many books, or wrote poems and painted pictures" (89). This leads Studs to ultimately reject these experiences, especially after he finds the words "STUDS LOVES LUCY . . . LUCY IS CRAZY ABOUT STUDS . . . I LIKE TO KISS LUCY—STUDS . . . STUDS KISSED LUCY A MILLION TIMES" written all over the neighborhood (91). He then vows to become "the iron man [who] would knock the laugh off the face of Mr. Anybody with the sweetest paste in the mush Mr. Anybody got" (92). Feelings of imagination, inquisitiveness, and love find little acceptance after this declaration except in the nostalgic memories of Lucy and Washington Park he periodically has as he grows older. While Carla Cappetti calls the Lucy and Washington Park episode a "private world of romance" (127), suggesting that Lucy rather than the park awakens these feelings in Studs, these feelings and ideas show up in the vacant lot and lake episodes recounted above, where Lucy is not present. Lucy also teases Studs for holding and expressing these feelings: "[H]e told her the wind was like the hand of a pretty girl, and when it touched the leaves, it was like that pretty girl stroking very fine silk. She laughed, and said that it was a very funny and a very silly thought for a person like Studs Lonigan to have" (88). Her response to Studs's epiphany ends up embarrassing him, furthering his resolve to reject the experience.

Nelson Algren's young Polish American male characters in *Never Come Morning* (1942) express an even more adamant skepticism of parks and playgrounds. At least part of this skepticism results from being constrained in their Northwest Chicago Polish neighborhood. When Bruno and his friends travel outside of his neighborhood to steal a slot machine at a road house, we learn that "Bruno had never been this far west of the Triangle before" (20). But this skepticism is also a consequence of urban values rooted in extreme forms of heteronormative masculinity, racial superiority, and economic self-interest. Like Studs, Algren's Bruno Bicek associates these spaces with the feminine realm: "He himself had never liked being on a playground, for fear the fellows would see him there. Playgrounds were for girls and sprouts" (27). Instead, Bruno and his friends prefer to hang out in the tunnels beneath the L and other hidden places: "The children of the poor preferred the crowded adventures of the alleyways to the policed safety of the playgrounds and settlements" (30). As in the pool hall, streets, and alleyways in Farrell's Studs Lonigan trilogy, Algren's tunnels and vacant buildings support destructive behaviors. In them, Bruno allows his friends to rape his girlfriend Steffi, kills a "Sheeny" Greek from another neighborhood for trying to join the rape, and tries to rob a drunk man, a crime for which he is eventually arrested.

In describing the lack of influence that parks and playgrounds have on their characters, Farrell and Algren call attention to the economic, social, and geographical constraints that result in narrow conceptions of place for working-class youths in urban neighborhoods.[4] In other words, they point towards a process that Martyn Lee has described as a "habitus of location." For Lee, urban spaces are embedded in "a set of relatively consistent, enduring and generative cultural (pre) dispositions" that "appear . . . as entirely spontaneous or natural forms of cognition" (132, 133). In this sense, the aggressive forms of masculinity and individualism valued in their neighborhoods can appear much more natural than alternative ways of conceptualizing the world experienced in urban pastoral landscapes like Washington Park. Because of this, Studs and Bruno find it difficult to escape the economic and social forces that help trap them in a downward spiral.[5] This isn't to say that Farrell and Algren depict these forces as completely deterministic. Like other uses of naturalism during the period, they also envision ways their characters begin to understand and, in some cases, resist the economic forces entrapping them (Pizer 7, 15). In the Studs Lonigan trilogy, the character Danny O'Neill eventually becomes able to recognize the economic and social forces structuring the lives of urban youth like himself. He comes to represent in the trilogy both the inverse of Studs's fall and the qualified optimism of 1930s naturalist fiction.[6] According to Charles Fanning, O'Neill illustrates an alternative trajectory towards knowledge, growth, and social consciousness by "choos[ing] the Park," using it to train "to become a professional baseball player" (xviii). This decision, the trilogy seems to suggest, helps lead him to attend college and become interested in radical socialist politics. While working at a filling station to make money for tuition, Danny vows that "*he would destroy the old world with his pen; he would help create the new world. He would study to prepare himself*" (italics in original, 453). For O'Neill, the marching workers and students that take to the streets towards the end of the trilogy's final novel, *Judgment Day* (1935), offer the kind of change necessary to cultivate a more advanced sense of interconnectedness that Studs experiences in the park. Instead of blaming the economic depression and the deterioration of their neighborhoods on Jews, Reds, and African Americans (as Studs and his father do), the marchers identify crass individualism, racism, and economic exploitation as the culprits.

If Farrell values urban pastoral spaces while pointing towards the difficulty of integrating them into the experiences of urban youth without more structural economic and social changes, Mike Gold depicts the lack of access to urban pastoral spaces in the Lower East Side as well as ways that children in the neighborhood attempt to create these spaces for themselves. Like Farrell, Gold sees radical economic and social changes as necessary to alleviate the conditions experienced by working-class urban children and their families. For Gold, experiences of urban pastoral spaces play a formative role in creating "a garden for the human spirit" that will nourish attempts to ensure social and economic changes in working-class neighborhoods (309). The Bronx Park mushroom-hunting trip young Mike and his family go on in Gold's *Jews Without Money* is often identified as the novel's primary urban pastoral interlude (Denning 246–47). But the vacant lots in Mike's neighborhood offer more unique and powerful forms of urban postpastoral experience and insights. The mushroom-hunting trip at Bronx Park primarily emphasizes the experiences of young Mike's immigrant parents, which are often infused with forms of nostalgia. In the park, his mother can relive her youth in the fields and forests of Hungary and show Mike and his sister an alternative to the "dry, dead mushrooms in [American] grocery stores" (153). Instead, she tells them that "a real mushroom should taste of its own earth or tree'" (154).

The children do enjoy their time in Bronx Park as seen in the effects the landscape has on Mike's imagination. For example, he calls the forest a "mysterious house," suggesting its ability to inspire feelings of wonder, escape, and connectedness to nonhuman animals: "The trees were like walls, their leaves made a ceiling. Clear, sweet voices sang through the house. These were the birds. The birds lived in the house. Little ants and beetles ran about under our foot" (153). But Gold is careful to remind us of Bronx Park's physical distance from where the family lives and its psychological distance from the children's daily experiences. Getting to the park is an obstacle in itself, as Mike and his family join the "[e]xcited screaming mothers, fathers sagging under enormous lunch baskets, children yelling, puking, and running under every one's legs . . . [in a] bedlam of legs and arms, sneezing, spitting, cursing, sighing—a super-tenement on wheels" (149–50). As Mike's father tells them, "In Rumania it is a little walk to the country . . . Here it is a fight for one's life. What a crazy land!" (150). His comment emphasizes the physical and psychological inaccessibility of the park, at least to the children who have little experience of fields and forests in their daily life and experiences. Mike's mother also continually expresses this to the children after they arrive at the park, and the episode ends with her telling them: "I'm so happy in a forest! You American children don't know what it means! I am happy!" (155). Not only does this comment conceal the problems the parents faced in Rumania that led them to immigrate to the US, it also rejects whatever feelings and ideas the children are experiencing, suggesting that they are unable to fully appreciate the fields and forests they encounter in the park. As Mike's comparison of the forest to a "mysterious house" suggests, the children do have unique and insightful experiences there. But the mother is correct that the park is physically distant from the children's everyday experiences—an occasional Sunday trip rather than easily accessible alternative to the crowded and dangerous tenements of the Lower East Side.

If the trip to Bronx Park suggests an archaic pastoral landscape largely inaccessible to Mike and other children in the Lower East Side, Gold creates an alternative strain of urban pastoralism by depicting the children's attempts to create their own "green" space in the empty lots of the neighborhood. Early in the novel, the narrator reveals that he and the children of the neighborhood exhibit a "hunger for country things" (40). He recalls being "amazed by . . . [the] miracle" of "grass struggling between the sidewalk cracks" (41). He continues, "We were amazed by this miracle. We guarded this treasure, allowed no one to step on it. Every hour the gang studied 'our' grass, to try to catch it growing. It died, of course, after a few days; only children are hardy enough to grow on the East Side" (41). For the narrator and his friends, the empty lots along Delancey Street become green spaces to cultivate and defend: "Air, space, weeds, elbow room, one sickened for space on the East Side, any kind of marsh or wasteland to testify that the world was still young and free" (46). While these lots are described as "[s]habby old ground, ripped up like a battlefield by workers' picks and shovels, little garbage dump lying forgotten in the midst of tall tenements . . . home of all the twisted junk, rusty baby carriages, lumber, bottles, boxes, moldy pants and dead cats of the neighborhood," they become through "the power of imagination . . . a vast western plane" where the neighborhood children "buried pirate treasure, and built snow forts . . . played football and baseball . . . [and] dug caves, and with Peary explored the North Pole" (46). The acts of imagination and care fostered by the lots are practices akin to what Alexander Wilson calls "restoration." For Wilson, restoration encompasses acts of "human intervention and care" on "disturbed" lands that seek to "heal, connect, and empower" as well as to "make intelligible our relations with each other and with the natural world" (17). In this sense, the lots facilitate alternative forms of place-sense by offering space to imagine a world outside of the overcrowded Lower East Side in ways that could serve to transform the neighborhood's conditions.

While the lots offer Mike a broader conception of the world around him, they do sometimes support a narrow sense of place in becoming spaces to defend from rival gangs like the "Forsythe Street boys" (47). This need to defend the vacant lot is later ascribed to the influence of Mike's first childhood hero, described as "a Messiah who would look like Buffalo Bill, and who could annihilate our enemies" (190). But by the end of the novel, the narrator realizes that neither his gang nor those of his rivals are any match for the economic forces that control the fate of their neighborhood, a realization that leads him to substitute the collectivity of the working class for the conservative individualism of dime novel depictions of Buffalo Bill: "But Schiff Parkway was an opponent we could not defeat. It robbed us of our playground at last" (48). Instead, the former vacant lots become "[a] long concrete patch . . . with anemic trees and lines of benches where jobless workers sit in summer" (48), a vision of urban development that anticipates gentrification in our own time. Mike and his friends return to their "crowded street," where one of them soon is decapitated by a horse car: "Later it [the head] was discovered under the car, hanging from a bloody axle" (49). The grotesqueness of the latter image particularly amplifies Gold's criticism of an economic system and urban design that packs people on top of each other and forces children to play in the street. In the final pages of the novel, the narrator comes to the realization after listening to a radical speaker that the "workers' revolution" is "the true Messiah" who "will destroy the East Side . . . and build there a garden for the human spirit" (309).

Both Farrell and Gold depict the function and effectiveness of urban pastoral spaces—whether in the form of parks or the residents' efforts to turn vacant lots into their own green spaces—as counterforces to narrow and uncritical forms of place-sense in working-urban neighborhoods during the period. While Farrell's characters often reject new understandings of place in their experiences of plants, trees, and open skies in vacant lots and parks, Gold's characters use these latter spaces to practice forms of restoration. With his vacant lots where urban children discover grass and imaginative freedom among discarded objects and building debris, Gold calls attention to ways such spaces can be used to create more spacious kinds of place-sense that helps recognize social and environmental connections and envision alternative forms of urban life.

Dumps

Like Gold, Tillie Olsen addresses the use of less traditional landscape as recreational spaces for urban children. In her unfinished novel, *Yonnondio: From the Thirties*, written in the 1930s but not published until 1974, Olsen depicts the role of a garbage dump in creating forms of place-sense for working-class children living in an Omaha meatpacking district.[7] For the children in the novel, the dump becomes both a place to scavenge for discarded goods and a playground. But more directly than the novels of Gold, Farrell, and Algren discussed above, *Yonnondio* calls attention to the environmental precariousness of urban working-class neighborhoods and their proximity to toxic landscapes. In the novel, the dump becomes a space to recognize what Rob Nixon calls the "slow violence" of capitalism on land and people. For Nixon, this kind of violence is often experienced by the poor and "occurs gradually and out of sight" (2, 4). In *Yonnondio*, the environmental toxicity of the dump inflicts slow forms of violence on the bodies of the working-class residents who live near it. As Martin V. Melosi points out, the open dumps of the period that small cities like Omaha favored were "notoriously unsanitary, attracting vermin, giving off offensive odors, threatening groundwater supplies, and posing fire hazards" (181). But besides illustrating forms of slow violence on working-class populations, the contaminated spaces and bodies depicted in *Yonnondio* also reveal the limitations of capitalism in containing the toxic environmental and social conditions it produces, which threaten to transgress their afforded boundaries.[8]

In the novel, the Holbrook family—which includes the young protagonist Mazie, her siblings Will and (eventually) Bess, and her parents Anna and Tom—move from a mining town in Wyoming to a tenant farm in South Dakota and finally to a working-class neighborhood in Omaha. Like Farrell and Gold, Olsen depicts the effects of urban pastoral spaces but largely finds these areas inaccessible. She also depicts these spaces, at times, as offering a false and even dangerous sense of safety and escape, as when Anna takes Mazie and her siblings to hunt for edible greens in the vacant lots and suburbs of Omaha. Eventually finding themselves in a wealthier neighborhood of the city, where they discover "[l]awns, flower beds and boarders, [and] children on bikes" (115), they stop to rest in a lot on "a stretch along the river bluff, yellow and green and white with flowers and grass and dandelion glory" (116). The pastoral landscape particularly affects Anna, who, in a burst of energy, informs the children about the various flowers and trees around them. She soon becomes intoxicated by the effects of the landscape, suggesting an anesthetic quality to the experience that distances her from the children and frightens Mazie: "A remote look was on her face, as if she had forgotten them, as if she had become someone else, was not their mother any more" (117). The scene takes on a further anesthetic tone as Anna begins "stroking Mazie's hair in a kind of languor, a swoon" (118). Anna's stroking combined with the idyllic scene creates a similar effect on Mazie: "Soft wove the bliss round hurt and fear and shame—the old worn fragile bliss, a new frail selfness bliss, healing, transforming" (119). While the pastoral landscape offers Mazie and Anna a temporary feeling of escape and safety in this scene, Olsen ultimately depicts their languor as a kind of precarious cocoon. In separating its pupa from the outside world, the cocoon ends up exposing them to danger. In other words, while their experience of the suburban empty lot offers Anna and Mazie escape from the oppressive conditions of Omaha and a feeling of connectivity to the natural world around them, it isolates them from each other and leaves them more vulnerable to the forces of modernity that continuously seek to penetrate their cocoon. Though Mazie attempts to prolong the feelings she associates with the rural landscape of South Dakota by walking around Omaha "in the full soft dream of the farm," she is constantly fighting a kind of pastoral psychosis: "But terrible moments of waking would come when the world that was about her would crash into her dream with terrible discordant music" (73). In these moments, she views the world around her through the "grotesqueness and crooked vision" of "nightmares" (73), experiences later described as "enter[ing] into her like death" (85). She eventually forces herself to shed the cocoon in order to maintain her sanity: "Stupid, she chastised herself grievingly, stupid. Who cares about the farm? Who wants to pick stupid weeds?" (118).

Mazie seems to be resisting what Leo Marx calls the "all-feeling," a term the critic introduces in his analysis of "The Mast-Head" chapter of Herman Melville's *Moby-Dick*. In the chapter, Ishmael nearly falls from the masthead after becoming hypnotized by the beauty of the ocean landscape around him.[9] For Marx, Ishmael struggles in the novel to find balance between a rejection and an overly romanticizing view of nature: "Ishmael is defining a complex pastoralism, a view of experience that matches the duality of nature. The possibility of green fields is meaningful, but only so far as it is joined to its opposite" (313). By fighting against the "all-feeling" created by her experience on the farm and reinforced by the empty lot, Mazie is attempting to create a more mindful sense of place in the Omaha urban landscape that helps her acclimate to her immediate surroundings.

Not only does Mazie experience forms of place-sense in the South Dakota rural and Omaha suburban landscapes, she also experiences them in the Omaha dump her family lives near. For Mazie and the other children in the area, the dump is a place to find useful objects that have been discarded: "Peerers, combers and excavators go treasure hunting. (They compete with old men and women looking for covering, furnishings, sustenance—anything usable, transformable, barterable, salable)" (121). But the dump also provides their primary forms of recreation and social interactions. They prefer the "adventure and fairy ground dump and city" to the "livedveryhappyeverafter fairy tales" of the library (126). Much like the characters of Gold's Lower East Side, the children imaginatively appropriate the discarded objects they find in the dump to create "strange structures" such as "lookout towers, sets, ships, tents, forts, lean-tos, clubhouses, cities and stores and train tracks, cabooses, pretend places" (121). In doing so, they attempt to create an alternative social order in which they find a more stable sense of place and identity: "Children—already stratified as dummies in school, condemned as unfit for the worlds of learning, art, imagination, invention—plan, measure, figure, design, invent, construct, costume themselves, stage dramas; endlessly—between tasks, errands, smaller children to be looked after, jobs, dailinesses—live in passionate absorbed activity, in rapt make believe" (121).

Anthony Dawahare calls the children's practice of imaginative and playful bricolage in *Yonnondio* a form of utopian consciousness that allows them to "subjectively negate class restraints and ... think utopianly" (268). He sees their creative use of the dump as exhibiting socialist forms of labor in which "workers, by an 'investment' of their creativity, are able to transform even the products of exploitation ... into visions of a better (less alienated) world" (269). For Dawahare, Olsen uses the term "selfness" to describe this process. But Dawahare misses a crucial aspect of the social and economic relations the children create in the dump. The children are certainly able to express empowering senses of place and identity by creating imaginative new forms out of the discarded objects in the dump, though often not in ways that promote selfness. As in the vacant lots of Gold's Lower East Side, the dump is described by Olsen's narrator as a battleground: "On the dump, territory is established, shifted, abandoned, fought over, combined" (121). The dump even has its own hierarchy with Jinella, one of the older children who uses the dump, on top. Collecting "shaving curls, moldering hats, raggy teddies, torn lace curtains ... fringes, tassels, stubs of lipstick, wrecks of high-heeled shoes and boots, [and] lavish jewelry Tiffany would never recognize" (127), Jinella recreates the space and objects she has claimed into a Hollywood film that focuses solely on her: "Luxuriously on her rug, pretend silk slinking and slithering on her body, turbaned, puffing her long pretend cigarette: Say vamp me, vamp me. I'm Nazimova. Take me to the roadhouse, I want to make whoopee. Hotcha. Never never never. O my gigolo, my gigolo. A moment of ecstasy, a lifetime of regret" (128). She will not even allow Mazie and the other children to enter her tent unless they contribute "something for the gunny sack" (117).

If Jinella is at the top of the dump hierarchy, Erina is at the bottom. A young girl who is epileptic and physically deformed, Erina particularly illustrates the effects of the polluted spaces on the human body. Together with the hot weather of a summer heat wave, Jinella's body works to visualize the toxicity of the dump and the nearby slaughterhouse. Using imagery that combines sight and smell, the narrator endows the toxicity of the "throbbing" heat with material presence, describing it as a "stench cooking down into the pavements" and making its way into the houses "like a great wave of vomit in the air" (129). The importance of smell as an indicator of toxicity is further magnified by the narrator's description of the dump's inescapable odors: "It smelled sewer, smelled garbage, smelled crap 'cep right at the river-bluff edge" (135). The heat and smell even have a visual effect on the bodies moving through dump. Erina's body particularly takes on strange and grotesque forms in the afternoon sun: "Wavering in the heat waves, dragging along, jerking funny; skinny with her bones sticking out like great knobs and the tiny arm stub that hung down and ended in a knob.... Flickering out her faded tongue and the spit slobbering down" (138). Because of her appearance, Erina frightens Mazie and the other children: "She will push me over the cliff, thought Mazie" (138). But they also fear that Erina will contaminate them: "Erina's breath was in Mazie's face; Mazie saw how the pus oozed from her eyes, stuck on her eyelashes; weed stickers—maybe lice—in her hair. *Go away, Erina; it's so hot and you are wavy like everything else. Last night I was your body. I was you. Go away*" (138).[10]

While Erina visualizes the toxicity of the dump and slaughterhouse, she also models forms of social and environmental consciousness for Mazie. Though Erina initially disgusts and frightens Mazie, she also instills in her a sense of empathy and wonder: a "sick-happy feeling to be with Erina, to listen to Erina" (139). This feeling stems from the deformed girl's ability to poetically and empathically respond to shared suffering and vulnerability in the world around her. Though her conception of the world partakes in an interpretation of Christianity that sees her illness and deformations as a product of sin—"I pray but God don't make me better and Pa and Tammysue socks me 'cause it means I was sinning too bad to get forgiven" (139)—she is able to empathize with other living creatures in ways that move beyond this outlook. For example, she tells Mazie, "Watch for the little ants. . . . Don't hurt their houses. They have to hurry and work so hard and carry heavy things and I sees them carry each other sometime" (139). For Erina, ants, like humans, suffer and can perform kind acts for each other. Erina's perspective helps Mazie see beyond "the running sores on her legs" and her "crying and slobbering" (138). It also leads her to do nice things for Erina, such as offering to steal ice for her or trying to get her a lemon cream soda from Jinella.

Erina's influence allows Mazie to begin recognizing the toxic effects of the dump on the working-class families that live near it. This nascent awareness is also expressed through Mazie's experience of a magazine that she finds in the dump. While flipping through it, she comes across a picture that initially frightens her: "[O]ut of one of the pages, a little girl's eyes stared at her, big eyes, black, almost holes, from her face lots and lots of lines going all kinds of ways, so much lines you couldn't look at them all but you had to try while your head got dizzier and dizzier. And scareder. It was something like you, like something" (136). While the picture of the distorted girl reminds Mazie of Erina in that their eyes are both like "black holes" (139), she also recognizes her own features, distorted by the conditions in which her family lives. Though the little girl in the picture and Erina both frighten Mazie, they also force her to confront her own relationship to the world around her. No longer able to imaginatively escape to the Dakota farm or join Jinella at the top of the dump hierarchy, Mazie begins developing the "selfness" Dawahare views the dump as fostering by recognizing her connection to the discarded objects and people that surround her. As objects/people that are consumed or used up, they hold little value in the social and economic order and are left to slowly decompose. But they also refuse to disappear. In this sense, the dump not only illustrates "slow violence" perpetrated on the poor working-class residents in the area, but it also suggests that toxicity is a byproduct of capitalism that can neither be fully contained or ignored. As the novel suggests through the fear of contamination represented by the toxic heat and Erina's deformities as well as the promise of organized resistance created in the hellish labor and living conditions of slaughterhouse workers, this toxicity threatens to transgress the boundaries afforded to it by dominant American economic interests.

As in Gold's *Jews Without Money*, the working-class characters of Olsen's *Yonnondio* begin to create forms of environmental and political awareness through their experiences of and engagement with the overcrowded, constraining, and polluted urban landscape they inhabit. While Gold and Olsen use parks, vacant lots, and/or urban dumps as the instigators of such thought, Richard Wright uses rats in *Native Son* to depict forms of social and environmental consciousness based in an awareness of shared vulnerability and collective struggle. In Wright's novel, rats not only offer new ways of identifying with nonhuman animals often considered dangerous pests; they also represent symbols of resistance and mobility and are used to critique attitudes towards human groups considered inhuman.

Rats and Native Sons[11]

In twentieth-century American urban pastoral landscapes, white power structures have often confined African Americans to peripheral slums where garbage, constrictive spaces, and dilapidated structures replaced the green parks, tree-lined avenues, and picturesque skylines of buildings and skyscrapers. African Americans have frequently been compared to violent beasts, despised pests, and comic primates in order to establish these slums as their "natural" habitat. Any unauthorized deviation from this habitat has been considered a fugitive breach on a highly controlled bucolic, white urban landscape—like an ape escaping its cage or a rat infiltrating a home. For Richard Wright, images of escape and infiltration are powerful tropes that undermine racial hierarchies in Chicago. In *Native Son* (1940), Wright uses transgressive "beasts" and "pests" to create his own urban postpastoral vision, one that includes human groups and animal species typically left out of the traditional pastoral city. In doing so, he critiques dominant anthropocentric conceptions of human and animal "pests" that underlie racism.[12]

Critics addressing the roles of animals in Wright's novel have typically focused on his allusions to apes. But the rat, another prominent animal in the novel, is also of central importance.[13] It becomes a symbol for the black "ecological burden-and-beauty paradox," representing both the impoverished conditions faced by urban African Americans and their abilities to transgress the arbitrary borders imposed upon them by urban whites.[14] In struggling against the containment practices that support dominant ways of ordering landscapes and controlling human and nonhuman "others," Bigger and the rat call attention to the social and environmental practices that create the slums in which they live. Furthermore, rats in the novel critique racial and biological categories rooted in cultural attitudes that deem African Americans as less than human. In drawing connections between Bigger and the rat, the novel suggests that neither is quite what s/he seems; a radical strangeness endues both with an irreducibility that pushes against how they are initially conceived. Finally, by directing focus onto the "neighbor species" that inhabit urban landscapes, the novel offers alternative ways of experiencing and understanding animals often thought of as pests.[15] In doing so, it highlights a more complex history of interactions between the urban poor and commensal animals like rats that have occasionally resulted in unique empathic experiences with such species as well as powerful forms of political consciousness and activism.

Though often ignored by ecocritics, *Native Son* has received more attention for its environmental awareness than the urban novels discussed in previous sections. According to Lawrence Buell, Wright's novel calls attention to the social and health effects of urban slums by depicting sparsely described and interchangeable enclosed spaces and using symbol-oriented events like Bigger's encounter with the rat in the novel's opening pages (*Writing* 138–39). The rat, for Buell, expresses "virtually all the *represented* squalor of the Thomases' apartment" (139). But the introduction of the rat does more than just reveal the economic hardship and living conditions of Bigger's family. The rat critiques racial and anthropocentric categories used to support narrow conceptions of what constitutes "humans," "animals," and "pests." Critics in animal studies often attempt to trouble these categories in order to push against narrow and destructive anthropocentric attitudes towards the environment and its inhabitants (both human and nonhuman). Timothy Morton identifies what he calls the "strange stranger" as a figure that marks continuities between humans and other creatures. He writes, "This stranger isn't just strange. She, or he, or it—can we tell? how?—is strangely strange" (41). For Morton, a sense of strangeness forces us to confront our initial expectations towards other beings, allowing us to see continuity while still recognizing difference. It can also help us perceive our initial conceptions of another being as projections of our own limited awareness and knowledge of the world (54). Morton argues that confrontations with strange strangers in literature creates an aesthetic experience that "unsettles and disgusts" rather than "mirror[s] our fantasies" of a "self-contained, harmonious" or "awe-inspiring, open" social and natural world (91–92). Joseph Entin sees a similar function in the work of depression-era writers and photographers. For Entin, "sensational modernists" (including Wright) use "aesthetics of astonishment" to call attention to "the historical and cultural contingency of images and figures" considered "natural and eternal" (17–18). In asking us to identify with human and nonhuman characters exhibiting an irreducible strangeness or difference, both Morton and Entin model forms of reading that acknowledges similarity *and* difference when identifying with what Entin calls "life on the margins" (18).

Both also reject forms of empathy that result in pity. Wright certainly attempted to avoid provoking pity when characterizing Bigger in *Native Son*. As mentioned in the previous chapter, Wright lamented the response to *Uncle Tom's Children*, promising to write a book that "no one would weep over" ("How 'Bigger'" 531). But if Wright consciously attempted to avoid writing a novel that would invoke pity and guilt in white readers, his bleak characterization of Bigger has often led critics to consider the character a vulgar stereotype. This was the criticism of James Baldwin, who called Bigger a confirmation of "the monster created by the American republic" (41). But Baldwin seems to miss a major aesthetic function of Bigger's characterization in the novel. Entin argues that "Wright was quite likely more aware of the dilemmas Baldwin describes than Baldwin seems to have recognized" (218). For Entin, the "deep-seated ambiguity" in Wright's depiction of "Bigger as a racial monster . . . ultimately unsettles the racial stereotypes the novel seems to reinforce" (218). Nowhere is this ambiguity more apparent, I would add, than in the role animals play in the novel.

As mentioned above, critics tend to focus on allusions to apes when discussing the role of animals in the novel. In "Bigger Thomas Reconsidered: 'Native Son,' Film and 'King Kong,'" Harold Hellenbrand identifies the influence of Edgar Allen Poe's 1841 story "The Murders in the Rue Morgue" and Ernest B. Schoedsack and Merian C. Cooper's 1933 film *King Kong* on Wright's depiction of Bigger. From Poe's story, he views Bigger's decapitation of Mary and his stuffing of her body in the furnace as alluding to the orangutan's brutal murder of Madame L'Espanaye and her daughter (87). And from Schoedsack and Cooper's *King Kong*, he sees Bigger's attempt to elude his pursuers by climbing a tenement rooftop water tower as alluding to Kong's ascent of the Empire State Building. One of Bigger's pursuers, he notes, even alludes to the mythical Kong when he exclaims, "Kill that black ape!" (92–93). To complicate these stereotypical depictions of apes and illustrate ways that Bigger's "savagery" is a product of a white "fantasy come to life," Wright imposes visible human features beneath his protagonist's ape mask (89). Entin also views Kong as a likely influence on Bigger. He sees this influence not only in how the giant ape expresses the "anxieties (and stereotypes) about racial difference and sexual transgression" held by white Americans, but also in the film's invitation for audiences to "sympathize with the colossal primate even as they fear him and applaud his demise" (217).

While I agree with the comparison Hellenbrand and Entin make between Bigger and Kong, the ape is only one animal in the novel that Wright appropriates for these purposes. The rat complements and even surpasses the ape in testing readers' ability to identify with Bigger by offering an animal that is more appropriate to the urban environment and human carelessness. As an exotic implant into the urban landscape, the ape is meant to obscure the conditions of African Americans living in cities. The rat, on the other hand, not only reflects the economic squalor of Bigger and his family, it also takes on a life of its own that pushes against the boundaries of "normalcy" and "strangeness." Furthermore, in his own violent struggles against entrapment, scarcity, fear, and disgust, Bigger takes on a kind of ratness that transforms him into a subject of empathy rather than an object of pity or fear.

In "How 'Bigger' was Born," originally published in the June 1940 issue of the *Saturday Review of Literature*, Wright describes initially feeling ambivalent over the inclusion of the rat in the opening pages of the novel. He writes, "I recalled that I'd seen many rats on the street, that I'd heard and read of Negro children being bitten by rats in their beds" ("How 'Bigger'" 539).[16] While Wright feared that the rat would "hog" the scene, he soon decided to let him/her "walk in . . . to disclose *only* Bigger, his family, their little room, and their relationships" (539). Despite his attempt to qualify the rat's presence in the opening scene of *Native Son*, the creature becomes a noticeable presence in Wright's other fictional works, particularly "The Man Who Lived Underground" (1944).[17] He also seems to have rodents in mind when in "How 'Bigger' was Born" he writes, "Why should I not, like a scientist in a laboratory, use my imagination and invent test-tube situations, place Bigger in them, and, following the guidance of my own hopes and fears, what I had learned and remembered, work out in fictional form an emotional statement and resolution of this problem?" (523). Though Wright is perhaps channeling Zola's "experimental novel" in this analogy, he also alludes to the use of rats and other rodents in scientific experimentation, which are often utilized for their physical, psychological, and dietary similarities to human beings. Wright certainly encountered rats and other lab animals at Chicago's Michael Reese Hospital where he worked in 1933 cleaning the labs and caring for guinea pigs used in laboratory experiments.[18]

Perhaps Wright's interest in and experience with the species influenced him to allow the rat more presence than he originally intended. The mimetic depiction of the rat as well as the dramatic ferocity Wright uses to describe his battle with Bigger leads critic Mary Allen to call the rat the "life that sets this mighty novel in motion" (143). From Bigger's first encounter with the species, Wright establishes the latter's ability to provoke fear and horror in Bigger's family: "A huge black rat squealed and leaped at Bigger's trouser-leg and snagged it in his teeth, hanging on" (*Native Son* 3). After kicking off the rat, Bigger dodges the creature as it leaps at him again. Not only does the rat's ferocity frighten Bigger and his family, the "hideousness" of its appearance also provokes disgust, particularly in response to the creature's teeth: "[I]t reared once more and bared long yellow fangs, piping shrilly, belly quivering" (Allen 143–44, Wright 4). But throughout his portrayal of Bigger's fight with the rat, Wright combines this fear and disgust with what Allen calls a "perverse dignity of life against the odds" (143). He particularly achieves this through images like the rat's "long thin song of defiance," "black beady eyes glittering," and "forefeet pawing in the air restlessly" (Wright 4). Each of these images help readers empathize with the creature, while still recognizing its strangeness. These feelings persist to the point that when Bigger finally kills the rat, he reacts in a way that seems unnecessarily violent and hateful: "He kicked the splintered box out of the way and the flat black body of the rat lay exposed, it two long yellow tusks showing distinctly. Bigger took a shoe and pounded the rat's head, crushing it, cursing hysterically: 'You sonofabitch!'" (4–5). Bigger's reaction to the dead rat introduces the explosive anger he will exhibit throughout the novel and foreshadows the hate his white pursuers and prosecutors project upon him after they discover Mary's body.

Though Bigger and the rat both struggle to survive in the scarce environment of the Black Belt tenements, there are a few allusions to rats in the novel, starting with similarities in their appearance and actions. The blackness, large size, and ferocity of the rat clearly allude to Bigger. Furthermore, his two major crimes—killing Mary and Bessie—occur at night, and he's forced to hide in a dilapidated tenement with other nocturnal creatures after Mary's bones are discovered in the Daltons' furnace. Upon entering the first vacant tenement with Bessie, he joins the world of rats and other so-called pests of the nighttime and shadows: "[H]e heard the scurrying of quick, dry feet over the wooden floors" (*Native Son* 266). Finally, his white pursuers become akin to exterminators who attempt to flush Bigger out into the open. As the 8,000 white policemen and volunteers steadily close the gauntlet over Bigger, searching every vacant and rented apartment in Chicago's Black Belt "under a blanket warrant from the mayor" (282), the space in which he can freely move about grows smaller and smaller. Like the rat he corners at the beginning of the novel, Bigger is eventually left "crawling" with only a couple options: to fight back or try to escape (307).

On their own, these allusions to rats or rat-like behavior only partially establish the species as a major creaturely trope in the novel. While the white world clearly considers Bigger a beastly predator, no one ever directly calls him a rat.[19] But one short encounter during Bigger's flight in the second part of the novel reestablishes connections between the species and Bigger. As Bigger searches for another tenement to hide in, he sees a rat similar in size and color to the one he kills at the beginning of the novel. Instead of feeling disgust and anger as in the previous encounter, Bigger now envies the rat's ability to easily move about and hide in the city: "He paused at a corner and saw a big black rat leaping over the snow. It shot past him into a doorway where it slid out of sight through a hole. He looked wistfully at that gaping black hole through which the rat had darted to safety" (*Native Son* 288). Here, the rat becomes a transgressive creature, easily able to cross over arbitrary boundaries, particularly those established to separate species and, in Bigger's case, race. As Bigger reflects, "They keep us bottled up here like wild animals.... He knew that black people could not go outside of the Black Belt to rent a flat; they had to live on their side of the 'line.' No white real estate man would rent a flat to a black man other than in the sections where it had been decided that black people might live" (288). In his envy of the rat's mobility, Bigger at least partially recognizes that these arbitrary lines mean little to the animal, who will cross boundaries to survive even at the fear of death. That the Daltons' neighborhood in Hyde Park-Kenwood, once one of "the oldest and . . . most exclusive suburbs of Chicago," was only a "block from the Black Belt" by the time Wright had written the novel (Jurca 102) speaks to the fear affluent white families felt at the precariousness of the boundaries they fought to protect.

The rat, in fact, has been used by working-class and civil rights activists as a positive symbol to protest unjust and unsanitary living conditions. During the mid-twentieth century Harlem rent strike, organizer Jesse Gray used the image of a rat as an emblem of power. "The tenants are like rats now,' he said. 'Rats feel their power, and they come out in broad daylight and just sit there. Once the tenants feel *their* power, they stop running, they're not afraid anymore. We've shown them—and they see now—that they have rights whether they live on Park Avenue or Lenox Avenue" (qtd. in Sullivan 62).[20] As Robert Sullivan explains, while Gray and the tenants initially pointed towards the tenements' infestation with rats as one of their grievances against Harlem landlords, they eventually began to use the creature as a symbol of power and defiance. Referring to January 1964, the month and year of what he calls the city's largest rent strike ever, Sullivan writes, "[T]he strike spread from Harlem to the Bronx and the Lower East Side, including Hispanic neighborhoods. Now, at protest rallies, the signs that said NO RENT FOR RATS and FREEDOM NOW and JAIL THE SLUMLORDS were accompanied by signs that said LAS RATAS" (63).

The symbolic use of the rat by strikers makes sense. As the rat is readily encountered in the city, its use becomes highly appropriate to symbolize material conditions and shared struggle in urban landscapes.[21] As a "neighbor species," rats occupy human development and live off human carelessness or waste, even if they are not always seen. Sullivan writes,

> Rats live in man's parallel universe, surviving on the effluvia of human society; they eat our garbage. I think of rats as our mirror species, revered but similar, thriving or suffering in the very cities where we do

the same. If the presence of a grizzly bear is the indicator of the wildness of an area, the range of unsettled habitat, then a rat is an indicator of the presence of man. (2)

In this passage, Sullivan reminds us that rats are most abundant in places that humans tend to ignore: alleyways, dumps, and lower income neighborhoods. The "rat problem" in these places, he explains, tend to have "less to do with the rat and more to do with the man" (2). Though still cognizant of the danger rats can pose to human beings, Sullivan offers a decidedly empathetic portrayal of them. "[I]n New York City," he writes, "the bulk of rats live in quiet desperation, hiding beneath the table of man, under stress, skittering in fear, under siege by larger rats" (3). Facing a similar predicament when hiding out in the empty tenements, perhaps this is why, as Mary Allen notes, Bigger shows a "rare sensitivity" toward creatures on a lower "scale of being" when on the run. She writes, "It is animals, not people, that come to his mind in his thought that he must 'meet his end like any other living thing upon the earth'" (145).

The ape, on the other hand, allows whites in the novel to conceal the real social and living conditions of African Americans in Chicago's Black Belt. Their characterization of Bigger as an ape belongs more to the exotic realm of Hollywood than it does to the urban environment of Chicago. We catch a glimpse of such representations when Bigger and Jack go see the film *Trader Horn* (1931) toward the beginning of the novel: "[Bigger] saw pictures of naked black men and women whirling in wild dances and heard drums beating" (*Native Son* 36). For Bigger—"hearing the roll of tom-toms and the screams of black men and women dancing free and wild, men and women who were adjusted to their soil and at home in their world, secure from fear and hysteria" (38)—these fictional and stereotypical representations of blacks as primitive serve to convince him that he and other African Americans don't belong in the environments created by white civilization. Among whites, blacks are, in the words of Bigger, just "hanging from a tree like a bunch of bananas" (34), a metaphor he uses to jokingly ridicule the sexual desire his friend Gus expresses while watching a group of wealthy, young white women shown in a newsreel. Bigger's joke, with its phallic image of hanging bananas, unintentionally portrays African Americans as sex-crazed apes ready to pounce on and rape white women. Similarly, the newspapers, Buckley, and the medical examiner use the ape metaphor to describe Bigger's actions against Mary, falsely claiming that he raped her before killing her. In this sense, the ape becomes a powerful interpellation, pushing Bigger to accept a false identity that ideologically positions him as inferior. His experiences with rats, on the other hand, offer moments that call such identification into question. Like the rat, he does belong in his environment and can cross the arbitrary boundaries set by whites.

Of the white characters in the novel, Bigger's lawyer, Max, comes closest to recognizing that his client's vicious murders are influenced by racism. According to Max, racism and hate have led Bigger to violently lash out at the whites and blacks around him. To illustrate the role his client has been given in society, Max turns to images of undesirable plants and monstrous carnivores, including "a weed under a stone" and a "corpse" that "leaps to kill" (*Native Son* 455, 457). Like the undesirable life forms these images conjure, Bigger has had to "defend himself against, or adapt himself to, the total natural world in which he lives" (461). Unable to gain access to what Max sees as the two pillars of American society—"personality and security" (472)—Bigger has been conditioned through social forces and his environment to express himself through anger, theft, and violence.

In order to get the courtroom to identify and empathize with Bigger, Max identifies Bigger's actions as analogous to those of the early colonists, who according to Max, arrived in the Americas "from lands where their personalities had been denied" (*Native Son* 452). He tells the court,

> These twelve million Negroes, conditioned broadly by our own notions as we were by European ones when we first came here, are

struggling within unbelievably narrow limits to achieve that feeling of at-home-ness for which we once strove so ardently. And compared with our own struggle, they are striving under conditions far more difficult. If anybody can, surely we ought to be able to understand what these people are after. (464)

Describing Bigger's act as "part of a furious blaze of liquid life-energy which once blazed and is still blazing in our land" (465), Max goes on to call it "an act of *creation*" (466). While Max's remarks to the court at first glance appear to rest on an idyllic and nostalgic understanding of America's past, Wright is careful to portray them as a rhetorical argument aimed at a specific audience for a particular situation. He does not use these remarks to valorize capitalism and pastoral versions of American mythic nationalism but to find ways to get white Americans to identify with Bigger as a human and an American pursuing the same goals of personality and security as them. Wright does include subtle economic and environmental critiques of capitalism in Max's speech, as when the lawyer identifies how the colonists and their progeny so thoroughly "conquered" the "wild land" of America: "But in conquering they *used* others, used their lives. Like a miner using a pick or a carpenter using a saw, they bent the will of others to their own. Lives to them were tools and weapons to be wielded against a hostile land and climate" (452). But these critiques are used to show the similarities between Bigger's act of creation (and destruction) and those that built America: "Did we not build a nation, did we not wage war and conquer in the name of a dream to realize our personalities and to make those realized personalities secure!" (465). But in making him seem more human to the white world, he ends up defining humanness according to their abstractions. The alternative, according to Max and this logic, is continued violence and destruction—Bigger, like "millions of others more or less like him, white and black" (*Native Son* 469), could eventually turn on their bourgeois masters. "Who knows," he asks the court, "when some slight shock, disturbing the delicate balance between social order and thirsty aspiration, shall send the skyscrapers in our cities toppling" (469). In using this image, Max ends up supporting the fear of otherness championed by white society.

In the end, then, Bigger becomes the exotic and brutal ape rather than the urban and transgressive rat. Locked in a cage and waiting to be executed, Bigger stares through his bars with a "faint, wry, bitter smile" (*Native Son* 502). The absence of the rat in the novel's closing pages forecloses any chance that Bigger might elude his fate. All that he's left with besides a "strange" and bitter smile is an even "stranger" realization: "What I killed for must've been good!" (501). While this reaction shocks Max and lends credence to Baldwin's charge that Bigger is a stereotype that supports caricatures of African Americans, the novel's ending is more nuanced than Baldwin's critique suggests. As Entin argues, the significance of sensational modernist texts by Wright and others rests in their failure "to imagine fully formed solutions to the problems that they present" (33–34). By "frequently leav[ing] readers in . . . [a] terrain of aesthetic, political, and emotional uncertainty" (34), these texts force us to examine often unquestioned beliefs and assumptions regarding what constitutes race, humanness, and animality. In doing so, they leave room for experiencing and acknowledging radical difference by resisting the possibility of projecting contingent categories onto characters like Bigger and the rat.

As with the novels of Farrell, Algren, Gold, and Olsen, *Native Son* examines the potential of urban pastoral experiences to create new forms of place that counter the deterministic forces and constrictive spaces that seek to trap working-class urban residents. But as in Hurston's work on black folklore, Wright's novel moves beyond the symbolic use of nonhuman animals by contesting assumptions concerning animal "predators" and "pests" in unique and surprising ways. In inverting connections between African Americans and animal species often considered "beasts" or "pests," *Native Son* models ways that depictions of animals can be used to critique human-animal binaries often used to support racial hierarchies. Viewing depictions of animals in this way can help envision social rights for exploited human groups *and* environmental rights for nonhuman species. In this sense, the novel helps expand urban pastoralism beyond the objects, human groups, and nonhuman species often associated with the pastoral city, creating versions of the mode that are more ecological and egalitarian in design.

Conclusion

The urban pastoral mode plays a central role in depression-era novels focused on urban landscapes. Whether used to highlight ways that working-class residents experienced and/or attempted to create new understandings of place in urban parks and other "green" spaces or to model ways that human-animal relationships can subvert narrow anthropocentric and racial categories, the mode became a powerful tool to highlight social and environmental crises in urban landscapes. In appropriating the mode for these purposes, Farrell, Algren, Gold, Olsen, and Wright anticipate the urban crises of the postwar era, exacerbated by white flight, deindustrialization, and urban public works projects. Their recognition of the racial and economic restrictions often limiting access to urban pastoral resources is also relevant to understanding ongoing forms of gentrification happening in many of today's large and small cities. Like the wilderness and the rural, cities became geographical landscapes through which depression-era authors sought to critique and reimagine dominant social and environmental relationships in the US. In addition to geographical landscapes, authors of the period also turned to the terrain of the technological, identifying ways that particular forms and uses of technology support economic, gender, racial, and environmental exploitation. Responding to the ecological disasters from the late 1920s to the early '50s, including the development and use of the atom bomb, these authors also recognized the unprecedented threat of technology on both the human and nonhuman worlds.

Chapter 4

Futuramas and Atom Bombs

Though not the financial success its planners had originally envisioned, the 1939 New York World's Fair attracted forty-five million visitors over its two-year run, making it the "best attended event in the United States during the first half of the twentieth century" (203). Referred to as "Dawn of a New Day" and "the World of Tomorrow," the fair offered visitors a glimpse of the future in the form of exhibits showcasing new commercial products by the leading corporations of the day, including a relatively new invention called television, as well as visions of future societies in exhibits like Democracy and General Motor's Futurama. The relative popularity of the fair illustrates an interest in the social and economic potential of technological progress during the period. Not only would technology, according to the fair, help streamline everyday tasks and chores, it would also help solve many of the major problems brought to light during the Depression.

For David E. Nye, the 1939–40 New York World's Fair appealed to the "technological sublime" in its depictions of the role technology could play in creating a better world. The technological sublime, according to Nye, does not rely on the terror of the Burkean sublime or the transcendent knowledge of the Kantian sublime. Instead, the "awe" induced by railroads, skyscrapers, bridges, and dams celebrated "the power of human reason, and . . . granted special privilege to engineers and inventors" (60). But underlying the period's fascination with the possibilities of the technological sublime lies a grotesque underside that questions the benevolence and morality attributed to an uncritical celebration of technology. For critics, these celebrations often obscured the social and environmental limitations and effects of some forms of technological progress. While the development and use of atomic bombs to end World War II would signal a major crisis in the technological sublime, the fair itself highlighted the contingency of the myth of the moral scientist and his/her benevolent technological inventions.

In this chapter, I argue that depression-era filmmakers and authors, particularly science fiction authors of the 1930s, '40s, and early '50s, critiqued forms of technology in similar ways as modern environmentalists like Rachel Carson, whose admonishment of indiscriminate uses of DDT and other pesticides in *Silent Spring* (1962) would highlight the destructive effects of technology on the natural world and the human body. In the first section of the chapter, I argue that the 1939–40 New York World's Fair use of the technological sublime obscured the economic, social, and environmental crises of the period. This extends even to the ground on which the fair was built, which was previously the Corona Ash Dump famously depicted in F. Scott Fitzgerald's *The Great Gatsby* as the "Valley of Ashes." But if the fair largely supported a version of progress and the future defined by the technological sublime, some exhibits, such as the American Institute of Planner's (AIP) documentary film, *The City* (1939), offered alternative depictions of technology that revealed the grotesque effects often underlying dominant understandings of technological progress valued by the fair planners. In the second section, I argue that science fiction authors Ray Bradbury and Judith Merril critiqued the technological sublime by appropriating what Istvan Csicsery-Ronay Jr. calls the "sf grotesque." Bradbury uses the grotesque to call attention to the major environmental and social consequences of imperialist forms of technology used for unchecked human expansion. Merril uses the mode to connect gender inequality and environmental destruction underlying the use and effects of the atomic bomb. In the third and final section of the chapter, I argue that George Schuyler appropriates aspects of the technological sublime to show how white civilizations have used technology to enslave black groups around the world. While Schuyler primarily depicts technology in ways that show its violent uses to construct racial power, he also hints at other uses of technology that are more socially egalitarian and environmentally sustainable.

By calling attention to the destructive capabilities of frequently celebrated technologies, the authors and filmmakers I will discuss in this chapter offer an early example of technology-critique, which would become central to environmentalists in the later part of the century. Similarly, the expression of ideas we would come to associate with modern environmentalism in "Golden Age" science fiction suggests that they were of greater importance to science fiction authors of this period than critics often realize. In depicting disorienting alien landscapes and grotesque victims of technology, these authors create novel and effective ways of envisioning the environmental consequences of forms of science and technology during the period. By suggesting ways that environmental exploitation and economic, racial, and gender inequality often underlie the technological sublime, they also, like other cultural artists of the period, recognize the importance of bringing together social and environmental issues. Finally, in envisioning more progressive forms of technology, some of these authors and filmmakers point to the important roles that technology *can* play in creating a more socially egalitarian and environmentally sustainable world.

"The World of Tomorrow"

In its uncritical, idealist notions of progress, the 1939 New York World's Fair largely represents what Lewis Mumford had over a decade earlier called a "utopia of escape" (15). For Mumford, this utopian mode is an "idle dream" that dispenses with "the real, limited, imperfect people" around us to create private forms of fantasy and escape. Mumford particularly associates the utopia of escape with modern forms of technology, which, he claims, are continually attempting to reproduce the "deep longing to return to and remain at rest in the mother's womb" (19). The 1939–40 New York World's Fair attempted to create a kind of escape by limiting contingency, tension, and difference through visions of "sanitized and safe" future worlds with "no poor neighborhoods, no traffic jams, no polluted streams, no smog, no ruins, no large factories, no industrial blight, no signs of war . . . no military installations . . . no racial tensions and no job discrimination" (Nye 213). But if the fair attempted to limit contingency and difference in its utopian vision of the future, some of its exhibits offered glimpses of the "sci fi grotesque." If the technological sublime illustrates a largely conservative experience that asks the viewer to celebrate and submit to human ingenuity and progress, the "grotesque" can work in literature and film to expose aspects of technological progress that the mind "is not sure it wants to know" (Csicsery-Ronay Jr. 186). The use of the grotesque at the fair is at least partially informed by a small minority of progressive scientists and critics who attempted to exert influence in the fair planning process (Kuznick 343). One alternative exhibit that made its way into the fair due to this influence was the short film *The City*, scripted by Lewis Mumford and co-directed by Willard Van Dyke and Ralph Steiner. Using aspects of the grotesque to highlight social and environmental conditions that countered the rational and unblemished landscape created by the technological sublime, *The City* challenged aspects of the fair's vision of progress.

Before turning to instances of the grotesque at the fair, it will be helpful to more fully describe the fair's vision of technology, progress, and urban living. Perhaps no exhibit represents this vision more closely than General Motors' extremely popular Futurama exhibit. In his novel *World's Fair* (1985), E. L. Doctorow describes the exhibit as "everyone's first stop" and recounts waiting in line "practically an hour" to experience it (323). Like other popular exhibits at the fair, the Futurama provided fairgoers "an olympian view of the future" by mimicking riding in an airplane, an experience most fairgoers had not yet experienced due to the relative newness of commercial air travel. To enhance this effect, the exhibit used dioramas and miniatures that fairgoers could look down on and take in more fully (Nye 202–203, 214). In the model world below, designed by American industrial designer and motorway enthusiast Norman Bel Geddes, visitors would see "multilane highways, power plants, farms for artificially produced crops, rooftop platforms for individual flying machines and autogyros, and various gadgets" (Morshed 74–75). Perhaps none of these was more prominent in the model than the multilane motorways, which connected the various landscapes and envisioned the prominence of the automobile in the future. The depictions of such motorways in cities would particularly resonate with visitors who might have just driven to the fair using the expressways built by Robert Moses. As Marshall Berman writes, "Spectators on their way to and from the fair, as they flowed along Moses' roads and across his bridges, could directly experience something of this visionary future, and see that it seemed to work" (303). Doctorow recounts a similar experience of the Futurama's prescience. He writes,

> [After] the show was over, and with your I HAVE SEEN THE FUTURE button in your hand you came out into the sun and you were standing on precisely the corner you had just seen, the future was right where you were standing and what was small had become big, the scale had enlarged and you were no longer looking down at it, but standing in it, on this corner of the future, right here in the World's Fair! (325)

Approximating the exhibit's futuristic landscape in the design of the space in and around the fair could help convince fairgoers to accept and value the promoters' vision of the future.

Though the model world in the Futurama envisioned major changes to different landscapes across the US, its depiction of the future city particularly drew upon the technological sublime in ways that exalted the moral vision of engineers and designers while obscuring or omitting people and places that didn't fit into its vision of urban living.¹ Largely based on the "center-oriented, geometrical" modernist urban design of Le Corbusier's "Radiant City" (Morshed 74), the city is populated by tall skyscrapers that divide the city into superblocks connected by expressways. As Robert Fishman argues, the great urban theorists of the period rooted their designs in "the technological innovations that inspired their age." For Le Corbusier, the skyscraper particularly influenced his design of the Radiant City (*Urban Utopias* 13). Associated with the "geometrical sublime," the modern skyscraper represents a form of the technological sublime, particularly in its ability to provide more totalizing perceptions of the urban landscape that cultivated a sense of "mastery" over people and objects residing below (Nye 106–7). In the model city of the Futurama, the tall skyscrapers "a quarter of a mile high . . . with convenient rest and recreational facilities for all" have "on many of the buildings . . . landing decks for helicopters and autogyros," while the parks beneath are "united into long green strips surrounding each community." The prominent use of parks and other green spaces in the city particularly appeals to a sense of "urban pastoralism," though the lack of model people used to populate them suggests these spaces play a more aesthetic than recreational function.² Furthermore, the parks and expressways have been used to replace "outmoded business sections and undesirable slum areas whenever possible" (*To New Horizons*). The latter particularly suggests the antisocial basis of the exhibit's urban pastoralism and use of the technological sublime, as it ignores problems associated with displaced workers and undesirable slum areas. Instead, the exhibit falls back on an uncritical "utopia of escape" rooted in idealistic versions of technology and modernist urban design that see them as ways to create a future without crime, pollution, poverty, and traffic.

The idea of urban pastoral displacement envisioned by the Futurama's urban landscape also describes the history behind the fair's construction. Before becoming the site of the 1939 New York World's Fair, Flushing Meadow Park in Queens was home to the Corona Ash Dump, a former marsh used by the Brooklyn Ash Removal Company from

1909 to 1934 to dump "millions of cubic yards of smoldering waste" (Mille 135). According to Benjamin Mille, the smoke from the dump often made it often necessary to use police officers to direct traffic at nearby intersections and complaints about the smell were reported "as far as four miles away" (177). The dump also served as the model for F. Scott Fitzgerald's "Valley of Ashes" in *The Great Gatsby* (1925). The ash heap, Nick Carraway informs us, "[is] a fantastic farm where ashes grow like wheat into ridges and hills and grotesque gardens; where ashes take the forms of houses and chimneys and rising smoke and, finally, with a transcendent effort, of ash-gray men who move dimly and already crumbling through the powdery air" (25). Fitzgerald's antipastoral treatment of the landscape uses pastoral images like "wheat" and "gardens" to highlight the grotesque quality of the objects and inhabitants of this landscape as compared to the highly ordered spaces of Manhattan and East and West Egg.[3] For Carraway, the ash dump is a grotesque landscape that everyone traveling between Long Island and Manhattan must stop at for "at least a minute" to sometimes "as long as half an hour" (26). While the ash dump works in the novel to symbolize the excess of the 1920s and the detritus of the American Dream, as suggested by an early title of the novel—*Among the Ash-Heaps and Millionaires* (Mille 135)—it also brings readers face to face with the excess waste of urban living in the modern age viewable in the ash and objects littering the dump as well as the workers and residents inhabiting the area. As such, the landscape works to (at least momentarily) counter what Brian Thill calls an "away-fantasy" in waste management. As Thill reminds us, waste elimination often takes the form of displacement as "waste becomes something for someone else to eliminate *for* you" and is "not actually . . . scrubbed from the world, just from your world, more or less" (29). While the ash heap in *The Great Gatsby* serves to expose residents and travelers to the highly toxic mounds of ash and other debris contaminating the landscape as well as the human populations forced to live and work there, the fair contributed to the away-fantasy in its highly ordered and clean landscape that displaced and hid the waste once covering the area.

New Yorkers moving in between Manhattan and Long Island would no longer have to confront the immense, toxic, and ugly waste that littered the former marsh.

If most fair exhibits supported the Futurama's vision of a highly ordered, technological landscape devoid of social and environmental issues, at least one exhibit tried to depict the grotesque underside of this vision. *The City* (1939)—outlined by Pare Lorentz, Lewis Mumford, directed and shot by Ralph Steiner and Willard Van Dyke, scored by composer Aaron Copland, and produced by Clarence Stein's Civic Films, a subsidiary of the American Institute of Planners (AIP)—also envisions a future city meant to alleviate some of the major issues of the period. While not as popular as GM's Futurama, the film "attracted large and enthusiastic crowds" (Gillette 42), representing a social-consciousness side of the fair (39).[4] Unlike the Futurama's futuristic urban landscape, *The City* proposes combining the modern city and the traditional rural New England village into a single design best illustrated by Greenbelt, Maryland, one of the New Deal's "Greenbelt towns." But what distinguishes *The City* most is its willingness to depict the major environmental and social issues of the day, including industrial pollution as well as urban alienation, traffic jams, and pedestrian casualties, often associating them with the kind of urban thought and views of technology supported by other exhibits at the fair.

Influenced by the British "garden city" movement, the film is divided into four sections, each addressing a different form of community.[5] While the first section of the film praises the traditional New England village's close-knit and democratic forms of community as well as its close relationship to the natural environment, the second and third sections critique different version of the modern city—including the industrial city (represented by Pittsburgh) and the metropolitan city (represented by New York)—for their unchecked pollution, individualism, and automobile culture. Finally, the film presents its version of the ideal urban community: a synthesis of the New England village and the conveniences of the modern city, represented by the Greenbelt garden city.

Of the four sections, the most interesting are the middle two for their powerful critique of the industrial and metropolitan city. In these sequences, the filmmakers call attention to forms of urban life and technology at the heart of the fair's celebration of the technological sublime. Using the steel-producing city of Pittsburgh to illustrate the environmental and social hazards of the industrial urban landscape, *The City* highlights the crowded and unhealthy living conditions for workers and their families who reside there. The billowing smoke stacks, molten iron and steel, and cargo trains define the landscape rather than the clean industrial spaces depicted in the Futurama's model world. As the narrator reflects, "Smoke makes prosperity, they tell you here. Smoke makes prosperity . . . no matter if you choke on it." The smoke, together with images of unpaved sidewalks, cramped living quarters, and exhausted, unhealthy residents, gives the industrial urban landscape a hellish quality, echoing James Parton's description of the city in 1868: "Hell with the lid off!" These images are more grotesque than sublime, countering what Nye calls the "industrial" sublime's ability to provoke "respect [for] the power of the corporation and the intelligence of its engineers" through its efficiently organized landscape and its "dynamism of moving machinery and powerful forces" (126). Instead of respect, the images in *The City* seek to produce revulsion for the condition of the landscape and its inhabitants. They also suggest an inability to contain the forces unleashed during steel production.[6] The images that open the section particularly comment on the difficulties of containing the molten iron. Transitioning from a blacksmith of the New England village leisurely hammering hot iron into a desired shape, the scene dramatically shifts to images of the blast furnace, where molten iron sprays from and overflows its containers. There's even a shot of molten slag making its way down an embankment into a ravine below and, perhaps, eventually into the river.[7]

If the second section of the film highlights the poor living and environmental conditions of the industrial city, the next section focuses on the alienation, antisocial behavior, and traffic congestion associated with metropolitan cities like New York. But the film also makes sure to show how the two types of cities are mutually reliant on each other. The second section's final scene cleverly uses a train to transition from the industrial to the metropolitan city, alluding to the relationship between the two urban landscapes. The prosperity of the latter is predicated on the misery of workers and residents in industrial cities, as the steel produced in places like Pittsburgh is used to reinforce the giant skyscrapers of New York and other large cities. In addition to connecting the two cities, the film's depiction of New York directly counters the technological sublimity of the skyscrapers, touted by other exhibits at the fair. Instead, *The City* often depicts skyscrapers from the street. The towering structures in these shots block out the sky and sunlight and threaten to entrap urban residents in a prison made of concrete, glass, and steel.

Besides enclosing its residents, the metropolitan city also, according to the film, transforms residents into antisocial automatons dictated by time and money. Urban workers are shown at crowded lunch counters, quickly eating their food rather than talking to their neighbors. The film depicts the preparation of their food as an assembly line operation, that moves from toaster to line cook to the customer's mouth, gradually picking up speed as the cycle repeats itself. Furthermore, the congested automobile traffic both inside and directly outside of the city counters the fair's uncritical attitudes towards expressways. Not only do these expressways frustrate commuters and rob them of hours of their time, they also threaten pedestrians crossing the street as well as children looking for places to play. In a scene that echoes the decapitation of one of young Mike's friends in *Jews Without Money*, *The City* includes the voices of operators reporting yet another instance of a car hitting a pedestrian.

The fourth section of the film introduces a vision of the city that the film supports. Synthesizing the New England village and the modern city, the Greenbelt city attempts to resolve some of the issues described above through more place-based and environmentally sustainable understandings of urban design and technology. The scenes take place in Greenbelt, Maryland, the fully functioning New Deal cooperative community planned in 1935 and settled in 1937. Like the Futurama, the Greenbelt town stresses the importance of modern technology for the garden city. One of the first things we see in this section is construction workers building a dam, followed by an airplane taking off. "Science tak[ing] flight at last for human purposes," the narrator tells us, as we catch our first glimpse of the Greenbelt town: clearings of low buildings and land that are "built into the countryside" and surrounded by thick forests. Unlike other depictions of urban life at the fair, *The City* attempts to appropriate science and technology as a tool for constructing new social and environmental relationships among urban residents. "The new city," the narrator tells use, "is organized to make cooperation possible between machines, and men, and nature. Each has its place." In basing its uses of science and technology in alternative social and environmental values, *The City* offers a powerful critique of the nature-dominating technological sublime (Nye 64).

One of the features of the city meant to spur social and environmental cooperation is the "belt of public land" kept green and undeveloped for the benefit of the residents, especially the children who "need the earth for playing and growing." Contrasting with the metropolis city in which children search in vain for open spaces, the greenbelt fields, forests, and rivers offer children safe places to play. Furthermore, unlike the Futurama's modernist city, which includes urban parks and public gathering places but keeps other parts of the city, particularly residential skyscrapers, densely packed, the garden cities attempt a more complete structural redesigning of the city in terms of space and landscape by "bringing the city into the country, bringing the parks and gardens into city." Like Farrell's *Young Lonigan* and Gold's *Jews Without Money*, *The City* suggests the limitations of urban parks without larger structural changes that include less dense neighborhoods and the promotion of values that engender a more open and cooperative sense of place.[8] Finally, the film ends (like the Futurama) by stressing that the green city is a real possibility: "Order has come. Order and life together. We've got the skill, we've found the way, we've built the cities. All that we know about machines, and soils, and raw materials, and human ways of living is waiting. We can reproduce the pattern and better it a thousand times. It's here. The new city. Ready to serve a better age. You and your children . . . the choice is yours." But unlike the Futurama, the fairgoer saw few signs of technology, design, and cooperative values that support this vision in and around the fair.[9]

If *The City* critiques the dominant social and environmental values of modern engineering and urban design, its vision occasionally falls short, first by adhering to the dominant racial and gender norms of the period. In terms of gender, women still do the housework and laundry. Furthermore, there are no people of color shown living in the garden city. According to Greenbelt, Maryland's 1996 National Register of Historic Places Registration Form, the plan for the town originally included 250 units for African Americans, but this part of the plan was eventually dropped. As such, the community takes on aspects of the "privileged" suburban escape from which the film tries to distance it. Jane Jacobs would later criticize garden cities for these very reasons in *The Death and Life of Great American Cities* (1961), calling them "different degrees of extended private life" for "middle class professionals and their families" who "set themselves distinctly apart from the different people in the surrounding city" (83, 84). Aside from Jacobs's later criticism, the vision exhibited by Greenbelt, Maryland, was also criticized by the filmmakers themselves. As Howard Gillette Jr. notes, co-directors Ralph Steiner and Willard Van Dyke were skeptical of the garden city design and resisted the ideas they saw forced upon them by garden city planners Clarence Stein and Henry Wright as well as by Mumford's script. Referring to the designs portrayed in Greenbelt, Maryland as "jails without locks" and "modern slums," Steiner stated, "What the city planners built resulted from all head and no heart and no eye. Stingy minds creating stingy houses" (qtd. in Gillett 75).[10]

Regardless of the potential political and aesthetic limitations of the Greenbelt city depicted in *The City*, the documentary identifies fundamental problems associated with modern urban life that its creators believed couldn't be fixed by replacing slums with expressways. Though the garden city depicted in the film is subject to its own omissions and difficulties, it offered a real urban alternative that was transformed, against the wishes of its planner, into the postwar suburb. Robert Fishman writes,

> It was not the communitarians but the speculators ... who ... adopt[ed] the "large-scale methods" that [Catherine] Bauer had called for, and they used them not to build the modernist collective dwellings Bauer and Mumford advocated, but more efficiently constructed versions of that monument of "individual Home Ownership," the single family suburban house. The collective architecture and planning of the New Deal "Greenbelt Towns" remained a curiosity, while the suburban house gained new impetus from the most modern methods of functional mass production. (177)

As US soldiers returned from the second World War, the dominant form of community became suburbs for many white, middle-class Americans, reestablishing dominant gender roles temporarily lifted by the war and leaving cities and their remaining residents to experience further economic, social, and environmental decline.

If the debates over technology and social engineering represented by the exhibits at the 1939 New York World's Fair offered one venue to critique aspects of the technological sublime that obscured major environmental and social issues, the science fiction genre offered another. Sci-fi authors during the 1930s, '40s, and early '50s identified and chiseled away at aspects of the technological sublime by defining and critiquing major contradictions underlying American society concerning race, gender, and the environment, especially after the devastating effects of the atom bomb became more known to the public. To highlight the contradictions hidden beneath the technological sublime, these authors more explicitly revealed its "grotesque" underside.

Science Fiction and the Grotesque

Science fiction has often held a contentious relationship to the technological advances and social values guiding western society. Looking back at the twentieth century, Lawrence Buell writes, "For half a century, science fiction has taken a keen, if not consistent interest in ecology, in planetary endangerment, in environmental ethics, in humankind's relation to the nonhuman world" (*The Future* 56). Buell and other critics largely attributes this concern to post-*Silent Spring* environmental thought (58), but "Golden Age" science fiction novels and stories of the 1930s, '40s, and early '50s also often directly engaged with major ecological issues of the day in socially progressive ways.[11] Critics have noted the left-leaning political allegiances of many writers in the genre during the 1930s and early '40s. In *The Cultural Front*, Michael Denning counts the Futurians—a fan club of science fiction writers including Isaac Asimov, Frederick Pohl, Damon Knight, and Judith Merril—among the radical literary groups that advocated and contributed to proletarian literature during the Depression (225–26). Members of the Futurians have also commented on the group's socially progressive vision. Damon Knight recalls that "several" Futurians joined the Young Communist League (YCL) in the 1930s (5).[12] Knight also points out that the group embraced the inclusion of women, who were often excluded from other sci-fi fan clubs during the period (21). Futurian science fiction editor and writer, Frederick Pohl, remarks on his four-year membership in the YCL, "Trade unionism, civil rights, an end to racial discrimination—no one now thinks of them as revolutionary. What the Communist Party and the YCL stood for in the 1930s, absent Moscow, looks pretty good right now" (54). Besides the Futurians, other science fiction writers held progressive social and economic ideas during the period. Robert Heinlein was a "radical liberal" during the 1930s and involved in leftist causes like Upton Sinclair's 1934 End Poverty in California campaign (Patterson Jr. 176). His early story "Misfits" (1939) involves a Civilian Conservation Corps-like government agency called the Cosmic Construction Corps that, according to its "enabling act," takes young troubled men into space "*for the purpose of conserving and improving our interplanetary resources, and providing useful, healthful occupations for the youth of this planet*" (italics in original, 509). Like Heinlein, James Blish, who was also associated with the Futurians, would also use depression-era subjects in his collection of "Okie" stories, published together in the 1950s as *Cities in Flight*. In the novelized stories, cities develop technologies that allow them to leave a declining earth to find better opportunities in the galaxy.

But beyond appropriating aspects of New Deal social and conservation programs in their attempts to envision future solutions to present issues, sci-fi authors of the early "Golden Age" also directly address the intersection of environmental and social issues by calling attention to the ecological effects of racism, imperialism, and gender inequality. To do so, these texts often critique the technological sublime by identifying the grotesque consequences of uncritical forms of scientific and technological progress. For Golden Age sci-fi writers, the grotesque became a popular mode to highlight the contingency of practices and beliefs resulting in destructive acts against land, human groups, and animal species. While Ray Bradbury connects imperial practices to environmental devastation and the genocide of indigenous populations, Judith Merril calls attention to ways that the effect of nuclear fallout exposes gender hierarchies that support forms of social and environmental exploitation.

As Gary K. Wolfe and David Seed have argued, Ray Bradbury restages the social and environmental effects of American frontier expansion on the planet Mars in *The Martian Chronicles* (1950).[13] Like the American West, Mars becomes a palimpsest as human explorers and settlers quickly change the environment. Technology plays a major role in creating these changes, particularly by establishing the means for earth explorers to reach Mars as well as in the changes they create on the Martian landscape.[14] If the railroad helped make Western imperialism possible in the US, the development of the spaceship in Bradbury's stories allow imperialism to extend to Mars (Wolfe 109). The accessibility of the planet due to technological advances initiates a trajectory of environmental exploitation that will result in the kind of resource scarcity that is occurring on Earth and find its ultimate resolution in war and the use of atomic weapons. In this sense, the use of atomic weapons is part of a larger disregard of the natural environment and human well-being rooted in uncritical support of technological and economic progress found in changes to the Mississippi River preceding the 1927 flood and the Great Plains preceding the Dust Bowl. For Bradbury, Mars is not an alien landscape where humans can escape from the issues they have created on Earth. On writing the novel, the author notes, "I decided that Mars would be nothing more nor less than a mirror in which Earth Man would be reflected, twice as large as life, with his wonders, beauties and terrors, his petty politics, his ravening greeds, and simple faiths. He would find no more and no less on Mars, than what he brought in his pocket and in his heart" (qtd. in Seed 52). Reflecting on two decades of ecological calamities on Earth, Bradbury uses Mars to illustrate the devastating effects that unchecked expansion and economic development can have on environments and the inhabitants who depend upon them.

Perhaps no story in the *Chronicles* foreshadows the social and ecological devastation that imperialist expansion has than "—And the Moon Be Still as Bright." First published in a 1948 issue of *Thrilling Wonder Stories*, the narrative follows a group of American explorers who arrive on Mars to find that all the Martians are dead, having contracted chicken pox from earlier human expeditions to the planet. Jeff Spender, the expedition's archaeologist, is dismayed that a million-year-old race finds its ultimate demise because of a "child's disease, a disease that doesn't even kill *children* on Earth" (Bradbury 51). Spender's identification of the effects of human disease on the Martians situates the story firmly in American colonial and frontier experiences in which European diseases helped wipe out large populations of indigenous peoples (Seed 68). Spender is also dismayed at his crew mates' indifference to the Martian landscape and culture, particularly after another crew mate, Biggs, tosses empty bottles of alcohol in the Martian canal and later vomits on a tile mosaic in a Martian city after drinking too much. The archaeologist soon leaves the expedition to go off on his own, but he returns a week later calling himself the "last Martian" and proceeds to kill five of the crew members, including a Native American crew member called "Cherokee" who he at first believes will sympathize with his actions. When Cherokee reacts in horror, Spender shoots him and flees from camp. Captain Wilder, the commander of the expedition who is friends with the archaeologist and sympathetic to his point of view, and his men eventually find the rogue archaeologist. After refusing to surrender to his former crew mates, Spender asks the captain to do what he can "to restrict tearing this planet apart" (68). While Spender is eventually killed in the shootout, a later story in the *Chronicles* suggests that Captain Wilder is given the unsavory job of exploring the outer universe for questioning his superiors' plans to develop Mars.

In calling himself the last Martian, Spender renounces his affiliation with human progress and expansion, processes he associates with genocide and environmental destruction, and allies himself with a culture he believes values nature. As he tells Captain Wilder, "They [the Martians] knew how to live with nature and get along with nature. They didn't try too hard to be all men and no animal" (66). Explorers and settlers from Earth, on the other hand, have and will continue to destroy the environment: "No matter how we touch Mars, we'll never touch it. And then we'll get mad at it, and you know what we'll do? We'll rip it up, rip the skin off, and change it to fit ourselves" (54). Later stories in *The Martian Chronicles* prove Spender's warnings correct. In the intercalary chapter "The Locusts," human ships and settlers arriving on Mars are compared to the biblical insect.

Upon landing, the narrator informs us that "the men with hammers in their hands [ran] to beat the strange world into a shape that was familiar to the eye, to bludgeon away all the strangeness, their mouths fringed with nails so they resembled steel-toothed carnivores, spitting them into their swift hands as they hammered up frame cottages and scuttled over roofs with shingles to blot out the eerie stars, and fit green shades to pull against the night" (78). In half a year, we learn, "a dozen small towns had been laid down upon the naked planet, filled with sizzling neon tubes and yellow electric bulbs" (78). Next, the narrator continues, come the "women . . . with flower pots" (78). Each layer of change seeks to make an "alien" landscape seem more familiar and productive. Even the names brought by settlers from Earth seek to change the landscape by thinking of it in terms of the usable resources they hope to extract:

> The old Martian names were names of water and air and hills. They were the names of snows that emptied south in stone canals to fill the empty seas. And the names of sealed and buried sorcerers and towers and obelisks. And the rockets struck at the names like hammers, breaking away the marble into shale, shattering the crockery milestones that named the old towns, in the rubble of which great pylons were plunged with new names: IRON TOWN, STEEL TOWN, ALUMINUM CITY, ELECTRIC VILLAGE, CORN TOWN, GRAIN VILLA, DETROIT II, all mechanical names and the metal names from Earth. (102–3)

Like the American West, explorers and settlers largely view the Martian landscape in terms of resources and wealth—as a continuation of economic and technological progress started on Earth.

While the previous stories allude to the environmental changes that the settlement and economic development of the Martian landscape promises to bring, the story "The Green Morning" focuses on the environmental effects of another kind of change inflicted on the landscape. In the story, an unhealthy young man from Earth named Benjamin Driscoll travels across the Martian landscape to plant and grow trees: "[T]rees and foliage, producing air, more air, growing larger with each season; trees to cool the towns in the boiling summers, trees to hold back the winter winds. There were so many things a tree could do: add color, provide shade, drop fruit, or become a children's playground, a whole sky universe to climb and hang from; an architecture of food and pleasure, that was a tree" (73). Against the hot, dry Martian landscape, Driscoll vows to wage a "horticultural war" to uncover the "mineral wealth hid[ing] in the soil, untapped because the old ferns, flowers, bushes, and trees had tired themselves out" (75). One night it begins to rain, and the next morning Driscoll awakens to find "thousands" of trees "great ... huge trees ... as tall as ten men" standing where he planted his seeds. The "fresh, pure, green, cold oxygen," flowing from the trees "like a moving current," causes the young man to faint. When he awakens, he finds that "five thousand new trees had climbed up into the yellow sun" (77). While some critics have seen Driscoll as a delusional character who hallucinates a pastoral vision of Mars (Seed 65), his attempts to wage a "horticultural war" on the landscape give his action a more diabolical cast. Kim Stanley Robinson, author of the *Mars Trilogy*, comes to a similar conclusion, seeing in the young man's actions a form of "violence" against the landscape. According to Robinson, the story even came to influence his own depiction of "terraforming" the planet in *Green Mars* (1993), the second novel in the trilogy (147). The act also alludes to Charles Dana Wilbur's popular and eventually debunked late nineteenth-century slogan "Rain Follows the Plow." Wilbur believed that cultivating arid land would change the climate of the area, bringing rain and more fertility to the soil (Smith 182). This practice would help contribute to the American Dust Bowl, as the sod on lands not suitable for crops was disrupted under the false belief that more crops would equal more rain. In this sense, the erratic growth of trees in Bradbury's story seems like a form of revenge against the violence perpetrated on the Martian landscape. The trees' spontaneous and seemingly unlimited ability to grow gives them the appearance of a grotesque "organic" monster, threatening to overtake the land and provide more oxygen than the human body can stand.

If "The Green Morning" envisions a nightmare that inverts the pastoral desires of western/Martian homesteaders by giving them too much of what they desire, other stories in the novel depict the consequences of unleashing nature's powerful forces through the atomic bomb. In stories like "The Off Season" and "The Watchers," the settlers on Mars watch the Earth burn due to an atomic war on the planet: "Part of it [Earth] seemed to come apart in a million pieces, as if a gigantic jigsaw had exploded. It burned with an unholy dripping glare for a minute, three times normal size, then dwindled" (143). In "The Watchers," the Earth burns for three hours before the fire goes out, leaving it burnt but still there. While these two stories depict characters viewing the explosion of atomic weapons on Earth from the distant safety of Mars, a later story, "There Will Come Soft Rains," shifts focus back to the home planet in the aftermath of nuclear war. The story depicts the hourly checklist of an automated house in Fresno, California, that continues to function despite the fact that its human owners have been killed by an atomic blast. When shifting to the garden to turn on the sprinkler system, we discover what has happened to the residents: "The entire west face of the house was black, save for five places. Here the silhouette in paint of a man mowing a lawn. Here, as in a photograph, a woman bent to pick flowers. Still further over, their images burned on wood in one titanic instant, a small boy, hands flung into the air; higher up, the image of a thrown ball, and opposite him a girl, hands raised to catch a ball which never came down" (167). The grotesque shadows provide an eerie reminder of the mother and children's last moments, like the shadows left by of residents in Hiroshima after the use of atomic weapons in 1945.

The story further suggests the uninhabitable state of the planet through its depiction of nonhuman and, in some cases, artificial animals. The family's dog, "once huge and fleshy, but now gone to bone and covered with sores" (168), returns home and becomes frantic when unable to find its owners: "It ran wildly in circles, biting at its tail, spun in a frenzy, and died" (168). All other life forms in the house are mechanical replicas, perhaps (like the dog) representing the family's need to connect with nonhuman animals in a future that holds less opportunities to encounter them.[15] Robot mice clean up the mud the dog leaves in the house as well as the dog itself after its death. The nursery includes walls on which hidden film projectors project animals and floors made "to resemble a crisp cereal meadow" on which "aluminum roaches and iron crickets" scurry across (168). Furthermore, the air in the nursery is filled with animal and nature sounds as well as "butterflies of delicate red tissue" (169). Despite the mechanical ecosystem in the house that persists as organic life struggles outside, not even these artificial lifeforms can survive. A tree, left lifeless by the blast or the preceding fallout, crashes through the window, spilling cleaning solvent into the stove and starting a fire. The house unsuccessfully attempts to put out the fire and is soon burnt to a single wall. The story ends with a mechanical voice that repeatedly tells the day to the lifeless landscape, as if to underscore the impermanence of humanity in the face of the powerful forces unleashed by the atomic and (soon after) hydrogen bomb.

If the 1939 World's Fair in New York attempted to create and capitalize on a new faith in the technological sublime, the development and use of atomic bombs in the following decade caused many Americans to question this faith. Together with the massive dust storms and flooding in the preceding decades, the atomic bomb would lay the foundation for the development of the modern environmentalist movement in the second half of the twentieth century. The immense, devastating, and largely uncontained power of the new weapon prevented a celebration of human ingenuity. As the effects of the bomb became better understood, the weapon undermined the belief that science and technological progress were "morally uplifting" (228). Revealing the contingency of "[n]ature and human existence" (228), the bomb became a "permanent, invisible terror that offers no [sublime] moral enlightenment" (253). While the US federal government initially used censorship and public relations campaigns to hide and downplay the devastation caused by the bomb both during and after the explosion, it soon became unable to successfully assuage the concerns Americans had about the weapon (253).[16] John Hersey's 1946 issue-length article in the *New Yorker*, "Hiroshima," offered a powerful counternarrative to the official discourse concerning the bomb by describing "the attack from point of view of the victims" (Sharp 444).

The development and use of nuclear weapons and energy helped transform science fiction in the 1940s from "marginal pulp fantasy and escapism . . . to a more authoritative, public discourse on the present, future, and alternative course of American history" (Newell and Lamont 12). If Bradbury used the genre to critique imperialist understandings of technology and progress, Judith Merril used the genre to challenge gender norms underlying dominant attitudes concerning technology, social hierarchy, and the environment (16). As Dianne Newell and Victoria Lamont argue, the postwar atomic age positioned the savagery unleashed by nuclear fission as a primitive, feminized force to be tamed by male scientists (14). Merril often inverted this view of nuclear fission, recasting it as a male response to a loss of control that has devastating effects on human landscapes and bodies. Published in 1948 in *Astounding Science Fiction*, Merril's "That Only a Mother" particularly highlights the grotesque effects of nuclear radiation on the human body while challenging gender norms. In the story, radioactive poisoning from a nuclear war of the near future is leading to the mutation of newborn children and a rash of infanticides by fathers horrified by their mutated babies' appearances. When the story opens, Margaret is worried that her baby will be born mutated, especially since her husband (Hank) was probably exposed to radiation while working at the Oak Ridge National Laboratory. Margaret gives birth while Hank is serving as a "technical lieutenant" in an ongoing nuclear war, and through her letters to Hank, we are informed that the baby (Henrietta) is born normal. But towards the end of the story, we find out that Henrietta was indeed born without arms or legs due to radiation exposure. As another consequence of her exposure, the baby's brain develops at an accelerated pace allowing her to intelligibly talk at eighteen months. When Margaret's husband returns from duty, he is horrified that his wife is unable to recognize the baby's mutations, and the story ends by suggesting that he kill Henrietta: "*She didn't know*. His hands, beyond control, ran up and down the soft-skinned baby body, the sinuous, limbless body. *Oh, God, dear God*—his head shook and his muscles contracted in a bitter spasm of hysteria. His fingers tightened on his child—*Oh God, she didn't know*" (73). Hank's reaction to the physically deformed yet highly intelligent infant reveals an irrational fear of whatever threatens the phallocentric ordering and containment of social life, the human body, and the nonhuman realm.

Merril's early story builds upon what Istvan Csicsery-Ronay calls the "female grotesque." For Csicsery-Ronay, the female body has often been associated with the "metamorphic physicality" of the grotesque. The word's origin, he points out, "refers back to dark and moist interior spaces" (193). He writes,

> Metaphoric energy is easily associated with the momentous, uncontrollable, and juicy changes that occur in the female body (at least compared with the conventional standard of the male body) in menstruation, pregnancy, childbirth, lactation, menopause. From the phallocratic male perspective, these physical processes are uncomfortably insistent; they distract, they interrupt, they stink, and they stain. They are seen as physical concomitants of women's grotesque mental processes: changeability, undependability, materialism, and inability to abstract from their immediate, personal situations. Women are prone to disease because they are too open to the world; they are liable to infect, because their interiors can flow out onto others. (193)[17]

Similarly, Merril's "That Only a Mother" questions the norms and practices projected onto women by men. As "more mind than body," Henrietta upsets the "very foundation upon which gendered identity is based" (Newell and Lamont 32). Her grotesque physical features further question gender normalcy. Henrietta's lack of appendages amplifies her lack of phallus, making her both more vulnerable *and* contagious in Hank's phallocentric point of view. Her accelerated knowledge also threatens the dominance of male intellect in American patriarchal society. To further upset gender hierarchies, Merril inverts the traditional mental qualities ascribed to males and females. For Newell and Lamont, Margaret's interactions with Henrietta are as rational as Hank's are hysterical. Noting that Merril uses the word "hysterical" to describe Hank's reaction, the two critics argue that Margaret accepts Henrietta because her understanding of "normalcy" has expanded in ways unavailable to Hank (32–33). They also go on to suggest that the relationship established between Margaret and Henrietta, particularly because the two are able to freely communicate due to the child's heightened mental abilities, envisions relationships built on "equality and exchange rather than hierarchy and dependence" (33). Hank's "hysterical" response, on the other hand, ends up reinforcing a status quo that has led to harmful gender relations and environmental conditions.

Published two years later, Merril's first novel, *Shadow on the Hearth* (1950), builds upon the critique of gender hierarchy introduced in "That Only a Mother" while calling attention to the atom bomb's destruction of the natural environment. In the novel, an unnamed enemy has dropped nuclear weapons on all the major cities in the US, including New York, outside of which Gladys Mitchell, the novel's protagonist, and her family live in a Westchester County suburb. Since her husband is in New York when the bombs are dropped, she is alone in their suburban house with her two daughters. Eventually, she gives refuge to her immigrant maid and a high school physics teacher known for his opposition to nuclear armament, both of whom are hiding from the authorities after being deemed as potential subversives. While Gladys's characterization as a housewife who desperately misses her husband and is mostly ignorant of world events and scientific principles supports gender hierarchies of the Cold War era, Merril crafts Gladys in this way to create a particular effect on the reader. As Newell and Lamont point out, "Merril herself did not identify with her heroine, who functions as representative of a domestic norm to which Merril did not aspire to conform" (35). To support this, they cite a 1950 letter from Merril sent to fellow science fiction author Fritz Leiber, informing him "that she didn't 'much care for women like Gladys, but . . . she was the inevitable personality through whose eyes the happenings could best be seen'" (qtd. in Newell and Lamont 35). Other differences between the two include Merril's knowledge of the science behind nuclear radiation, gained through correspondence with atomic scientists and writers of the day, including John Hersey, David Bradley, and Philip Morrison (34). Gladys, on the other hand, rejects her daughter's suggestion that they look at her son's science fiction magazines to get some ideas for what to do in this situation, replying, "We wouldn't know what to look for" (23). Furthermore, unlike Gladys, Merril was raised by a "mother who was a suffragette, an ardent, idealistic Social Democrat, and a New York Zionist." She, herself, became a Trotskyite in the 1930s and '40s, an antiwar protestor in the 1960s and '70s, and antinuclear activist in the 1970s (25).

Though Gladys does often conform to common gender norms during the period, she also sometimes subtly transgresses the gender, political, and environmental hierarchies of the postwar era. In fact, Merril endows Gladys with a sense of agency, intellect, and courage largely missing in depictions of female characters of the period. She is adaptable, often willing to examine her own lack of knowledge and assumptions, and protects her house from looters as well as a gas leak in the basement. She also acts as a foil to her patriarchal neighbor, Jim Turner. Turner has been put in charge of the neighborhood and is characterized as overly sure of himself and the masculine, nationalist world he represents: protective of women and suspicious of outsiders. Often treating Gladys like a child and making subtle sexual passes at her, the novel suggests that men like him are responsible for the nuclear disaster and relish the chance "to act out their right-wing fantasies of domination and control" (Booker 71). Like Hank in "That Only a Mother," Turner's fear of outsiders and female agency suggests that masculine rational thought is really a hysteric response to a perceived lack of control.

In addition to rejecting the domineering presence of Turner and the masculine world he represents, the novel also critiques the atom bomb's effects on the human body and the environment. One of Gladys's daughters is exposed to radiation after retrieving a toy from outside, and part of the narrative concerns the mother's attempt to find a doctor for her. Though the novel omits the graphic effects of radiation included in the earlier story, radiation poisoning is depicted as a real and volatile danger to the human body, spreading unchecked from the urban explosion sites to the surrounding suburbs. Furthermore, Merril highlights the effects of nuclear bombs on the natural environment, a consequence not addressed in the earlier story. In a scene that anticipates Rachel Carson's famous opening in *Silent Spring* (1962), Gladys looks out of the window and notices, in the aftermath of the explosion, that "[i]t was so quiet. Not even birds . . . *No birds!*" (85). Then she sees them: "three sparrows on their backs and toothpick legs turned pleading to the sky; another across the lawn; a few more farther away. Those that hadn't died had gone. Where?" (85).[18] Though Carson addresses the effect of pesticides like DDT, rather than atom bombs, on the bird population of an anonymous American town, the scenes echo each other in their insistence on the apocalyptic effects that both technologies can have on humans *and* nonhumans.[19] Furthermore, the development and testing of nuclear weapons had a crucial effect on Carson who cited the detonations of atom and hydrogen bombs in the Bikini Islands from 1946 to 1958 as a major influence on the development of her environmental ideas (Lear 220).[20] In this sense, the "white granular power" that "had fallen like snow upon the roofs and the lawns, the fields and streams" could allude to DDT, radioactive dust, and the Dust Bowl, creating a lineage of human-made environmental disasters through the image of dust from the 1930s to the early '60s and the birth of the modern environmentalism (Carson 3).

For Merril and Bradbury, contingency and otherness disrupt uncritical understandings of technological and economic progress. By focusing on the devastating consequences of frontier conquest and/ or nuclear technology on their characters and landscapes, Merril and Bradbury join other authors of the period in recognizing intersections between social and environmental issues during and after the Depression. Except for *The Martian Chronicle*'s occasional depiction of the largely absent and non-racialized Martians as well as its inclusion of "Way Up in the Middle of the Air," a story about black southerners who attempt to escape racial oppression by migrating to Mars, neither Bradbury nor Merril focus on ways that science and technology have often been used to limit the access that African Americans and other persons of color have to environmental resources, knowledge, and benefits.[21] For George Schuyler, the speculative nature of science fiction becomes a way to reimagine the effects and possibilities of technology from a black perspective.[22]

The Black "Technological Sublime"

In George Schuyler's *Black Empire*, the ingenious and ruthless Dr. Belsidus leads an army of black engineers, scientists, and soldiers, referred to in the novel as the "Black Internationale" to retake Africa from white colonial forces and turn it into a powerful and technologically advanced black empire. Originally serialized in the *Pittsburgh Courier* from 1936 and 1938, the novel combines aspects of the technological sublime and grotesque to restage the subjugation of black populations by imagining how African Americans might master and turn technological advances against white nations. As Amor Kohli argues, "*Black empire* respects the power of the 'machine of white civilization,' but refuses to accept what they supposedly suggest about the legitimacy of their creators' position of supremacy" (44). While the novel may appear to celebrate technology in its depiction of black scientific and engineering ingenuity, the ambivalent implementation of the technological sublime also calls attention to the grotesque uses that technology has played in the hands of white "civilization." In other words, the novel highlights the grotesque underside of technology's awe-inspiring power by mimicking and surpassing the same violent and destructive methods used by white nations to subjugate people of African descent around the world.

Schuyler's treatment of technology in the novel is informed by ongoing critical debates over how serious we are supposed to take the author's depiction of black insurrection and empire building. The debate usually centers around Schuyler's reaction to the popularity of the serial. In a letter to a staffer at the *Pittsburgh Courier*, he mused, "I have been greatly amused by the public enthusiasm for 'The Black Internationale,' which is hokum and hack work of the purest vein. I deliberately set out to crowd as much race chauvinism and sheer improbability into it as my fertile imagination could conjure. The result vindicates my low opinion of the human race" (qtd. in Hill and Rasmussen, 260). Some critics, like John Gruesser, take Schuyler at his word, claiming that he creates an "anti-utopia" in *Black Empire* to reveal the "dangers of race chauvinism." For Gruesser, the society promised by Dr. Belsidus in the novel "is just as fascistic and repressive as the colonial governments he ousts" (683). Much of the novel supports Gruesser's conclusion, especially at the end of the first section of the novel, "The Black Internationale," when Dr. Belsidus declares himself a dictator. Celebrating their initial victories in taking back Africa from the colonial powers, he tells his followers, "There is still need of consolidating our power, of making Africa a political and industrial entity . . . Until this is accomplished, you need a strong, a ruthless, an intelligent leader. Negroes are not yet used to freedom, and so for a time we must have dictatorship, but that will depend upon you and the manner in which you carry out my orders. For, as you know, I will not tolerate disobedience or inefficiency or laziness" (141). The price for disobedience, as we learn time and time again in the novel, is torture and death. Furthermore, we later learn that Dr. Belsidus has implemented a clinic that practices eugenics by eliminating the sick and "unfit," a practice that Carl Slater, the protagonist of the narrative who becomes Belsidus's secretary and confident, finds reprehensible (148).

On the other hand, some critics are skeptical of Schuyler's response, instead viewing the serials as more serious than the author would have them. Robert A. Hill and R. Kent Rasmussen, who edit the most recent publication of *Black Empire*, claim that the novel and other "pulp serials" Schuyler wrote during the period, "possess profound thematic affinities with his contemporary 'serious' essays, affinities that transcend the 'genre gap' and suggest ... an overarching commonality of literary purpose and concern" (260). They argue that the author included "just about everything that he knew or felt about race, psychology, pedagogy, international politics, history, war, technology, health, and modern science" in the novel, allowing "us a self-portrait of the author and his times, seen through the medium of melodramatic fiction" (261). Amor Kohli also resists seeing the novel as "hokum," instead claiming that a major thematic concern of the novel is a meditation on the "often-attractive pull of 'hokum,' in spite of one's knowledge to the contrary" (46). While Kohli agrees with Gruesser's assertion that the novel exhibits an anti-utopian thrust because of the duplicitous nature of pulp themes in the novel, he also claims that "*Black Empire* refuses, ultimately, to completely suspend utopian possibility" (47). For him, the dystopian aspects of the novel are overshadowed by "the wonder and celebration felt in the purported achievement of utopia and the new advances that were made possible by black industry and genius" (47). Kohli rightly emphasizes the confluence of dystopian and utopian impulses in the novel and offers a compelling rejoinder to critics like Yogita Goyal who see the Belsidus's campaign as "an instance of colonial power in black face" (27). While we should be skeptical of Belsidus's ideas, it seems reductive to see the novel as merely critiquing Pan-Africanism and black imperialism. This is especially so, as even Goyal notes, since the "powerful role of parody, masking, and doublespeak in Schuyler's prose" problematizes attempts to reduce the novel to any static meaning or position (26). Belsidus, himself, seems to resist this position when telling his delegates at a banquet celebrating their victory over a joint European force, "You must not make the mistake of the white man and try to enslave others, for that is the beginning of every people's fall. You must banish race hatred from your hearts" (257). This isn't to say that the dictator plans to relinquish his power, as he promises to "lead . . . [them] to a higher civilization than Europe has ever seen" (258). But his words counteract his usual draconian language and methods, perhaps the result of Carl's "moral restraint" (Hill and Rasmussen 286). For Hill and Rasmussen, Carl and Belsidus "represent different aspects of Schuyler's ideological weltanschauung, particularly regarding . . . revolutionary ideology, black liberation, and black power" (286), as well as, I would add, technology.

Instead of arguing over whether the novel's utopian or dystopian impulses win out in Schuyler's depiction of Pan-African insurrection, perhaps the better solution involves following Kohli's line of analysis and identifying ways that the two impulses work together to create an early example of what Tom Moylan calls the "critical utopia" (10). For Moylan, the critical utopia does not offer a "blueprint" of social change but a "more recognizable and dynamic" social vision that includes "the continuing presence of difference and imperfection within society itself" (10–11). In marking the historical influence of white imperialism on black insurrection in the novel, Schuyler is not offering a utopian blueprint for a Pan-African empire; instead, he calls attention to the legacy of violence and control experienced by people of African descent around the world at the hands of Europe and America.

While critics have documented the science fictional aspects of *Black Empire*, they have had less to say about Schuyler's attitudes towards science and technology in the novel. In terms of science fiction, Hill and Rasmussen argue that *Black Empire* shares several "themes" associated with the genre that include "'far traveling,' the wonders of science, man and the machine, progress, man and the future, war, genetics, cataclysm, man and his environment, superpowers, genius, and man and religion" (307). Perhaps no sci-fi theme is as prominent in the novel as the role of futuristic technologies. These include new and "revolutionary devices" of the time, including "television, short-wave radio, and facsimile machines" (Hill and Rasmussen 308). They also, as we shall see, include technologies that have the possibility to radically transform the way humans understand social and environmental relationship. In regards to Schuyler's attitudes towards science and technology, only one of the author's two biographers comments on the role of science in Schuyler's novels. On the author's earlier novel, *Black No More* (1931), which focuses on a process invented by a black scientist that turns African Americans white, Jeffrey B. Ferguson writes, "[S]cience merely provides another arena for human folly, one all the more ridiculous for its exalted status as a privileged discourse of truth and as a repository of all-too-human fantasies of total Faustian control" (228). Isiah Lavender sees a similar view of science as connecting both *Black No More* and *Black Empire*. Both, he claims, use "scientific extrapolation by mad scientists to pose solutions to the color line" (108). But Schuyler may have been more open to and excited about the possibilities of technology, particularly new developments in alternative energy sources. In a 1931 article, he celebrated the work of French inventor Georges Claude, who had "invented a method of utilizing the differences in temperature of tropical waters to generate electricity" (qtd. in Hill and Rasmussen 306). Remarking on the vast social effects such an invention would create, he writes, "Think how a chain of power plants like that, getting power free of charge, will revolutionize our civilization!" (qtd. in 306). While Claude's invention did not *revolutionize* energy production during the period—both prototypes were destroyed by ocean waves in the 1930s—Schuyler's interest in it complicates his attitudes towards technology. On the one hand, Schuyler depicts ways that technological power has allowed white civilization to dominate black races. On the other hand, his depictions of technology suggest alternative uses beyond war and commercialism.

Science and technology takes two forms in the novel. First, they become ways to create new kinds of weapons. Foreseeing the utterly debilitating force of atomic and hydrogen bombs, black scientists in the novel develop a weapon that will disable any machine that it points at. As Professor Portalba, a Brazilian scientist working for Dr. Belsidus, explains, "Ze machine ... ees in reality two machines in one. Eet ees first of all an atom smasher, a huge cyclotron, which generates an atomic or proton beam which can disintegrate any metal. Secondly, it ees a developer of a radio beam which possesses the faculty of stopping the propellers of machines and rendering batteries and connections useless'" (244–45). While Belsidus responds to the weapon "as pleased as a boy with a new bag of marbles" (244), Carl initially feels "awed by the awful potentialities of this machine" (255). The weapon is used at the end of the novel, first to disable a joint British and French air and navy fleet that threatens the African continent after Belsidus and his army reconquer it: "There was a low hum all along the line. It grew louder and louder. The crews retreated a couple of hundred feet from the machines. Gradually they grew red, then orange, and the voltage was stepped up. The myriad spines that made them resemble some sort of futuristic porcupines were like livid hairs. The proton rays darted out of the nozzles toward the lines of ships scarcely two miles away" (249). While the description of the weapon draws from a more pulp version of science fiction, its ability to fully disable the enemy anticipates the overpowering effects of the atomic bomb in the following decade. Like "Fat Man" and "Little Boy," the weapon brings the war to a swift end. Furthermore, in his depiction of the Black Internationale's awe-inspiring ultimate weapon, Schuyler does not omit the effects of the weapon on its victims. From two miles, it appears like nothing much is happening on the targeted ships. But through field glasses, the observers witness the "[s]ailors ... running frantically about the ships" as well as an "uncanny procession" of explosions levied by the black air force fighters attacking the defenseless ships (249). While magnifying the effects of the weapon may function in the novel to describe the delight that members of the Black Internationale take in watching the colonizers suffer, Schulyer may also be calling attention to the unobserved consequences that modern weaponry has on human beings.

If the first form of technology developed by black scientists and engineers in the novel is used for destructive purposes, the second form points towards more social and, to some degree, environmental ends. Using sunlight and "liquid chemical food," scientists grow larger and better quality food, removing the dangers of "soil erosion" and "plant disease" (49). Carl Slater describes walking "through . . . plots of tomato plants fifteen and twenty feet high" (55). They also create "sun engines" that use the sunlight captured through "highly polished aluminum mirrors" to create electricity and heat through steam power (53). To produce electricity during "short or cloudy" days, the engines are later attached to "big silos" that "store up heat at extremely high temperatures and . . . retain it almost without loss for years" (160). As Sam Hamilton, one of the Black Internationale's most prominent chemists, tells Carl, "There have been other solar engines but this surpasses them all. It only costs $100 to make and it seems to last indefinitely" (53). Later, when Carl tours a larger facility of the engines in Africa, a scientist tells him, "There's no place in the world that has more sunshine than Africa and the supply is inexhaustible and eternal" (160). While renewable energy interests have spiked in recent decades, it's important to note the interest in the subject during the 1930s and '40s that may have influenced Schuyler's depiction of these forms of technology.[23] In this sense, *Black Empire* initiates a conversation/debate about technology in similar ways as the 1939 New York World's Fair. While both often illustrate the potential negatives of scientific and technological innovations during the period, they also offer a progressive undercurrent that envisions more socially and environmentally conscious forms of technology.

Besides Claude's experiments with ocean thermal energy conversion, the residual uses of wind and water mills, and the popularity of hydroelectric dams in the American South and West, engineers and entrepreneurs experimented with other forms of renewable energy production during the period. Perhaps the closest to Schuyler's sun engines, minus the electricity, was William J. Bailey's solar water heater, based in Los Angeles. While solar water heaters went back to the late nineteenth century, trapping sunlight through glass panels that heated water in a box, Bailey devised a way to store hot water to use at night and other times the sun did not shine. As Alexis Madrigal explains, "His system used the natural tendency of hot water to rise—because it's lighter—and cold water to fall. The series of pipes he called 'Sun Coils' circulated water through the pipes surely through the movement induced by solar heating. The hotter water eventually moved into a storage tank that was placed above the flat, glass-covered collector. The colder water fell and was circulated through the system again" (86). According to Madrigal, Bailey's Day and Night Solar Heater Company, which produced and sold the heater, was financially successful in the 1920s, until the discovery of natural gas and consolidation of gas industries in Southern California during the early twentieth century made natural gas the cheaper option. In 1930, Madrigal notes, Bailey's company sold only forty solar heaters (85–87).

In addition to Bailey's solar water heater, George Keck, an architect perhaps best known for his "House of Tomorrow" display at the 1934 Chicago World's Fair, also experimented with solar forms of heating, using window panes that would heat houses in the late 1930s and '40s. These "Thermopane windows," as they were called, included "two sheets of glass with a layer of air sandwiched in between . . . [that] acted as an insulator, keeping heat from escaping from the house while still allowing sunlight in" (91). Keck's design was also initially popular, with suburban subdivisions in Chicago and New York utilizing aspects of it by the late 1940s. A report commissioned by President Harry Truman in 1950, *Resources for Freedom*, noted the potential of solar homes in future natural resource practices (92). Like Bailey's solar water heaters, Keck's solar homes soon fell out of favor with home builders due to their aesthetic uniformity and higher costs (93–94). In exploring the electrical possibilities of solar heaters, Schuyler added a novel idea to an innovative and more-environmentally sustainable form of energy.[24] Along with the developments of Bailey and Keck, the author's "sun engine" symbolizes a road not taken—an alternative to the practices that have contributed to the environmental and social crises of our time, particularly as energy continues to rise in both financial and environmental costs.

Schuyler depicts renewable forms of technology in *Black Empire* as creating economic self-sufficiency for people of African descent. They also have the potential to develop more sustainable uses of natural resources and new ecological relationships to the world around them. But Schuyler also depicts ways that uses of these technologies reflect dominant Euro-American practices of domination. The Black Internationale develops the sun engines, liquid gardens, and other innovative scientific discoveries and machinery primarily for militaristic and industrial ends. Much of the food grown at the farm is sold in the market, presumably to help Dr. Belsidus's organization raise money to retake Africa and defeat the Euro-American armies. Even the appearance of the sun engine resembles a "great battery of glass anti-aircraft guns" (52), and the machine is later developed into a larger apparatus that can provide the tremendous energy needed to power the Black Internationale's ultimate weapon. But the tension between social and militaristic uses of technology in the novel speaks to debates during the period over the function science should play in the community. Carl Slater's more diplomatic and community-oriented vision of the Black Internationale appears to be gaining ground in the final pages of the novel, as even the remorseless Dr. Belsidus asks his followers to banish race hatred from their hearts. But the fanatical leader and his technological sublime vision of black-made machinery working for the good of the black empire still resonates loudly as the novel closes. As such, the novel retains its awareness of the imperialistic uses of technology, while nodding to potential alternative understandings of technology's role in the community.

Conclusion

While the 1939 New York World's Fair marked a celebration of the technological sublime, it also highlighted a growing awareness of the industrial and militaristic appropriations of science and technology and their social and environmental effects. Critics of the fair and science fiction authors called attention to the racial, gender, and/or environmental exploitation often accompanying forms of technological progress celebrated by the fair. The filmmakers and writers involved with *The City* critiqued the social and environmental impacts of the modern industrial and metropolitan cities, while Bradbury connected the legacy of frontier expansion to the human and ecological catastrophe of nuclear warfare. Like Bradbury, Judith Merril also called attention to the human and environmental consequences of atomic bombs while inverting gendered understandings of the weapon. Finally, Schuyler pointed to the role of science and technology in conquering people of African descent, while at the same time envisioning alternative forms of technology that we would today consider to be renewable. Though the 1960s often stands as the birth of the modern environmentalist movement under the banner of Rachel Carson's critique of DDT in *Silent Spring*, all the ingredients were present by the late 1940s for critiquing indiscriminate uses of technology from an environmentalist perspective—especially after the effects of nuclear radiation became better known. For depression-era authors and filmmakers, the grotesque became a powerful aesthetic and political mode to visualize and critique the technological sublime and the forms of environmental, economic, racial, and gender exploitation it often supported.

Conclusion

In *The Green Depression*, I've argued that depression-era American literature (and some films) depict ideas that would become associated with environmentalism in the second half of the twentieth century. To support this argument, I've focused on authors from the period whose work echoes changes in conservationist thought, in three areas in particular. Witnessing the severity of the period's dust storms, widespread flooding, and use of atom bombs, depression-era authors began to more fully articulate the apocalyptic effects that humans can have on the environment. They also depicted the inherent value and ecological importance of nonhuman nature, particularly animal "predators" and "pests" under attack by overzealous hunters, ranchers, and government officials in the first half of the twentieth century. Finally, many authors of the period made connections between environmental issues and forms of economic, racial, and gender inequality, anticipating what we now refer to as "environmental justice." To show the reach of environmental thinking during the period, my first three chapters focused on a different geographical landscape: the wilderness, rural, and urban. In my last chapter, I identified debates over technology during the period that would influence environmental understandings of technological progress in the second half of the century. In closing, I would like to offer a few final thoughts regarding the historical and cultural legacy of depression-era ecoliterature as well as point towards further work that can be done on the subject.

While we often attribute the beginnings of the "modern" environmentalist movement to the David Brower-led defeat of the Echo Park Dam protests in the 1950s or the publication of Rachel Carson's *Silent Spring* in 1962, the ideas that would become central to the movement circulated in American culture and conservationist thought in the 1930s and '40s. Early deaths and historical exigencies may have played a role in stalling their more widespread acceptance. Many of the figures associated with the major transitions in conservationist thought during the period had passed away by the end of the 1940s. On November 10, 1939, Robert Marshall died at the age of thirty-eight of unknown causes while asleep on a train to New York (Glover 267). Less than a decade later, Aldo Leopold died of a heart attack while fighting a fire on a neighbor's land near his shack in the sand county region of central Wisconsin. The marine biologist and ecologist Ed Ricketts, Steinbeck's friend and teacher, also died in 1948 after a train struck his car. The bombing of Pearl Harbor by Japan on December 7, 1941, largely "deprioritized" Roosevelt's conservation policies, though his "conservation gains" preceding the war remained unchanged (Brinkley 517). The president would die a few years later on April 12, 1945 (575). One wonders how the history of environmentalism may have been different if these major contributors to conservation and early environmental thought had lived longer or if the war had not interrupted Roosevelt's conservationist programs and policies.

That said, the expression of environmental ideas during the period would live on, influencing future generations of environmental-minded activists and authors. Rachel Carson got her start in the 1930s working for the Bureau of Fisheries, eventually becoming head of public relations for the Fish and Wildlife Service in 1940 (Brinkley 467). Carson's first report on DDT was published in a memo for the Service in 1946, which led conservationist Rosalie Edge to add the insecticide to her "poison" file and later call attention to the use of DDT at Westchester County golf clubs (Furmansky 241, 243–44). Maurice Broun, the curator of Edge's Hawk Mountain, would provide Carson decades worth of data on birds that would prove integral to her research (247). The activism of the Wilderness Society, co-founded by Marshall, Leopold, and others in 1935, would eventually culminate in the Wilderness Act of 1964 (Sutter 6–7). And Leopold's *A Sand*

County Almanac would, together with Carson's *Silent Spring*, became one of the environmentalist movement's "bibles" (Lannoo 149).

While historians have begun identifying the historical influence of depression-era politicians, activists, and scientists on environmentalism in the later twentieth century, finding ecocritical scholarship on depression-era literary works and films is more difficult. Some such scholarship has been done on individual authors and regions. But since many authors did not explicitly identify themselves with conservationist or ecological thought, readers and critics tend to interpret their works in terms of the predominant social politics, aesthetic movements, and/or literary genres of the period. As a corrective to this, *The Green Depression* seeks to begin a conversation on the importance of nature, ecology, and environmental justice in depression-era culture. While I've focused on the literary works, films, and issues that have stuck out to me in my understanding of environmental thought during the period, other questions need to be examined concerning the ecological importance of work from the period. First, while I currently address the work of African American, Native American, and working-class male and female writers, it is important to examine how Latinx, Asian American, and other ethnic artists of the period understand and contribute to environmental thought in their work, especially due to the multiethnic dimension of 1930s literature (Denning xv). How do authors like Josefina Niggli, Lin Yutang, Miné Okubo, and William Saroyan depict nature and/or environmental thought in their work? What connections do they envision between environmental and social issues? And what continuities *and* differences does their work have with other texts addressed in *The Green Depression*?

Next, how do artists of other cultural mediums besides literature and film—particularly photography, painting, and music—explore ecological issues during the period? How do photographers like Ansel Adams and Ben Shahn, painters like Diego Rivera, Chiura Obata, and Miné Okubo, and musicians like Woody Guthrie, Huddie "Lead Belly" Ledbetter, and Aaron Copland depict nature, ecology, and/or environmental justice? And what unique perspectives do the particularities of their mediums contribute to understanding humanity's relationship to the natural world and/or issues concerning environmental justice? Third, in what ways can the digital humanities help us better understand how literary and other cultural works used words like "nature," "ecology," and "environment," as well as how critics and other audiences received these words? What other aspects of depression-era ecoliterature can the digital humanities help illuminate? Finally, what role did other geographical landscapes and cultural genres of the period play in depicting intersections between environmental and social issues? For example, how did depictions of highly manicured suburbs in literary works during the period support, model, and (in some cases) contest racial, gender, and environmental hierarchical structures at work in these emerging landscapes. How did depictions of the "supernatural" and "monstrous" in Universal Studio's monster films of the 1930s and '40s and the horror fiction of H. P. Lovecraft and C. L. Moore reinforce and/or critique conceptions of the "natural" and the "human" used in support of dominant racial, gender, and environmental hierarchies and practices?

Further analysis of literature, film, and other cultural forms from the 1930s and '40s by ecocritics and environmental humanists can also help us envision more sustainable relationships with the Earth, its inhabitants, and each other in our own time. Thus far in the twenty-first century, Americans have faced Hurricane Katrina, the Great Recession, the BP oil spill, Superstorm Sandy, the Flint, Michigan, water crisis, the Dakota Access Pipeline, and historic flooding and wildfires across the US. These and other similar events have stressed the continuing convergence of environmental, economic, and racial issues that grow even more volatile under the influence of climate change. Our current historical moment eerily echoes the environmental, economic, and political "crises of authority" of the 1930s and '40s, so much so that Sen. Ed. Markey of Massachusetts and Rep. Alexandria Ocasio-Cortez of New York introduced the "Green New Deal" in February of 2019. The resolution, focused on fighting climate change and economic injustice, is an obvious reference to Roosevelt's New Deal, which was also often "green" in its attempts to reverse years of unsustainable deforestation and agriculture and create more opportunities for Americans to access green spaces by creating and maintaining urban, state, and national parks. Recent filmmakers have recognized connections between the two periods too, among them Andrew Stanton's Pixar film *Wall-E* (2008), Ken Burns's documentary *The Dust Bowl* (2012), and Christopher Nolan's sci-fi film *Interstellar* (2014). Each of these works draw upon the Dust Bowl's legacy in understanding climate change and other contemporary environmental issues.[1]

Recognizing similarities *and* important distinctions between the two periods, how else might depression-era political and environmental thought influence our response to climate change, pollution, water access, and mass extinction as well as current forms of economic, racial, and gender inequality. What would a contemporary Civilian Conservation Corps and Works Progress Administration look like? In what ways might government help protect and restore wilderness landscapes and natural resources on public lands while protecting the rights of indigenous groups? How might it help rebuild cities while maintaining diverse and affordable neighborhoods and accessible parks? How else has depression-era ecoliterature and film informed contemporary understanding of nonhuman predator and pests, urban design, wilderness preservation, and other issues explored (or overlooked) in the preceding chapters?

These and other questions suggest the abundance of further work that can (and should) be done on the role of environmentalist thought in cultural works of the period. *The Green Depression* only scratches the surface.

Notes

Introduction

1. Other cities between the Great Plains and the East Coast were also covered with dust from this storm. Chicago experienced "twelve million tons of dust" (Egan 5), and in Boston and Scranton, "dust fell like snow" (151). As Timothy Egan notes, "[d]ust in Chicago, Boston, Manhattan, Philadelphia, and Washington gave the great cities of America a dose of what the people in the little communities of the High Plains had been living with for nearly two years" (152).

2. While Donald Worster published his groundbreaking work, *The Dust Bowl*, in 1979, a slew of other historians within the past decade have also recognized the importance of environmental thought and issues during the period. Worster and Egan focus on the Dust Bowl, while Phillips concentrates on shifts in agricultural conservation methods started by the New Deal. Maher examines the role of the Civilian Conservation Corps (CCC) in popularizing and expanding conservationist thought to the American public, while Brinkley focuses on a range of FDR's contributions to environmental thought.

3. See *Steinbeck and the Environment: Interdisciplinary Approaches*, eds. Susan F. Beegal, et al. (University of Alabama Press, 2007); *Faulkner and the Ecology of the South*, eds. Joseph R. Urgo and Ann J. Abadie (University Press of Mississippi, 2007); and *Clear-Cutting Eden: Ecology and the Pastoral in Southern Literature*, Christopher Rieger (University of Alabama Press, 2009).

4. Leopold's famous essay "Thinking Like a Mountain," included in *A Sand County Almanac* (1949), contains one of his most poignant critiques of the federal government's predator eradication programs in the early twentieth century. Edge helped establish Hawk Mountain in Pennsylvania to protect and collect research on hawks and other birds of prey, research that Rachel Carson drew upon for *Silent Spring*.

5. In doing so, Leopold, Marshall, and other wilderness activists associated with the Wilderness Society anticipated Edward Abbey's critiques of "industrial tourism" in the 1960s. See Abbey's essay, "Polemic: Industrial Tourism and the National Parks," in *Desert Solitaire: A Season in the Wilderness* (1968).

6. The CCC also participated in predator eradication, clearing ranges of nonhuman competition (Flores 95).

7. According to Cappetti, the Chicago School sociologists often supported, though occasionally challenged, dominant understandings of "other" racial, ethnic, and economic groups living in Chicago, while literary authors associated with these sociologists often "creatively undermined these stereotypes" (16).

8. Though not included in *The Green Depression*, John Steinbeck's work was influenced by the marine biologist and author Edward Ricketts (Lannoo 25). Steinbeck would write about his experience accompanying Ricketts on a trip in 1940 to collect and study marine life in the Gulf of California in *The Log from the Sea of Corez* (1950). Ricketts's book *Between Pacific Tides* (1939), which illustrates his "concern with ecological holism" (Lannoo 36), became "a classic in the literature of marine biology," sold "more than a thousand copies," and "received excellent peer reviews in several high-profile journals" (41). For more on the contributions of Steinbeck and Ricketts to the development of environmental thought, see *Steinbeck and the Environment: Interdisciplinary Approaches*, eds. Susan F. Beegel, Susan Shilinglaw, and Wesley N. Tiffney, as well as Michael Lannoo, *Leopold's Shack and Ricketts's Lab: The Emergence of Environmentalism*.

9. These myths include Smith's "garden of the world" and "plantation myth," David Nye's "technological sublime," Annette Kolodny's "land-as-woman," and James Machor's "pastoral city."

10. In *Marxism and Literature*, Raymond Williams uses the terms "dominant," "residual," and "emergent" to describe the role that culture plays in supporting or contesting a particular social and economic order. Dominant and residual elements of culture, in particular, work like "myths" by reinforcing the beliefs and values that allow the status quo to continue. In critiquing and/or appropriating the dominant and residual, many of the authors I will address attempt to create or articulate the "new meanings and values, new practices, new relationships and kinds of relationships" that Williams associates with the emergent (123).

11. For ways that African Americans and women have appealed to pastoral thought, see Buell, *The Environmental Imagination*, 42–44 and 44–49.

12. In his 1984 article "Pastoralism in America," Marx does expand his analysis of complex pastoralism beyond high literature to interrogate how complex pastoralism can inform issues of social justice.

13. Though Gifford's use of "post" limits the pastoral's ability to develop in response to ongoing and future historical changes, his attempt to update pastoralism to make it more current to the contemporary discourse of environmental justice is helpful for using the term beyond its traditional applications. Christopher Reiger's "ecopastoral," which seeks to describe "new versions of human/nature relationships" in depression-era southern literature (3), is perhaps a more useful name in defining a form of pastoralism rooted in ecological/environmentalist thought.

14. Denning claims that ghetto pastorals differ in their mixture of naturalism and pastoralism, some relying more on one than the other: "One could . . . arrange the ghetto pastorals along a spectrum from pastoralism to naturalism, from the

sentimental human comedy of William Saroyan to the visions of hell in Nelson Algren" (251).

15. Denning's understanding of pastoralism is informed by the English literary critic William Empson, who defined the genre as "putting the complex into the simple" (Empson 11).

16. For book-length treatments of environmental thought in African American literature, see Paul Outka, *Race and Nature from Transcendentalism to the Harlem Renaissance* (Palgrave Macmillan, 2008) and Kimberly Ruffin, *Black on Earth: African American Ecoliterary Traditions* (University of Georgia Press, 2010). Articles include Michael Bennett's "Anti-Pastoralism, Frederick Douglass, and the Nature of Slavery" in *Beyond Nature Writing: Expanding the Boundaries of Ecocriticism* (University Press of Virginia, 2001) as well as Lawrence J. Oliver's "Apocalyptic and Slow Violence: The Environmental Vision of W. E. B. Du Bois in Darkwater" and Michael J. Beilfus's "Ironic Pastorals and Beautiful Swamps: W. E. B. Du Bois and the Troubled Landscapes of the American South," both of which are included in the *Interdisciplinary Studies in Literature and Environment* (Summer 2015).

17. See Barbara Foley's *Radical Representations: Politics and Form in U.S. Proletarian Fiction, 1929–1941* (Duke University Press, 1993); Michael Denning's *The Cultural Front: The Laboring of American Culturing in the Twentieth Century* (Verso, 1998); Joseph Entin's *Sensational Modernism: Experimental Fiction and Photography in Thirties America* (University of North Carolina Press, 2007); and Morris Dickstein's *Dancing in the Dark: A Cultural History of the Great Depression* (W. W. Norton & Company, 2010).

18. See Gary Canavan's edited collection *Green Planets: Ecology and Science Fiction* (Wesleyan, 2014) and Michael Bennett's collection, *The Nature of Cities: Ecocriticism and Urban Environments* (University of Arizona Press, 1999). For an analysis of urbanism's influence on modern American poetry, see Julia E. Daniel's *Building Natures: Modern American Poetry, Landscape Architecture, and City Planning*.

Chapter 1: The Last Frontier

1. Marshall would even lament the effects of *Arctic Village* on Wiseman. Returning to visit the town in 1938, he found that about half of the older residents had either moved or died and that "six radios, one automobile, and two or three airplanes a week disturbed the peace of the village" (Cole xii). According to Terrence Cole's 1991 preface, the popularity of *Arctic Village* played a large part in bringing about these changes, as it led to tourism in the area during the summer months (xxi).

2. Salten's novel and Disney's film are very different. In the novel, violence and cruelty among animals are interwoven into everyday life in the forest. While early

drafts of the film were closer to Felix Salten's original novel, the later cuts of the film removed almost all traces of cruelty among animals and most of the more sadistic acts of human hunters. According to Cartmill, the trickery and callousness of Salten's human characters is more pronounced in the early scripts and sketches for the film. In one scene, Bambi's mother is shot after she "declares her faith in the possibility of human faith" (173). Later in the scene, Bambi, thinking he hears his mother calling him, discovers that it is only a hunter with a deer call. Shot by the hunter, Bambi comes close to death but ends up surviving. Cartmill sees the "outbreak of World War II" as one possible reason for the tense and misanthropic tone of the early drafts (171). See Cartmill, 170–78.

3. Walt Disney attempted to get around early critiques by insisting that the film depicted German, rather than American, hunters. Since the original novel depicted German hunters and the US had just entered the war against Nazi Germany, his response was generally accepted (Cartmill 179). For a range of hunter and anti-hunter responses to the film, see Cartmill, 178–82.

4. He writes,

[T]he rhythms of *Bambi* are largo and maestoso. A dreamy languor pervades the film. The animated deer move through the forest with deliberate and sentient delicacy; autumn leaves fall with stately precision through shifting patterns of light to nestle weightlessly into the forest floor. The timeless, floating quality that results from all this minutely controlled slow movement makes a statement about the natural order that is more powerful than anything in the film's written continuity. (170)

5. I'm thinking here of the crows in *Dumbo* (1941), Honest John the Fox and Gideon the Cat in *Pinocchio* (1940), Br'er Fox and Br'er Bear in *Song of the South* (1946), the Siamese cats in *Lady and the Tramp* (1955), King Louie and his apes in *Jungle Book* (1967), and the hyenas in *The Lion King* (1994).

6. In the novel, violence and cruelty are interwoven into the everyday lives of forest animals. Instead of exchanging courtesies with each of the animals' families, as the newborn fawn does in the film, the novel's Bambi witnesses "a ferret killing a mouse . . . [c]rows attack[ing] a sick baby hare . . . a [mortally wounded] squirrel who escapes from a ferret . . . [and] [a] wounded fox [who] develops an infection for days" while following his mother through the forest (Cartmill 163).

7. The Fish and Wildlife Service, which the BBS turned into in 1940 after transferring from Agriculture to the Department of Interior, continues to spend "140 million of our taxpayer dollars a year" protecting agribusiness from nonhuman predators, killing "4 million in 1999 . . . 1.5 million a year in the early 2000s . . . 5 million in 2008 and well past 4 million in 2013" (Flores 172–73).

8. Wolves and coyotes were not the only predator species under siege during early conservationism. Birds of prey also came under attack by hunters, often funded by federal and state programs. In the early 1930s, the BBS proposed

poisoning pelicans in Yellowstone Park to help anglers catch more fish (Furmansky 141). In eastern Pennsylvania's Kittatinny Ridge, the Pennsylvania Game Commission encouraged and paid hunters to shoot thousands of migrating hawks and eagles, as well as any bird fitting the description, that stopped there each year due to "an anomaly of topography and weather" (151). Rosalie Edge would help end the practice by turning the ridge into a hawk sanctuary that became known as Hawk Mountain. See Dyana Z. Furmansky, *Rosalie Edge: Hawk of Mercy* (University of Georgia Press, 2009), 167–83.

9. While Walt Disney Studios' feature-length animated films often ignored or caricatured some nonhuman predator species, the studio did produce a sympathetic series of animated and live-action films on the coyote during the 1960s and '70s. According to Dan Flores, Disney (the man) may have been drawn towards "defending" the species after interacting with them at his Palm Springs home in the late 1950s (186). Disney's coyote films include *The Coyote's Lament* (1961), *Chico, the Misunderstood Coyote* (1961), *A Country Coyote Goes to Hollywood* (1965), *Concho, the Coyote Who Wasn't* (1966), *The Nashville Coyote* (1972), and *Carlo, the Sierra Coyote* (1974). See Flores's *Coyote America: A Natural and Supernatural History* (Basic Books, 2016), 151–52, 186–87.

10. As John F. Reiger notes, the rise of sportsmen's magazines and clubs in the 1870s and '80s constitute the origins of conservationism in the US. By successfully lobbying for game limit laws and publishing articles in sportsmen journals like *Forest and Stream* in favor of conserving lands through national forests and parks, American hunters helped establish conservation practices that would help curb the environmental damage created by overdevelopment and overhunting (4).

11. Leopold's recognition of the effects that environmental damage could have on human populations illustrate the relevancy of his ideas beyond "deep ecology" with which they are often associated.

12. Because of its focus on "the interaction of humans with their environment" (Urgo 7), Faulkner's work has lent itself to ecocritical readings. For Joseph R. Urgo, Faulkner's use of the word environment "contains . . . everything we now mean by the term ecology—the sum total of the found and built worlds of human existence, as well as the inherited nature of the human subject which is constructed into and out of that environment" (9–10). For a variety of ecocritical essays on a range of Faulkner's work, see Urgo and Ann J. Abadie's edited collection *Faulkner and the Ecology of the South* (University Press of Mississippi, 2004), a publication of essays presented at the Thirtieth Annual Faulkner and Yoknaptawpha Conference in 2003.

13. Contemporary historians are not the only ones to attribute the massive flooding to human development. Leading conservationists, authors, and filmmakers of the time also recognized the connection. Gifford Pinchot called the levees-only approach one of the "most colossal blunders in civilized history" (qtd. in Parish 43). New Orleans author Lyle Saxon also suggested the human culpability in the flooding in *Father Mississippi: The Story of the Great Flood of 1927*, a book-length account published, according to Parish, "before floodwaters had even subsided" (44).

14. For Culvin, categories that deem animals killable also extend to racial categories. Southern African Americans who transgress the status afforded to them by whites are often compared to animals, leaving them subject to forms of violence and death (97). I will return to Faulkner's depiction of the racial use of the nonhuman animal category in the next chapter.

15. Two edited collections of essays, Robert E. Fleming's *Hemingway and the Natural World* (1999) and Kevin Maier's *Teaching Hemingway and the Natural World* (2018), have laid the foundation for ecocritical reevaluations of Hemingway's attitudes towards the natural world. For many authors in these collections, Hemingway is often critical of attitudes and practices associated with hunting and land use.

16. Hemingway also describes the hunting codes he follows in a series of essays published by *Esquire* magazine in 1934, later collected in William White's 1967 edited collection of the author's journalistic writings, *By-Line: Ernest Hemingway*. These articles include "A. D. in Africa: A Tanganyika Letter" (April 1934), "Shootism Versus Sport: The Second Tanganyika Letter" (July 1934), and "Notes on Dangerous Game: The Third Tanganyika Letter" (July 1934).

17. As Charlene M. Murphy has argued, "Hemingway's writing and correspondence reveal a man who was thoughtful about the animals he killed, a man who hunted and fished for a prey he loved and respected" (166).

18. Roosevelt would publish an account of this safari in *Life-Histories of African Game Animals* (1914), co-written with zoologist Edmund Heller. Glickman ascribes the view of hyenas as gluttonous, stupid, and comic to the Kaguru of Tanzania in East Africa. For a summary of their views on hyenas, see Glickman, 525–26.

19. Charlene M. Murphy writes, "From the start of his writing career, Hemingway was keenly aware of man's destruction, and he repeatedly returned to this theme for at least thirty years" (165). For an overview of environmental awareness in Hemmingway's fiction and nonfiction, see Murphy, 165–66.

20. Hemingway often uses the Gulf Stream to illustrate the power and indifference of nature. The Gulf Stream, he writes in *Green Hills of Africa*, "has moved, as it moves, since before man" and "will flow, as it has flowed, after the Indians, after the Spaniards, after the British, after the Americans and after all the Cubans and all the systems of governments, the richness, the poverty, the martyrdom, the sacrifice and the venality and the cruelty are all gone" (149).

21. As del Gizzo argues, Hemingway also critiqued dominant racial discourse by frequently claiming to have Native American blood, an insistence that countered "cultural taboos about miscegenation and blood mixing" during his lifetime (501).

22. Influenced by his father's legal work defending the civil rights of fellow Jewish Americans as well as "Catholics, Indians, Japanese, blacks, and socialists" (11), Marshall advocated a frontier outlook endowed with a strong dose of racial, religious, and political tolerance. The importance Marshall placed on protecting civil

liberties is further demonstrated by his appointment as chairman of the ACLU's Washington branch as well as his work to alleviate discrimination in recreational facilities (resorts, campgrounds) leased from the Forest Service (Glover 152, 229).

23. According to Egan, One Bull offered to do this if a Sioux medicine bag was returned to the tribe (123). Similarly, McNickle's final novel, *Wind from an Enemy Sky* (1978), concerns the attempt to reconcile a tribal feud caused by the adoption of agriculture by some members of the tribe through the return of a tribal medicine bag. When the tribe finds out the medicine bag has been severely damaged by the neglect of a museum, all attempts to reconcile the feud, as well as relationships between white Americans, are shattered.

24. Though historian Graham D. Taylor sees the Indian New Deal as sometimes creating "a genuine sense of Indian self-determination," he sees it as ultimately due to its "imposed [reforms] upon the Indians, who did not see these elaborate proposals as answers to their own wants and needs" (xiii). Chief among these was tribal organization, which Collier saw as the primary answer to Native American self-determination. A strong proponent of "community organization as a means for changing and reforming American society as a whole," he failed to "recognize the difficulties of applying this approach to the allotted reservations" (13).

Chapter 2: Back to the Land

1. A scenario perhaps best articulated by King Vidor's feature film *Our Daily Bread* (1934) and Ralph Steiner and Willard Van Dyke's short documentary film *The City* (1939), both of which depict alternative communities infused with rural values and landscapes.

2. For a discussion of how frontier agricultural practices and policies led to these environmental disasters in the South and Great Plains, see Worster, *Dust Bowl*, 80–94, and Saikku, 36.

3. For an overview of these practices and their effects, see Cowdrey, 76–80.

4. William H. Major sees a similar form of pastoralism in the work of New Agrarianism. In *Grounded Vision*, he writes,

> The best agrarian writing looks at the past and tries to salvage what was worthy, but it also sees much that was not (racism, entrenched patriarchy, loss of topsoil) and that should be discarded. The pastoral idyll to which many Americans (and not just agrarians) remain in thrall may have been a largely fictional creation—and one that is conveniently used to beat up on the present—but to impart to that particular fiction the elements of material life that *did* function well is also to mistreat history. (22)

Likewise, Jennifer K. Ladino identifies a form of nostalgia that "can be a mechanism for social change, a model for ethical relationships, and a motivating force for social and environmental justice" (8). This "counter-nostalgia," as she refers to it, "revisits a dynamic past in a way that challenges dominant histories and reflects critically on the present" (16). For a more detailed explanation of "counter-nostalgia," see *Reclaiming Nostalgia*, 14–17.

5. What Kimberly Ruffin calls the black "ecological burden-and-beauty paradox" (2).

6. Son of LeRoy Percy, an influential Mississippi lawyer, banker, planter, and senator in the late nineteenth and early twentieth centuries, William Alexander Percy would become known not only for *Lanterns on the Levee*, which still remains in print today, but also for "sponsor[ing] young artists and writers, makin[ing] the Percy home in Greenville a salon visited by people of international renown, and encourag[ing] northern scholarship about the Delta" (Barry 293). Though not associated with the Agrarians, Percy was well regarded by Ransom and others in the group for his poetry and defense of the agrarian way of life (Barry 296).

7. See Keyling, 7–13.

8. In some cases, they were considered less valuable than animals as depicted in William Attaway's novel *Blood on the Forge* (1941). When Big Mat asks Mr. Johnson, the owner of the land where Mat and his black sharecropping brothers and wife live and work, for the guts of a hog he slaughters, the latter gives the choice parts to the rest of his hogs and the remainder to Mat.

9. The novel also depicts the banks as culpable in the demise of the farmer's ability to live off of his crops: "He [Jeeter] had done all the work, furnished the mule and the land, and yet the loan company had taken all the money the cotton brought, and made him lose three dollars" (106). On the whole, the novel depicts tenant farming as a dying agricultural system; even Captain John, who owns the land that Jeeter farms, has given up and left for Augusta.

10. Ironically, Jeeter and his wife Ada are killed at the end of the novel due to one of these field burnings. The fire spreads to their house during the night killing them in their sleep.

11. While Big Boy does not actually attack the lynch mob, he does imagine himself holding "off a whole mob wid a shotgun" hands as he hides in the pit (266). He even envisions killing the white mob members with his bare hands: "He caught one by the neck and choked him long and hard, choked him till his tongue and eyes popped out. Then he jumped upon his chest and stomped him like he had stomped that snake" (267). Though graphic in nature, Big Boy's imagined use of violence does not even approach the level of violence towards Bobo he soon witnesses.

12. But as in "Big Boy Leaves Homes," the story's ending calls attention to a contingent understanding of humanity that underlies white ways of ordering the world. For the Heartfields, Mann never becomes human, even after he helps save their lives at the risk of his own. For the officers and soldiers, Mann is just another looting and violent African American who deserves nothing less than the swift sentence of death.

13. Interestingly, Wright seems more reliant on aspects of pastoralism in his depiction of urban landscapes in *Native Son*. See the next chapter.

14. The closest Wright comes to envisioning new relationships between whites and blacks occurs at the end of "Fire and Cloud," in which poor whites and blacks march together to protest a southern town's unwillingness to provide relief to African Americans during the Depression. Led by Taylor, a black preacher, and two organizers from the Communist Party USA, the march symbolizes racial unity in the face of economic strife: "Taylor trembled when he saw them join, swelling the mass that moved towards the town. He looked ahead and saw black and white marching; he looked behind and saw black and white marching" (219). Together they become a "many-limbed, many-legged, many-handed crowd" of different colors that allows them to overcome the fear of acting alone (219). But "Fire and Cloud" is the only story in *Uncle Tom's Children* that holds out such a possibility, a hope that the next story, "Bright and Morning Star," seems less optimistic due to its depictions of a white informant who betrays the party's organizing activities.

15. For recent calls to see Hurston as an environmental author, see Cynthia Davis, "The Landscape of the Text: Locating Zora Neale Hurston in the Ecocritical Canon," in *Florida Studies: Proceedings of the 2005 Annual Meeting of the Florida College English Association*, ed. Steve Glassman (Cambridge Scholars Press, 2006); and Scott Hicks, "Zora Neale Hurston: Environmentalist in Southern Literature," in "*The Inside Light*": *New Critical Essays on Zora Neale Hurston*, ed. Deborah G. Plant (Praeger, 2010).

16. The dog's use by plantation owners to track down escaped slaves perhaps attributes to the ambiguous role they play in these stories. According to historians and critics Tyler Parry and Charlton Yingling, the use of dogs to "intimidate and control African Americans" continued after slavery, persisting in the use of K-9s by white police offers in civil rights protests during the 1950s and '60s as well as Black Lives Matter protests in the present. See Parry and Yingling, "The Canine Terror," *Jacobin*, May 19, 2016.

17. While Tea Cake is eventually attacked by a dog, we find out later that the dog was rabid.

Chapter 3: The Postpastoral City

1. For Machor, the work of nineteenth-century American writers like Hawthorne and Whitman "turned the ideal upon itself and in the process disclosed its contradictions." In doing so, they "illuminate both its limitations and value as a cultural idea" (203).

2. For a description of my use of literary naturalism in *The Green Depression*, see the introduction.

3. For Entin, aesthetics of astonishment also has roots in modernist aesthetics. He writes, "These explosive motifs were designed not only to startle audiences into a new awareness of destitution, discrimination, and conflict, but also to spark meditation on the ways in which aesthetic forms support—and perhaps might help undermine—hegemonic structures of power" (2).

4. In *Building Natures: Modern American Poetry, Landscape Architecture, and City Planning*, Julia E. Daniel identifies a similar ambiguity over urban parks in the poetry of Wallace Stevens and William Carlos Williams, particularly after the onset of the Depression. Both authors' works recognize that "[t]he failure of realizing the democratic telos of the American city park mirrors wider failures in the democratic and environmental ideals that characterize American city planning at large" (86, 88–89). See Daniel, chapters 2 and 3.

5. While Studs begins the trilogy in a better financial situation than Bruno, the onset of the Depression and his failing health severely affect his class standing by the end of the trilogy.

6. Though Farrell uses Danny O'Neill as a peripheral character in the Studs Lonigan trilogy, he would become central to five of Farrell's later novels, including *A World I Never Made* (1936), *No Star Is Lost* (1938), *Father and Son* (1940), *My Days of Anger* (1943), and *The Face of Time* (1953).

7. The dump became a popular trope in other works of the period as well, including William Wellman's *Wild Boys of the Road* (1933) and Gregory La Cava's *My Man Godfrey* (1934).

8. The slaughterhouse where Mazie's father works also certainly contributes to the "slow violence" perpetrated on the working-class families of Omaha's packinghouse neighborhoods as well as more fast forms of violence on the workers themselves. In terms of the latter, we hear of workers dying of heart attacks in the 108-degree "hog room" as well as a "SAFETY sign torn from the wall" by steam that has been "plastered onto . . . [the] swollen belly" of one of the workers (145, 146). But since the dump becomes the primary space through which we view the effects of pollution on the neighborhood children, I will focus on it in what follows.

9. See Marx, *The Machine in the Garden*, 290–92. For another example of Ishmael and others experiencing the "all-feeling," also see 303–305.

10. Comparing descriptions of dumps in Olsen's *Yonnondio* and Gregory La Cava's film *My Man Godfrey* (1936) further suggests the toxicity highlighted in Olsen's novel. La Cava's film opens in a New York municipal dump alongside the East River where unemployed men, including the film's protagonist Godfrey, live and wait for "the prosperity just around the corner." The film suggests that society has forgotten the men just as it has forgotten the mounds of empty cans that surround them, a connection made stronger when two wealthy sisters arrive at the dump looking for a "forgotten man" to bring back on their scavenger hunt. To show the value of the men, Godfrey eventually comes up with an idea to turn the dump into a posh nightclub called "the Dump" and use the residents as valets and waiters to serve the wealthy customers. He even plans to build housing for the employees at the nightclub. But watching La Cava's *My Man Godfrey* through contemporary eyes, one can't help but imagine the probable toxicity in the ground beneath the Dump, seeping into the East River as well as the customers and employees at the nightclub. While the film anticipates the early and mid-twentieth century practice of repurposing dumps and landfills into new developments,

it doesn't foresee the issues that civil engineers had with building on former landfills, which often caused severe structural issues and contamination issues (Melosi 184–85). Besides attempting to hide or displace the potentially dangerous waste objects of the dump, Godfrey's solution also attempts to cover over the class divides of American capitalism exposed by the Great Depression. In this sense, the nightclub is just a more comfortable version of the slum tourism represented by the scavenger hunt, allowing the rich to experience the dump without being affected—or at least not in ways they can detect—by the smells of garbage and sights of homeless men. Covering up the dump by burying the garbage and repurposing the people who lived there doesn't seem possible in *Yonnondio* as the dump exudes a toxicity such solutions are unable to fully alleviate or cover up. Nor do any politicians or enlightened businessmen seem interested in alleviating the conditions of workers and their families living in the houses near the slaughterhouse and dump. If change is to come, the novel suggests, it must come from the workers themselves through collective organizing and struggle. While describing the working conditions at the slaughterhouse, the narrator momentarily takes on the voice of a future worker and describes the kind of organizing necessary to create change: "[I]ndividual revolt was no good kid, no good at all, you had to bide your time and take it till there were enough of you to fight it all together on the job, and bide your time, and take it till the day millions of fists clamped in yours, and you could wipe out the whole thing, the whole goddamn thing, and a human could be a human for the first time on earth" (Olsen 79).

11. A version of this section was published as "'That sonofabitch could cut your throat': Bigger and the Black Rat in Richard Wright's *Native Son*" in the spring 2016 special issue of the *Journal of Midwest Modern Language Association* (vol. 49, no. 1): *Fugitive Environmentalisms*.

12. While Richard Wright and Zora Neale Hurston were often highly critical of each other's work, they both use nonhuman "predators" and "pests" to subvert stereotypes projected upon African Americans and particular nonhuman animal species.

13. The rat in *Native Son* has been the subject of at least one ecocritical article. Monika Geilern focuses on the rat's role in highlighting the environmental injustice of the Thomas family's living conditions as well as critiquing preservationist assumptions about the environmental value of interactions between humans and nonhumans. See Geilern, 97–107. In my reading of the opening rat scene, as well as of a later appearance of the rat that Geilern misses, the species takes on a more empathic quality, both as a living being struggling to survive and as a symbol for qualities valued by Bigger, including mobility and defiance.

14. For a discussion of Kimberly Ruffin's "ecological burden-and-beauty paradox," see the previous chapter.

15. O'Connor uses the term "neighbor species" to refer to "commensal" animals living in and around human development, "whether as agreeable companions, undesirable vermin, or merely part of the everyday scenery" (11). Unlike Donna Haraway's "companion species," neighbor species are not domesticated parts of

everyday human lives, but neither "are they truly wild or free-living" (Haraway 16, O'Connor 11).

16. Robert Sullivan, author of *Rats: Observations on the History and Habitat of the City's Most Unwanted Inhabitants*, confirms this tendency of rats: "Rats often bite young children and infants on the face because of the smell of food residues on the children. (Many of the approximately 50,000 people bitten by rats every year are children)" (6).

17. In the story, the black protagonist, Fred Daniels, hides in the sewer after he is falsely accused and made to confess to a murder. Daniels connection to rats becomes particularly apparent as he digs through walls in order to access the buildings connected to the sewer.

18. A fight that broke out between two of his fellow workers that knocked over some of the lab's guinea pig cages became the subject of the stories "What You Don't Know Won't Hurt You" (1942) and "The Man Who Went to Chicago" (1961). See Michel Fabre, 93–94 and 248–49, and Allen, 145–47.

19. Bigger's prosecuting attorney, Buckley, uses some form of "beast" at least thirteen times to refer to him during his closing remarks at the trial. Though he mostly uses the more general term "beast" in the speech, he also uses various "beastly" animals to describe Bigger, including a "half-human black ape" (476), a "black lizard" (476), a "black mad dog" (477), and "a coiled rattler" (482). Of these animals, he seems to focus on the ape comparison, as he makes it at least three times.

20. Sullivan calls it "one of a very small number of pro-rat comments . . . in the annals of New York City history" (62).

21. In this sense, the species shares an ability to resist full containment with the toxicity Olsen sees as emanating from Omaha's dump and slaughterhouse.

Chapter 4: Futuramas and Atom Bombs

1. Changes to other landscapes also relied on a vision of technology that flaunted its ability to resolve their major issues. Of the rural, the narrator remarks, "The farmer in 1960 works in greater security, for science and research have helped him to control many of the risks of agriculture. Hours of work have been shortened with almost universal electrification of rural areas. Fruit trees bear abundantly under individual glass housing. Orchards are protected against disease and insects. Science even influences pollination by artificial feeding." In industrial landscapes, technology has created better living and working conditions for workers while making production more efficient: "Industrial communities have gone ahead by multiplying the conveniences and comforts of living. Hundreds of comfortable homes for workers. All people benefited by broadening their scope of living, gaining by advanced means of communication and new methods of work. Here is a thriving and prosperous steel town. Notice the furnaces glowing . . . river and rowing mills."

2. As Nye notes, the Futurama and other exhibits using miniaturized landscapes "effectively omitted human beings as visible parts of the future," replacing them with "new machines, futuristic cars, idealized landscapes, and streamlined buildings" (221). When human beings did appear in the models, Nye continues, they did so "as tiny stick figures, without faces, discernible clothing styles, or visible class status" (221). In this depiction, Nye concludes, the "individual had no apparent obligations or social ties," negating for fairgoers "any attempt to grasp social relations" (221).

3. In 1923, Fitzgerald had the same experience as his fictional travelers, experiencing the ash dump daily when "commuting between Great Neck and Manhattan to rehearse a new play" (Miller 135).

4. According to Gillette, "[T]he fair drew the interests both of businessmen hoping to boost the city's economy out of Depression doldrums and social critics seeking to communicate a reform message to a broad audience." Mumford's biographer, Donald L. Miller, also claims that the film was very popular among fairgoers and critics when shown at the fair. See Miller, 366.

5. The "garden city" design, originated by Ebenezer Howard in England, was later adopted by American urban critics and planners like Catherine Bauer, Lewis Mumford, Henry Wright, and Clarence Stein, and implemented by the New Deal in its Greenbelt town program.

6. In this sense, the images of the uncontainable molten iron approach Edmund Burke's conception of the sublime. For Csicsery-Ronay, the Burkean sublime differs from the Kantian sublime by omitting the "access to the Transcendental Ego" that contains the fear and dread caused during sublime experiences (151). The Burkean sublime also, unlike the Kantian version, often includes "the categories of the monstrous and the excessive that shock the ego beyond repair and order" (152). These characteristics lead Csicsery-Ronay to associate Burke's sublime with the grotesque.

7. In his novel *Blood on the Forge* (1941), William Attaway also depicts the inability of the industrial landscape to contain aspects of the steel-making process, further supporting the grotesque industrial vision of *The City*. After fleeing Kentucky to work at a steel mill outside of Pittsburgh, the three central characters experience the harsh working and environmental conditions of industrial landscapes. As a fellow black worker named Smothers, crippled by an accident in the mill, tells them, "I kin hear when cold steel whisper all the time and hot roll steel cream like hell. *It's a sin to melt up the ground,* is what steel say. *It's a sin.* Steel bound to git ever'body 'cause o' that sin. They say I crazy, but mills gone crazy 'cause men bringin' trainloads of ground in here and meltin' it up" (150). Smother's words turn prophetic when Big Mat and Melody witness an explosion at the mill that kills fourteen men, including Smothers, and leaves Chinatown blind: "The down there came a blinding flash. Straight up into the sky it went, shooting its reflection to the far shore of the Monongahela. For a moment the windshield of the car filled with light. A mushroom cloud, streaked with whirling red fire, followed the flash. Under its giant bulk the blast furnace stood like black pop bottles.

Then the sound boomed over the car in a big wind. The windshield rattled" (157). Attaway's image of the explosion is eerily prophetic of the dropping of Big Boy and Little Man on Hiroshima and Nagasaki just a few years after the publication of his novel.

8. For discussions of urban pastoralism in the novels of Farrell and Gold, see previous chapter.

9. Sunnyside, Queens, a garden city neighborhood designed by Stein and Wright as well as developer Alexander Bing in the 1920s, is perhaps one exception.

10. Some of the critiques levied on the film by its directors stemmed from their assumptions regarding the aesthetic function of documentary film. While Willard Van Dyke, the film's co-director, saw film as a medium through which "young hopeful artists . . . felt that their art could make a difference" (qtd. in Gillett 75), he did not think it should be used for propaganda. In a 1973 interview at SUNY Buffalo, Van Dyke took pains to differentiate his views on film from the British propagandist filmmaker John Grierson: "He had a kind of contempt for art. He was a propagandist, and I thought that the two worked together. I thought there was no reason in the world not to have art in propaganda. Certainly, I was interested in social change, but I was also interested in the aesthetics of my medium, and the two of them were good together, but he [Grierson] didn't agree" (qtd. in Gillett 75). Similarly, Steiner rejected the belief that film could engagingly "present complex ideas." In an interview also at SUNY Buffalo, Steiner said, "Maybe the historians (like Mumford) can, but the film maker simply rubs his nose in hard visual facts. Most of the visuals come out of nose and eyes to reality and the lens to reality. If we had been the thinkers and sociologists we'd made a film that would have gone straight into the ash can—a dreary, dry thing" (qtd. in Gillett 77).

11. Other work examining environmental thought in science fictional works from the early 1960s to the present include Ursula K. Heise's *Sense of Place and Sense of Planet: The Environmental Imagination of the Global* (Oxford University Press, 2008); Patrick D. Murphy's "The Non-Alibi of Alien Scapes: SF and Ecocriticism" in *Beyond Nature Writing: Expanding the Boundaries of Ecocriticism*, eds. Karla Armbruster and Kathleen R. Wallace (University Press of Virginia, 2001), 263–78; and Eric Otto's *Green Speculations: Science Fiction and Transformative Environmentalism* (Ohio State University Press, 2012).

12. On the political affiliations of the Futurians, Frederick Pohl writes, "The Futurians weren't political, though some of its members surely were. . . . Most of the Futurians were simply not interested. What held us together was science fiction, and a common desire to write it" (57). On attempting to recruit science fiction fans in general to the YCL, Pohl writes,

> I don't think our failure was because Communism was so outrageous an idea for science-fiction fans. It may even have been that it was not outrageous enough. Science-fiction fans, like science-fiction writers, are about the most obstinately individual people alive, and they do get into strange things. Preach-

ing Marxism, we were competing with Technocrats, Esperantists, Single-Taxers, New Dealers, Ham-and-Eggers, and even one or two self-labeled Fascists. None of them were making much headway, either. (55)

13. Bradbury's literary biographer, David Seed, argues that *The Martian Chronicles* is a "composite novel" rather than a collection of short stories, in that it organizes the "miscellany" of the various stories with central themes that run throughout the collection (51). Many of the stories I will address in this section were published earlier in various science fiction magazines.

14. Historian Daniel R. Headrick argues for a similar understanding of the beginnings of colonialism. For him, "technological changes were indispensable to the expansion of Europe in the nineteenth century and profoundly affected its timing and location" (234). In claiming this, Headrick is not interested in making a technological deterministic understanding of colonialism, which sees the latter as only a product of developments in technology. Instead, he argues that "the appearance of a new technology can reinforce or trigger a motive by making the desired end possible or acceptably cheap" (234).

15. A scenario developed in Philip K. Dick's later novel *Do Androids Dream of Electric Sheep?* (1968).

16. For a discussion of how the US government kept information from its citizens concerning the effects of atomic bombs on the residents of Hiroshima and Nagasaki, see Lifton and Mitchell, 3–64.

17. C. L. Moore's "Shambleau" (1933) is one of the most engaging stories on the "female grotesque." In the story, Moore amplifies the grotesqueness of the female body by associating it with an alien race of female, snaked-headed vampires called the Shambleau who, the story suggests, served as an inspiration for the snake-headed monster in Greek mythology. Trapping the rugged and masculine space pirate Northwest Smith in "her living cloak" of worm-like hair (21), a single Shambleau feeds upon his life force, a process that deeply affects him: "[H]e stood, rigid as marble, as helplessly stony as any of Medusa's victims in ancient legends were, while the terrible pleasure of Shambleau thrilled and shuddered through every fiber of him; through every atom of his body and the intangible atoms of what men call the soul, through all that was Smith the dreadful pleasure ran" (21). While Smith is eventually saved from the embrace of the alien vampire by his partner Yarol, he becomes deeply changed by the experience (Bredhoft 374). When Yarol makes him promise to shoot any Shambleau he encounters in the future, Smith can only reply in a "wavered" voice, "I'll—try" (32). While some critics see Moore as ultimately unable to resolve the dilemmas surrounding gender relations depicted in the story (Rosinksy 72), Thomas A. Bredehoft convincingly argues that Yarol's shooting of Shambleau does not completely contain the female grotesque depicted in the story. For Bredhoft, Smith's encounter with Shambleau has "changed" him (374). Not only is Smith unable to fully commit to Yarol's promise, his "very language has been altered" from a sense of self-certainty and power to

"speeches . . . replete with . . . dashes and syntactic dislocations" (379). The uncertainty symbolized by these new "linguistic patterns" suggest, as Bredehoft goes on to explain, that Smith has "moved away from the [masculine] center, becoming more like the boundary-threatening Shambleau than like . . . [Yarol]" (380).

18. Anticipating a future without birds in "A Fable for Tomorrow," Carson writes,

> There was a strange stillness. The birds, for example—where had they gone? Many people spoke of them, puzzled and disturbed. The feeding stations in the backyards were deserted. The few birds seen anywhere were moribund; they trembled violently and could not fly. It was a spring without voices. On the mornings that had once throbbed with the dawn chorus of robins, catbirds, doves, jays, wrens, and scores of other bird voices there was now no sound: only silence lay over the fields and woods and marsh. (2)

19. In addition to livestock and birds, humans also experience the "strange blight" that ascends over the American town in "A Fable for Tomorrow." Carson writes, "The farmers spoke of much illness among their families. In the town the doctors had become more and more puzzled by new kinds of sickness appearing among their patients. There had been several sudden and unexplained deaths, not only among adults but even among children, who would be stricken suddenly while at play and die within a few hours" (2).

20. As William Souder notes, the discovery of DDT's potential use as an insecticide in 1939 coincided with the beginnings of the "arms race": the letter Einstein signed and delivered to FDR proposing that the US take advantage of recent developments in nuclear fission to start developing a new weapon more powerful than any ever used (238). Souder writes, "DDT and nuclear fission were to become the twin agents of a great change of heart and will. In virtual lockstep, the two technologies, deadly and yet beguiling, were perfected in war and then loosed on a world living uneasily at peace" (264). For an in-depth overview of the concurrent development of nuclear weapons and DDT and their effects on the development of Carson's thought, see Souder, chapter 9, "Earth on Fire."

21. Bradbury's "Way Up in the Middle of the Air" does highlight ways that African American inequality supports white supremacy during the period. In a remark to a prominent white citizen in the town named Teece who spends the story railing against and trying to stop the mass exodus, a young African American boy named Silly asks him, "[W]hat you goin' to do nights from now on?" (99). The boy's question refers to the practice of lynching and, as Elisabeth Anne Leonard argues, reveals how much "racism depends on the presence of those it hates" (257). Without the presence of an "inferior" people from which they distinguish themselves, she explains, the white citizens experience an identity crisis that exposes the absurd logic of racism. Though Leonard commends the story for this insight as well as addressing racial inequality when so many texts in the genre ignore it

(254), she does admonish Bradbury for his problematic use of black "stereotypes" in his depictions of African Americans in the US (257).

22. In exploring the various roles of technology in *Black Empire*, George Schuyler becomes an early practitioner of what Mark Dery refers to as "Afrofuturism," a term he uses to identify "[s]peculative fiction that treats African-American themes and addresses African-American concerns in the context of twentieth-century technoculture—and, more general, African-American signification that appropriates images of technology and a prosthetically enhanced future" (180). Since Dery coined the term in his 1993 article "Black to the Future: Interviews with Samuel R. Delany, Greg Tate, and Tricia Rose," originally published in *South Atlantic Quarterly*, Afrofuturism has gained traction among critics of African American literature and culture, resulting in two anthologies of black science fiction: *Dark Matter: A Century of Speculative Fiction from the African Diaspora*, ed. Sheree R. Thomas (Warner Aspect, 2000); and *Dark Matter: Reading the Bones*, ed. Sheree R. Thomas (Warner Aspect, 2004).

23. I don't want to suggest that Schuyler had environmental ends in mind with these kinds of technologies, as he seems to value them for their efficiency and ability to free African American populations from white-controlled energy sources. Their environmental value is primarily of interest to critics and readers in the present, who get a glimpse of early speculations of "green" technologies and their potential uses.

24. The presence of wind energy also contributed to the period's interest in renewable energy. By the end of the 1930s, the Jacobs Wind Electric Company had developed "a truly reliable" wind generator (Righter 93).

Conclusion

1. Burns's film is a two-part documentary on the historic dust storms of the 1930s that includes photographs and videos of the storms, interviews from residents in the area, and interviews with Donald Worster, Timothy Egan, and other historians who have written about the Dust Bowl. Nolan's *Interstellar* uses resident interviews from Burns's documentary, images of dust storms, and references to dust storm-related illnesses like "dust pneumonia" to depict a future world in which climate change has prevented humanity from producing enough food for survival. And in Stanton's *WALL-E*, the title character, a robot, must take refuge from periodic dust storms as he stacks skyscraper-high mounds of garbage in preparation for the return of humanity.

Bibliography

Primary Sources

Algren, Nelson. *Never Come Morning*. Four Walls Eight Windows, 1987.
Attaway, William. *Blood on the Forge*. New York Review Books, 2005.
Bambi. Dirs. Bill Roberts, David Hand, etc. Perf. Hardie Albright, Stan Alexander, Bobette Audrey. Walt Disney, 1942.
Bradbury, Ray. *The Martian Chronicles*. Bantam Books, 1970.
Caldwell, Erskine. *Tobacco Road*. Signet, 1982.
The City. Dir. Ralph Steiner and Willard Van Dyke. Perf. PostClassical Ensemble, 1939.
Davidson, Donald, et al. *I'll Take My Stand: The South and the Agrarian Tradition*. Louisiana State University Press, 1958.
Doctorow, E. L. *World's Fair*. Fawcett Publications, 1986.
Farrell, James T. *Studs Lonigan*. University of Illinois Press, 1993.
Faulkner, William. *Go Down, Moses*. Vintage International, 1990.
Federal Works Administration. *Final Report on the WPA Program, 1935–1943*. Government Printing Office, 1943.
Gold, Mike. *Jews Without Money*. Carroll & Graf, 1984.
Gone with the Wind. Dir. Victor Fleming. Perf. Vivien Leigh, Clark Gable, Olivia de Havilland, Leslie Howard. Warner Brothers, 1939.
Heinlein, Robert A. "Misfit." *The Past Through Tomorrow: "Future History" Stories*. Putnam, 1967.
Hemingway, Ernest. *Green Hills of Africa*. Scribner, 1996.
Hurston, Zora Neale. *Dust Tracks on a Road*. *Hurston: Folklore, Memoirs, & Other Writings*. Library of America, 1995, 557–808.
Hurston, Zora Neale. "Go Gator and Muddy the Water." In *Go Gator and Muddy the Water: Writings by Zora Neale Hurston from the Federal Writer's Project*. Ed. Pamela Borelon, W. W. Norton & Company, 1999.
Hurston, Zora Neale. *Mules and Men*. *Hurston: Folklore, Memoirs, & Other Writings*. Library of America, 1995, 1–268.
Hurston, Zora Neale. *Their Eyes Were Watching God*. Harper Perennial Modern Classics, 2006.
Interstellar. Dir. Christopher Nolan. Perf. Matthew McConaughey, Michael Caine, Anne Hathaway. Warner Brothers, 2013.

Jacobs, Jane. *The Death and Life of Great American Cities*. Modern Library, 1993.
Jezebel. Dir. William Wyler. Perf. Bette Davis, Henry Fonda, George Brent. Warner Brothers, 1938.
Leopold, Aldo. "Coon Valley: An Adventure in Cooperative Conservation." In *A Sand County Almanac & Other Writing*. Ed. Curt Meine. Library of America, 2013.
Leopold, Aldo. "Thinking Like a Mountain." In *A Sand County Almanac*, 129–33. Oxford University Press, 1968.
Marshall, Robert. *Alaska Wilderness: Exploring the Central Brooks Range*. Ed. George Marshall. University of California Press, 2005.
Marshall, Robert. *Arctic Village: A 1930s Portrait of Wiseman, Alaska*. University of Alaska Press, 1991.
McNickle, D'Arcy. *The Surrounded*. University of New Mexico Press, 1978.
Merril, Judith. *Shadow on the Hearth*. Doubleday, 1950.
Merril, Judith. "That Only a Mother." In *Women of Wonder, The Classic Years: Science Fiction by Women from the 1940s to the 1970s*. Ed. Pamela Sargent, 65–73. Harcourt Brace & Company, 1975.
Moore, C. L. "Shambleau." In *The Best of C. L. Moore*. Ed. Lester Del Rey, 1–32. Ballantine Books, 1975.
My Man Godfrey. Dir. Gregory La Cava. Perf. William Powell, Carole Lombard, Alice Brady. Universal, 1936.
Olsen, Tillie. *Yonnondio: From the Thirties*. Dell, 1977.
Our Daily Bread. Dir. King Vidor, Pare Lorentz, et al. Perf. Tom Keene, Karen Morley, Barbara Pepper. United Artists, 1934.
Percy, William Alexander. *Lanterns on the Levee: Recollections of a Planter's Son*. Louisiana State University Press, 1977
Schuyler, George S. *Black Empire*. Northeastern University Press, 1991.
Steinbeck, John. "To George Albee (1933)." In *Steinbeck: A Life in Letters*. Ed. Elaine Steinbeck and Robert Wallsten, 79–82. Viking Press, 1975.
Steinbeck, John. *The Grapes of Wrath*. Penguin Books, 2002.
To New Horizons. General Motors Corporation. Internet Archive, 1940.
Wallace, Henry A. *New Frontiers*. Reynal & Hitchcock, 1934.
Wright, Richard. "How Bigger Was Born." *Native Son*. Harper Perennial, 1993.
Wright, Richard. "The Man Who Lived Underground." *Eight Men*. Harper Perennial, 2008.
Wright, Richard. *Native Son*. Harper Perennial, 1993.
Wright, Richard. *Uncle Tom's Children*. *Richard Wright: Early Works*. Library of America, 1991, 221–441.

Secondary Sources

Allen, Mary. *Animals in American Literature*. University of Illinois Press, 1983.
Astro, Richard. *John Steinbeck and Edward F. Ricketts: The Shaping of a Novelist*. University of Minnesota Press, 1973.

Baldwin, James. *Notes of a Native Son*. Beacon Press, 1955.
Barry, John M. *Rising Tide: The Great Mississippi Flood of 1927 and How It Changed America*. Simon & Schuster, 1997.
Barthes, Roland. *Mythologies*. Trans. Annette Lavers. Hill and Wang, 1972.
Bennett, Michael. "Anti-Pastoralism, Frederick Douglass, and the Nature of Slavery." In *Beyond Nature Writing: Expanding the Boundaries of Ecocriticism*. Eds. Karla Armbruster and Kathleen R. Wallace, 195–210. University Press of Virginia, 2001.
Berman, Marshall. *All That Is Solid Melts into Air: The Experience of Modernity*. Penguin, 1983.
Booker, M. Keith. *Monsters, Mushroom Clouds, and the Cold War: American Science Fiction and the Roots of Postmodernism, 1946–1964*. Greenwood Press, 2001.
Brinkley, Douglas. *Rightful Heritage: Franklin D. Roosevelt and the Land of America*. HarperCollins Publishers, 2016.
Buell, Lawrence. *The Environmental Imagination: Thoreau, Nature Writing, and the Formation of American Culture*. Belknap Press of Harvard University Press, 1995.
Buell, Lawrence. *The Future of Environmental Criticism: Environmental Crisis and Literary Imagination*. John Wiley & Sons, 2005.
Buell, Lawrence. *Writing for an Endangered World: Literature, Culture, and the Environment in the U.S. and Beyond*. Belknap Press of Harvard University Press, 2003.
Burke, Kenneth. *The Philosophy of Literary Form: Studies in Symbolic Action*. University of California Press, 1973.
Campbell, Edward D. C. *The Celluloid South: Hollywood and the Southern Myth*. University of Tennessee Press, 1981.
Cappetti, Carla. *Writing Chicago: Modernism, Ethnography, and the Novel*. Columbia University Press, 1993.
Cartmill, Matt. *A View to a Death in the Morning: Hunting and Nature Through History*. Harvard University Press, 1993.
Catton, Theodore. *American Indians and National Forests*. University of Arizona Press, 2016.
Clark, Suzanne. "Roosevelt and Hemingway: Natural History, Manliness, and the Rhetoric of the Strenuous Life." In *Hemingway and the Natural World*. Ed. Robert E. Fleming, 55–67. University of Idaho Press, 1999.
Clark, Thomas D. *The Greening of the South: The Recovery of Land and Forest*. University of Kentucky Press, 2004.
Cole, Terrence. "Preface." *Arctic Village: A 1930's Portrait of Wiseman, Alaska*. University of Alaska Press, 1991.
Colvin, Christina M. "'His Guts Are All out of Him': Faulkner's Eruptive Animals." *Journal of Modern Literature* 38, no. 1 (2014): 94–106. JSTOR, doi:10.2979/jmodelite.38.1.94. Accessed June 4, 2016.
Cowdrey, Albert E. *This Land, This South: An Environmental History* (revised edition). University Press of Kentucky, 1996.

Cronon, William. *Nature's Metropolis: Chicago and the Great West*. W. W. Norton & Company, 1991.

Cronon, William. "Revisiting the Vanishing Frontier: The Legacy of Frederick Jackson Turner." *The Western Historical Quarterly* 18, no. 2 (1987): 157–76. JSTOR, doi:10.2307/969581. Accessed Feb. 5, 2016.

Csicsery-Ronay, Jr., Istvan. *The Seven Beauties of Science Fiction*. Wesleyan University Press, 2008.

Daniel, Julia E. *Building Nature: Modern American Poetry, Landscape Architecture, and City Planning*. University of Virginia Press, 2017.

Dawahare, Anthony. "'That Joyous Certainty': History and Utopia in Tillie Olsen's Depression-Era Literature." *Twentieth Century Literature* 44, no. 3 (1998): 261–75. Accessed Oct. 30, 2012.

del Gizzo, Suzanne. "Going Home: Hemingway, Primitivism, and Identity." *Modern Fiction Studies* 49, no. 3 (2003): 496–523. JSTOR, doi:10.2307/441809. Accessed Feb. 17, 2017.

Denning, Michael. *The Cultural Front: The Laboring of American Culture in the Twentieth Century*. Verso, 1993.

Dery, Mark. "Back to the Future: Interviews with Samuel R. Delany, Greg Tate, and Tricia Rose." *Flame Wars: The Discourse of Cyberculture*. Ed. Mark Dery, 179–222. Duke University Press, 1994.

Dickstein, Morris. *Dancing in the Dark: A Cultural History of the Great Depression*. W. W. Norton & Co., 2009.

Entin, Joseph B. *Sensational Modernism: Experimental Fiction and Photography in Thirties America*. University of North Carolina Press, 2007.

"Environment." *Oxford English Dictionary* (third edition), 2008.

Fabre, Michel. *The Unfinished Quest of Richard Wright*. Trans. Isabel Barzun. William Morrow & Company, 1973.

Fekete, John. *The Critical Twilight: Explorations in the Ideology of Anglo-American Literary Theory from Eliot to McLuhan*. Routledge & Kegan Paul, 1977.

Fishman, Robert. *Bourgeois Utopias: The Rise and Fall of Suburbia*. Basic Books, 1989.

Fishman, Robert. *Urban Utopias in the Twentieth Century: Ebenezer Howard, Frank Lloyd Wright, and Le Corbusier*. MIT Press, 1982.

Flores, Dan. *Coyote America: A Natural & Supernatural History*. Basic Books, 2016.

Furmansky, Dyana Z. *Rosalie Edge, Hawk of Mercy: The Activist Who Saved Nature from the Conservationists*. University of Georgia Press, 2009.

Gabler, Neil. *Walt Disney: The Triumph of the American Imagination*. Knopf, 2006.

Geilern, Monika. "Of Parasites and Humans: Encounters with Nature in Richard Wright's *Native Son* and Charles Johnson's *Dreamer*." In *Restoring the Connection to the Natural World: Essays on the African American Environmental Imagination*. Ed. Sylvia Mayer, 97–116. Transaction Publishers, 2003.

Giesen, James C. *Boll Weevil Blues: Cotton, Myth, and Power in the American South*. Chicago University Press, 2011.

Gifford, Terry. *Pastoral*. Routledge, 1999.
Gillette, Jr., Howard. *Civitas by Design: Building Better Communities, from the Garden City to the New Urbanism*. University of Pennsylvania Press, 2010.
Glickman, Stephen E. "The Spotted Hyena from Aristotle to the Lion King: Reputation is Everything." *Social Research* 62, no. 3 (1995): 501–37. *JSTOR*, http://www.jstor.org/stable/40971108. Accessed March 13, 2017.
Glover, James M. *A Wilderness Original: The Life of Bob Marshall*. Mountaineers, 1986.
Goyal, Yogita. "Black Nationalist Hokum: George Schuyler's Transnational Critique." *African American Review* 47, no. 1 (2014): 21–36. *Project MUSE*, https://muse.jhu.edu/article/561893. Accessed Dec. 14, 2016.
Green, Tara T. *Reimagining the Middle Passage: Black Resistance in Literature, Television, and Song*. Ohio State University Press, 2018.
Gruesser, John C. "George Schuyler, Samuel Brooks, and Max Disher." *African American Review* 27, no. 4 (1993): 679–86. *JSTOR*, http://www.jstor.org/stable/3041906. Accessed Jan. 11, 2017.
Haraway, Donna J. *When Species Meet*. University of Minnesota Press, 2008.
Headrick, Daniel R. "The Tools of Imperialism: Technology and the Expansion of European Colonial Empires in the Nineteenth Century." *Journal of Modern History* 51, no. 2 (1979): 231–63. *JSTOR*, http://www.jstor.org/stable/1879216. Accessed April 10, 2017.
Hediger, Ryan. "Hunting, Fishing, and the Cramp of Ethics in Ernest Hemingway's *The Old Man and the Sea*, *Green Hills of Africa*, and *Under Kilimanjaro*." *Hemingway Review* 27, no. 2 (2008): 35–59, *Project MUSE*, https://doi.org/10.1353/hem.0.0011. Accessed March 16, 2017.
Hediger, Ryan. "Pity and the Beasts: Teaching Hemingway Stories via Sympathy for Animals." *Teaching Hemingway and the Natural World*. Ed. Kevin Maier, 141–51. Kent State University Press, 2018.
Hellenbrand, Harold. "Bigger Thomas Reconsidered: 'Native Son,' Film and 'King Kong.'" *Journal of American Culture* 6, no. 1 (1983): 84–95. doi:10.1111/j.1542-734X.1983.0601_84.x. Accessed Nov. 8, 2013.
Hemenway, Robert E. *Zora Neale Hurston: A Literary Biography*. University of Illinois Press, 1978.
Hicks, Scott. "Zora Neale Hurston: Environmentalist in Southern Literature." In *"The Inside Light": New Critical Essays on Zora Neale Hurston*. Ed. Deborah G. Plant, 113–26. Praeger, 2010.
Hill, Robert A. and Rasmussen, R. Kent. "Afterword." In *Black Empire*, 259–323. Northeastern University Press, 1991.
Hine, Robert V., and Faragher, John Mack. *The American West: A New Interpretive History*. Yale University Press, 2000.
Jurca, Catherine. *White Diaspora: The Suburb and the Twentieth-Century American Novel*. Princeton University Press, 2001.
Kazin, Alfred. *On Native Grounds: An Interpretation of Modern American Fiction*. Harcourt Brace Jovanovich, 1982.

Kelley, Robin D. G. *Hammer and Hoe: Alabama Communists During the Great Depression.* University of North Carolina Press, 1990.

Kohli, Amor. "But That's Just Mad! Reading the Utopian Impulse in *Dark Princess* and *Black Empire*." *The Black Imagination: Science Fiction, Futurism, and the Speculative.* Eds. Sandra Jackson and Julie E. Moody-Freeman, 35–50. Routledge, 2011.

Kolodny, Annette. *The Lay of the Land: Metaphor as Experience and History in American Life and Letters.* University of North Carolina Press, 1975.

Kuznick, Peter J. "Losing the World of Tomorrow: The Battle Over the Presentation of Science at the 1939 New York World's Fair." *American Quarterly* 46, no. 3 (1994): 341–73. JSTOR, http:www.jstor.org/stable/2713269. Accessed May 26, 2015.

Ladino, Jennifer K. *Reclaiming Nostalgia: Longing for Nature in American Literature.* University of Virginia Press, 2012.

Lannoo, Michael J. *Leopold's Shack and Ricketts's Lab: The Emergence of Environmentalism.* University of California Press, 2010.

Lavender, Isiah. *Race in American Science Fiction.* Indiana University Press, 2011.

Lear, Linda. *Rachel Carson: Witness for Nature.* Mariner Books, 2009.

Lee, Martyn. "Relocating Location: Cultural Geography, the Specificity of Place and the City Habitus." *Cultural Methodologies.* Ed. Jim McGuigan, 126–41. SAGE Publications, 1998.

Leighninger Jr., Robert D. "Cultural Infrastructure: The Legacy of New Deal Public Space." *Journal of Architectural Education* 49, no. 4 (1996): 226–36. JSTOR, doi:10.2307/1425295. Accessed Sept. 25, 2014.

Leonard, Elisabeth Anne. "Race and Ethnicity in Science Fiction." *The Cambridge Companion to Science Fiction.* Eds. Edward James and Farah Mendlesohn, 253–63. Cambridge University Press, 2003.

Levine, Lawrence W. *Black Culture and Black Consciousness: Afro-American Folk Thought from Slavery to Freedom* (thirtieth anniversary edition). Oxford University Press, 2007.

Lifton, Robert J. and Mitchell, Greg. *Hiroshima in America: Fifty Years of Denial.* G. P. Putnam's Sons, 1995.

Lydenberg, John. "Nature Myth in Faulkner's 'The Bear.'" *American Literature* 24, no. 1 (1952): 62–72, Accessed March 13, 2017.

Machor, James L. *Pastoral Cities: Urban Ideas and the Symbolic Landscape of America.* University of Wisconsin Press, 1994.

Madrigal, Alexis. *Powering the Dream: The History and Promise of Green Technology.* Da Capo Press, 2011.

Maher, Neil M. *Nature's New Deal: The Civilian Conservation Corps and the Roots of the American Environmental Movement.* Oxford University Press, 2008.

Major, William H. *Grounded Vision: New Agrarianism and the Academy* (e-book). University of Alabama Press, 2011.

Marx, Leo. *The Machine in the Garden: Technology and the Pastoral Ideal in America.* Oxford University Press, 1970.

Marx, Leo. "Pastoralism in America." In *Ideology and Classical American Literature*. Ed. Sacvan Bercovitch and Myra Jehlen, 36–69. Cambridge University Press, 1986.
McCarthy, B. Eugene. "Models of History in Richard Wright's *Uncle Tom's Children*." *Black American Literature Forum* 25, no. 4 (1991): 729–43. JSTOR, doi:10.2307/3041719. Accessed April 2, 2017.
McElvaine, Robert S. *The Great Depression: America, 1929–1941*. Times Books, 1993.
Melosi, Martin V. *Garbage in the Cities: Refuse Reform and the Environment*. University of Pittsburgh Press, 2005.
Mille, Benjamin. *Fat of the Land: Garbage of New York the Last Two Hundred Years*. Four Walls Eight Windows, 2000.
Miller, Ronald L. *Lewis Mumford: A Life*. Weidenfeld and Nicolson, 1989.
Morshed, Adnan. "The Aesthetics of Ascension in Norman Bel Geddes's Futurama." *Journal of the Society of Architectural Historians* 63, no. 1 (2014): 74–99. JSTOR, doi:10.2307/4127993. Accessed April 16, 2017.
Morton, Timothy. *The Ecological Thought*. Harvard University Press, 2012.
Mumford, Lewis. *The Story of Utopia*. Viking Press, 1962.
Murphy, Charlene M. "Hemingway's Gentle Hunters: Contradiction or Duality?" In *Hemingway and the Natural World*. Ed. Robert E. Fleming, 165–74. University of Idaho Press, 1999.
Mykle, Robert. *Killer 'cane: The Deadly Hurricane of 1928*. Cooper Square Press, 2002.
Newell, Dianne, and Lamont, Victoria. *Judith Merril: A Critical Study*. McFarland & Company, 2012.
Nicholls, David G. *Conjuring the Folk: Forms of Modernity in African America*. University of Michigan Press, 2000.
Nixon, Rob. *Slow Violence and the Environmentalism of the Poor*. Harvard University Press, 2011.
Nye, David E. *American Technological Sublime*. MIT Press, 1994.
O'Connor, Terry. *Animals as Neighbors: The Past and Present of Commensal Species*. Michigan State University Press, 2013.
Outka, Paul. *Race and Nature from Transcendentalism to the Harlem Renaissance*. Palgrave Macmillan, 2008.
Owens, Louis. "The Red Road to Nowhere: D'Arcy McNickle's 'The Surrounded' and 'The Hungry Generation.'" *American Indian Quarterly* 13, no. 3 (1989): 239–48. JSTOR, doi:10.2307/1184435. Accessed Feb. 25, 2016.
Parker, Dorothy R. *Singing an Indian Song: A Biography of D'Arcy McNickle*. University of Nebraska Press, 1992.
Parrish, Susan Scott. "Faulkner and the Outer Weather of 1927." *American Literary History* 24, no. 1 (2012): 34–58.
Patterson, Jr., William H. *Robert Heinlein: In Dialogue with His Century* (vol. 1). Tom Doherty Associates Book, 2010.
Phillips, Sarah T. *This Land, This Nation: Conservation, Rural America, and the New Deal*. Cambridge University Press, 2007.

Pick, Anit. *Creaturely Poetics: Animality and Vulnerability in Literature and Film.* Columbia University Press, 2011.

Pizer, Donald. *Twentieth-Century American Literary Naturalism: An Interpretation.* Southern Illinois University Press. 1982.

Reiger, Christopher. *Clear-Cutting Eden: Ecology and the Pastoral in Southern Literature.* University of Alabama Press, 2009.

Reiger, John F. *American Sportsmen and the Origins of Conservation* (third edition). Oregon State University Press, 2001.

Righter, Robert W. *Wind Energy in America: A History.* University of Oklahoma Press, 1996.

Robinson, Kim Stanley. "Martian Musings and the Miraculous Conjunction." *Visions of Mars: Essays on the Red Planet in Fiction and Science.* Eds. Eric S. Rabkin, Howard V. Hendrix, and George Edgar Slusser, 146–51. McFarland & Company, 2011.

Ruffin, Kimberly N. *Black on Earth: African American Ecoliterature Traditions.* University of Georgia Press, 2010.

Saikku, Mikko. *This Delta, This Land: An Environmental History of the Yazoo-Mississippi Floodplain.* University of Georgia Press, 2005.

Seed, David. "The Subject of Mars." In *Ray Bradbury*, 45–82. University of Illinois Press, 2015.

Simek, Stephanie L., Belant, Jerrold L., et al. "History and Status of the American Black Bear in Mississippi." *Ursus* 23, no. 2 (2012): 159–67. *BioOne*, http://dx.doi.org/10.2192/URSUS-D-11-00031.1. Accessed July 26, 2019.

Sharp, Patrick B. "From Yellow Peril to Japanese Wasteland: John Hersey's 'Hiroshima.'" *Twentieth Century Literature* 46, no. 4 (2000): 434–52. *JSTOR*, doi:10.2307/827841. Accessed Jan. 2, 2017.

Smith, Henry Nash. *Virgin Land: The American West as a Symbol and Myth.* Harvard University Press, 1950.

Smith, Kimberly K. *African American Environmental Thought: Foundations.* University Press of Kansas, 2007.

Soper, Kate. *What is Nature: Culture, Politics and the Non-Human.* Blackwell, 1998.

Souder, William. *On a Farther Shore: The Life and Legacy of Rachel Carson.* Crown Publishers, 2012.

Sullivan, Robert. *Rats: Observations on the History and Habitat of the Cities Most Unwanted Inhabitants.* Bloomsbury USA, 2004.

Sutter, Paul S. *Driven Wild: How the Fight against Automobiles Launched the Modern Wilderness Movement.* University of Washington Press, 2002.

Taylor, Graham D. *The New Deal and American Indian Tribalism: The Administration of the Indian Reorganization Act, 1934–45.* University of Nebraska Press, 1980.

Thomas, Brennan M. "A Forest Fable: Elements of Allegory and Americana in Disney's *Bambi*." *Americanization of History: Conflation of Time and Culture in Film and Television.* Ed. Kathleen McDonald, 42–60. Cambridge Scholars Publishing, 2011.

Trachtenberg, Alan. "Myth and Symbol." *Massachusetts Review* 25, no. 4 (1984): 667–73. *JSTOR*, http://www.jstor.org/stable/25089609. Accessed April 20, 2017.

Wardi, Anissa Janine. *Water and African American Memory: An Ecocritical Perspective*. University Press of Florida, 2011.

Weaks-Baxter, Mary. *Reclaiming the American Farmer: The Reinvention of a Regional Mythology in Twentieth-Century Southern Writing*. Louisiana State University Press, 2006.

Williams, Raymond. *The Country and the City*. Oxford University Press, 1973.

Williams, Raymond. *Marxism and Literature*. Oxford University Press, 1988.

Wills, Garry. *John Wayne's America*. New York: Touchstone, 1998.

Wilson, Alexander. *The Culture of Nature: North American Landscape from Disney to the Exxon Valdez*. Blackwell Publishers, 1992.

Wise, Benjamin E. *William Alexander Percy: The Curious Life of a Mississippi Planter and Sexual Freethinker*. University of North Carolina Press, 2012.

Wolfe, Gary K. "The Frontier Myth in Ray Bradbury." *Ray Bradbury*. Ed. Harold Bloom, 103–23. Chelsea House, 2001.

Worster, Donald. *Dust Bowl: The Southern Plains in the 1930s*. Oxford University Press, 1982.

Worster, Donald. *Nature's Economy: A History of Ecological Ideas* (second edition). Cambridge University Press, 1995.

Index

Abbey, Edward, 173n5
Adams, Ansel, 169
African American folklore, 9, 15, 61, 87–93, 96–97, 128
African Americans: and cities, 101, 117–18, 123–24; and colonialism, 17, 132–33, 157–60, 165; and environmental thought, 18, 76, 77–78, 87; and flooding, 68, 69, 80–86, 94–96; and the New Deal, 6, 7; and science fiction, 157, 160–61, 189n22; and sharecropping, 68, 73–74, 77; and the South, 15, 61, 68–70, 73, 76–97; and stereotypes, 16, 68, 78–79, 85, 117, 119, 120, 125–26, 128, 188n21; and technology, 157–58, 160–63, 165
Afrofuturism, 189n22
agrarianism, 62, 179n4
Agricultural Administration Agency (AAA), 7
Algren, Nelson, 110, 128, 129; and literary naturalism, 106; *Never Come Morning*, 15–16, 105; and place, 102, 105–6, 128; and sociology, 9; and urban parks, 101, 105
Allen, Mary, 121–22, 125
American Indian Federation (AIF), 55
American Indians: and conservationist thought, 49; and the Dust Bowl, 51–52, 179n23; and the frontier, 14, 43–52, 56–57, 147; and the Indian Reorganization Act, 8, 43, 52–56, 57; and the New Deal, 6

American Institute of Planners (AIP), 132, 138
"—And the Moon Be Still as Bright" (Bradbury), 146–47
animal studies, 118
antipastoral, 15, 61, 75, 76, 77, 81, 86, 137
Arctic Village (Marshall), 22, 42, 175n1
Asimov, Isaac, 144
atom (atomic) bomb, 4, 6, 146, 150–52, 161, 166, 167, 186n7, 187n16; and Carson, 156, 188n20; and gender, 17, 132, 145, 152, 153–56; and the human body, 9, 17, 129, 152–53, 156; and the natural world, 17, 129, 156; and science fiction, 150–51, 152–53, 154–55, 156; and the technological sublime, 151; and US censorship, 151–52
Attaway, William, 180n8, 185n7

Bailey, William J., 163–64
Baldwin, James, 119, 128
Bambi (Disney), 14, 22–23, 24–28, 175n2
Bambi: A Life in the Forest (Salten), 24, 27, 175n2
Bauer, Catherine, 143, 185n5
"Bear, The" (Faulkner), 29, 31–34
Bel Geddes, Norman, 135
Berman, Marshall, 135
"Big Boy Leaves Home" (Wright), 77–80, 180n11
Black Empire (Schuyler), 17, 157–63, 165, 189n22

201

Black No More (Schuyler), 161
Blish, James, 145
Blood on the Forge (Attaway), 180n8, 185n7
Boas, Franz, 9
boll weevil songs, 93–94
BP oil spill, 170
Bradbury, Ray: and African Americans, 188n21; and the atom bomb, 17, 150–51, 156–57, 166; and the frontier, 17, 132, 145–50, 152, 156–57, 166; *The Martian Chronicles*, 17, 145–51, 187n13, 188n21
Bradley, David, 155
"Bright and Morning Star" (Wright), 77, 181n14
Brinkley, Douglas, 4, 173n2
Bronx Park, 107–8
Broun, Maurice, 168
Brower, David, 4, 167
Buell, Lawrence, 12, 32, 102, 103, 118, 144
Bureau of Biological Survey (BBS), 7, 28, 176n7
Bureau of Fisheries, 168
Bureau of Indian Affairs (BIA), 49, 52, 53, 54, 55–56, 57
Burgess, Ernest, 9
Burke, Edmund, 185n6
Burns, Ken, 19, 171, 189n1
Butler, Octavia, 18–19

Caldwell, Erskine: and the antipastoral, 15, 61, 73, 75–76, 86, 96; *Tobacco Road*, 75–76, 86–87
Cappetti, Carla, 104, 174n7
Carson, Rachel, 4, 9; and Hawk Mountain, 168, 173n4; and nuclear testing, 156, 189n20; *Silent Spring*, 132, 156, 166, 167, 169, 173n4, 188n18, 188n19
Cartmill, Matt, 25, 26, 27, 176n4
Chicago School of Sociology, 9, 174n7
Chicago World's Fair (1934), 164

Cities in Flight (Blish), 145
City, The (Steiner and Van Dyke), 9, 132, 134, 138–43, 166, 179n1, 186n19
Civic Films, 138
Civilian Conservation Corps (CCC), 6–7, 21, 145, 171, 173n2
Civil War, 70, 74
Civil Works Administration (CWA), 99
Claude, George, 161
climate change, 170, 171
Cole, Terrence, 175n1
Collier, John, 43, 52, 53, 54, 55, 179n24
colonialism: and Africa, 38, 40–41, 157–60, 165, 166; and the American frontier, 17, 24, 42, 43, 48, 145–50, 166; and technology, 17, 146, 157–58, 187n14
Communist Party USA, 181n14
conservation: and American Indians, 49; changes in, 4, 6, 28, 59, 88, 97, 168, 173n2; and hunters, 33, 35–36, 177n10; and predators, 28; and preservation, 7–8; and wilderness, 57
Cooper, Merian C., 120
Copland, Aaron, 138, 169
Corona Ash Dump, 132, 136
Cronon, William, 4, 42
Csicsery-Ronay, Istvan, Jr., 132, 133, 153, 185n6
Cultural Front, The (Denning), 144
Culvin, Christina, 69, 178n14

Dakota Access Pipeline, 170
Daniel, Julia E., 182n4
D'Arcy McNickle Center for American Indian and Indigenous Studies, 56
Dawahare, Anthony, 113–14
Dawes Act, 43, 53
DDT, 132, 156, 166, 168, 188n20
Death and Life of Great American Cities, The (Jacobs), 142
deep ecology, 177n11

del Gizzo, Suzanne, 40, 178n21
"Delta Autumn" (Faulkner), 29, 30, 33
Denning, Michael, 5–6, 12, 13, 101–2, 144, 174n14
depression-era authors/works, 5–6
Dery, Mark, 189n22
Dick, Philip K., 187n15
Dies, Martin, 56
Disney, Walt: and animals, 14, 26, 27, 57, 175n2; and hunting, 22–23, 24, 25, 27–28, 176n3; and predators, 27, 177n9
Doctorow, E. L., 134, 135
"Down by the Riverside" (Wright), 68, 80–86, 95, 180n12
Du Bois, W. E. B., 74
Dumbo (Disney), 176n5
Dust Bowl: and American Indians, 51–52, 173n23; causes of, 3–4, 22, 39, 149; and contemporary interest, 18–19, 22, 39, 171, 189n1; effects of, 3–4, 173n1; and other environmental disasters, 146, 156, 167
Dust Bowl, The (Burns), 19, 171, 189n1
Dust Tracks on the Road (Hurston), 87
dystopia, 158–59, 160

ecopastoral, 60, 88, 174n13
Edge, Rosalie, 3–4, 5, 7, 25, 168, 173n4, 177n8
Egan, Timothy, 4, 52, 173n2, 179n23, 189n1
Einstein, Albert, 188n20
Empson, William, 175n15
End Poverty in California (EPIC), 145
Entin, Joseph, 102, 119–20, 181n3
environmentalism: and Carson, 4, 9, 132, 156, 166, 167–68, 169, 188n20; development of, 4, 5, 18, 21, 97, 151, 167–68; and the postpastoral, 100; and technology, 9, 132, 151, 156, 166
environmental justice, 5, 24, 100, 167, 169, 170; and African Americans, 80, 95–97, 128–29; and American Indians, 43

Fanning, Charles, 106
Farrell, James T., 9, 102, 110, 129; and the Studs Lonigan trilogy, 106, 182n6; and urban pastoralism, 15–16, 101, 103–7, 110, 128; *Young Lonigan*, 15–16, 103–5, 141
Faulkner, William: and deforestation, 14; and ecocriticism, 33, 177n12; *Go Down, Moses*, 14, 29–34, 68–69; and the Great Mississippi Flood of 1927, 29–30; and hunting, 9, 14, 23, 28–29, 31–33, 34, 39; and predators, 31–33, 96; and race, 68–69, 178n14; and wilderness, 35, 41, 57
Fekete, John, 65
female grotesque, 153, 187n17
Ferguson, Jeffrey B., 161
Finney, Carolyn, 78
"Fire and Cloud" (Wright), 77, 181n14
Fish and Wildlife Service, 168, 176n7
Fishman, Robert, 136, 143
Fitzgerald, F. Scott, 11, 132, 137, 185n3
Fleming, Victor, 60
Flint, Michigan, water crisis, 170
Flores, Dan, 177n9
Florida Negro, The (Hurston), 88
frontier, 14–15, 23, 59, 62, 179n2; and Africa, 35, 39; and American Indians, 41–46, 49, 51–54, 56–57; and the Dust Bowl, 22, 39, 51–52; and science fiction, 17, 145–50, 157, 166
Futurama (General Motors), 131, 134–36, 138, 141, 142, 184n1, 185n2
Futurians, 144–45, 186n12

garden city, 8, 138, 139, 141, 142, 185n5
garden myth ("garden of the world"). *See* myths and symbols
Geilern, Monika, 183n13
gentrification, 109, 129

ghetto pastoral, 13, 101–2, 103, 174n14
Giesen, James C., 93–94
Gifford, Terry, 13, 100, 174n13
Gillette, Howard, Jr., 142, 185n4
Glickman, Stephen E., 36, 37, 178n18
Go Down, Moses (Faulkner), 14, 29–34, 39, 69
"Go Gator and Muddy the Water" (Hurston), 88
Gold, Mike: *Jews Without Money*, 16, 107–10, 116, 140, 141; and urban parks, 107–8; and urban pastoralism, 16, 101, 107–10, 113, 114, 128, 129; and vacant lots, 108–10
Gone with the Wind (film), 15, 63–64, 70–71
Goyal, Yogita, 159
Gray, Jesse, 124, 184n20
Great Depression, 5, 6, 8, 157, 182n4, 183n10; and the New York World's Fair, 131; and science fiction, 144–45; and the South, 58, 63, 64
Great Gatsby, The (Fitzgerald), 11, 132, 137–38
Great Mississippi Flood of 1927: causes of, 30, 146; and Faulkner, 30–31; influence of, 4, 6, 167; and Percy, 67; and Wright, 80, 81
Great Recession, 170
Green, Tara T., 80, 83, 84, 86
Greenbelt, Maryland, 141, 142
Greenbelt towns, 138, 139, 140–41, 143, 185n5
Green Hills of Africa (Hemingway), 14, 23, 35–41, 42
Green Mars (Robinson), 149
"Green Morning, The" (Bradbury), 148–50
Green New Deal, 170–71
grotesque: and gender (female grotesque), 153–54, 187n17; and literary naturalism, 102, 115; and science fiction (sci fi grotesque), 134, 144, 145, 148–50, 152–54, 157–58, 187n17; and technology, 131–32, 137, 138, 139, 144, 145, 152–54, 157–58, 166
Gruesser, John, 158, 159
Gulf Stream, 178n20
Guthrie, Woody, 169

Haraway, Donna, 183n15
Hawk Mountain, 168, 173n4, 177n8
Hawthorne, Nathaniel, 181n1
Headrick, Daniel R., 187n14
Hediger, Ryan, 35
Heinlein, Robert, 145
Hellenbrand, Harold, 120
Heller, Edmund, 178n18
Hemingway, Ernest: and Africa, 35, 37–41; and conservation, 34–36, 41, 178n16, 178n19; and ecocriticism, 178n15, 179n19; and the frontier, 39, 40; *Green Hills of Africa*, 14, 23, 35–41, 42; on the Gulf Stream, 178n20; and hunting, 9, 23, 34–39, 41, 178nn16–17; and predators, 14, 23, 28–29, 36–39, 96; and race, 40–41, 178n21; and wilderness, 14, 23, 41, 57
Hersey, John, 152, 155
Hetch Hetchy Valley, 7
Hicks, Scott, 88
Hill, Robert A., 159, 160
Homestead Act, 64
Howard, Ebenezer, 8, 185n5
"How 'Bigger' Was Born" (Wright), 119, 121
Hurricane Katrina, 170
Hurston, Zora Neale: and animals, 87–93, 95, 96, 181n17; and anthropology, 9, 89; and black folklore, 15, 61, 87–93, 94, 128; *Dust Tracks on a Road*, 87; and ecocriticism, 181n15; and flooding, 94–96; *The Florida Negro*, 88; and hoodoo, 88, 92; *Jonah's Gourd Vine*, 94; *Mules*

and Men, 89–93; and pests, 92–93, 94, 96, 128, 183n12; and predators, 89–92, 94, 96, 128, 183n12; and race, 68, 73, 87, 95–96; *Their Eyes Were Watching God*, 68, 73, 94–96, 181n17; and Wright, 95, 128, 183n12

I'll Take My Stand (Southern Agrarians), 15, 62
Indian Reorganization Act ("Indian New Deal"), 23, 43, 45, 52, 55, 179n24
Interstellar (Nolan), 19, 171, 189n1

Jacobs, Jane, 142
Jews Without Money (Gold), 16, 107–10, 116, 140, 141
Jezebel (film), 15, 71–73
Jonah's Gourd Vine (Hurston), 94
Judgment Day (Farrell), 106
Jungle Book, The (Disney), 176n5

Kant, Immanuel, 185n6
Kazin, Alfred, 13
Keck, George, 164
Kelley, Robin D. G., 7, 74
King Kong (Schoedsack and Cooper), 120
Kitunda, Jeremiah M., 37–38
Knight, Damon, 144–45
Kohli, Amor, 157, 159, 160
Kolodny, Annette, 70–71, 174n9
Kreyling, Michael, 65

La Cava, Gregory, 182n10
Ladino, Jennifer, 179n4
Lady and the Tramp (Disney), 176n5
La Farge, Oliver, 55
Lake Okeechobee flood (1928), 95
Lamont, Victoria, 152, 154–55
"land-as-woman." *See* myths and symbols
Land Utilization Project, 54

Lanterns on the Levee (Percy), 15, 62–63, 66–67, 69–70, 180n6
Lavender, Isiah, 161
Le Corbusier, 136
Ledbetter, Huddie "Lead Belly," 94, 169
Lee, Martyn, 105–6
Leiber, Fritz, 155
Leonard, Elisabeth Anne, 188n21
Leopold, Aldo: and the CCC, 7; and conservation, 5, 7–8, 9, 25, 41; death of, 168; and the Dust Bowl, 29, 177n11; and environmentalism, 168–69; and hunting, 23, 34, 39; and "land ethic," 33; and predators, 5, 23, 25, 28–29, 31, 32, 90, 96, 173n4; *A Sand County Almanac*, 168–69; "Thinking Like a Mountain," 29, 31, 173n4; and wilderness, 22, 34, 39, 41, 57, 173n5
Levine, Lawrence W., 89
Lin Yutang, 169
Lion King, The (Disney), 176n5
literary naturalism, 13, 49, 100, 101–2, 106, 121, 174n14, 181n2
"Locusts, The" (Bradbury), 147–48
Lomax, Alan, 94
"Long Black Song" (Wright), 77, 78
Lorentz, Pare, 138
Lovecraft, H. P., 170

Machor, James, 99–100, 174n9, 181n1
Madrigal, Alex, 164
Maher, Neil, 4, 21, 173n2
Major, William H., 179n4
"Man Who Lived Underground, The" (Wright), 121, 184n18
"Man Who Went to Chicago, The" (Wright), 184n18
Markey, Ed, 170
Marshall, Robert: *Arctic Village*, 22, 42, 175n1; and the CCC, 7–8; and conservation, 7–8, 22; and death, 168; and the frontier, 22, 42–43, 175n1;

and the Indian Reorganization Act, 54–55; and politics, 22, 42, 178n22; and wilderness, 173n5
Martian Chronicles, The (Bradbury), 17, 145–51, 157, 187n13
Marx, Leo, 10–12, 112–13, 174n12
McCarthy, B. Eugene, 77
McCarthy, Joseph, 56
McNickle, D'Arcy: and American Indians, 14–15, 23, 41–42, 43–54, 55–57; and the BIA, 52–54, 55–56; and the Dust Bowl, 51–52; and the frontier, 14–15, 23, 41–42, 43–54, 56; influence of, 56; and literary naturalism, 49; and the Newberry Library, 56; *The Surrounded*, 14, 23, 42, 43–52; and wilderness, 46–49, 55; *Wind from an Enemy Sky*, 179n23
Melosi, Martin V., 111
Melville, Herman, 11
Merril, Judith: and atom bombs, 9, 17, 145, 152–53, 154–57, 166; and the Futurians, 144; and gender, 17, 132, 145, 152–56, 166; and the grotesque, 132, 153–54; politics of, 144–45, 155; *Shadow on the Hearth*, 17, 154–56; "That Only a Mother," 17, 152–54
Mille, Benjamin, 137
Miller, Donald L., 185n4
"Misfit" (Heinlein), 145
"Mississippi Boweavil Blues" (Patton), 93–94
Mississippi River, 67
Moby-Dick (Melville), 11, 112–13, 182n9
Moore, C. L., 170, 187n17
Morrison, Philip, 155
Morton, Timothy, 102, 103, 118–19
Moses, Robert, 8, 99, 135
Moylan, Tom, 160
Mules and Men (Hurston), 9, 89–93
Mumford, Lewis: and *The City* (film), 9, 134, 138, 142, 143, 186n10; and the garden city, 8, 142, 143, 185n5; on utopia, 133–34
"Murders in the Rue Morgue, The" (Poe), 120
Murphy, Charlene M., 178n19
My Man Godfrey (La Cava), 182n10
myths and symbols, 10, 174n9; garden of the world (Smith), 59, 62, 65, 70, 73, 174n9; land-as-woman (Kolodny), 70–71, 174n9; pastoral city (Machor), 99–100, 117, 129; plantation myth (Smith), 64, 65, 66, 70; technological sublime (Nye), 17, 131–40, 143–44, 145–58, 160–63, 165–66

Native Americans. *See* American Indians
Native Son (Wright): and apes, 117, 120, 125–26, 128, 184n19; and Baldwin, 119; and ecocriticism, 117–18, 183n13; and rats, 16, 101, 117–18, 120–24, 128, 183n13; and urban pastoralism, 117, 180n13
Never Come Morning (Algren), 15–16, 105, 106
New Agrarianism, 179n4
Newberry Library, 56
New Deal: and African Americans, 6, 7; and agriculture, 7, 59; and American Indians, 6, 53, 54, 55; and conservation, 6–7; and the frontier, 42; and the Greenbelt towns, 138, 141, 143, 185n5; and the Green New Deal, 170–71; and science fiction, 145; and scientists, 8–9; and urban parks, 8, 99
Newell, Dianne, 152, 154–55
New York World's Fair (1939): *The City* (film), 138–43; and the Corona Ash Dump, 136–38; GM's Futurama, 134–36; and technology, 16–17, 131–32, 133, 143, 151, 163, 165–66, 185n4; and urban pastoralism, 136

Nicholls, David G., 89
Niggli, Josefina, 169
Nixon, Rob, 16, 111, 116
Nolan, Christopher, 19, 171, 189n1
nuclear fallout. *See* atom (atomic) bomb
Nye, David, 17, 131, 139, 174n9, 185n2

Obata, Chiura, 169
Ocasio-Cortez, Alexandria, 170
O'Connor, Terry, 183n15
"Off Season, The" (Bradbury), 150
Okubo, Miné, 169
Olsen, Tillie: and dumps, 16, 113–17, 182n10, 184n21; and urban pastoralism, 16, 101, 110, 111–13, 128; *Yonnondio*, 16, 110–17
Our Daily Bread (Vidor), 179n1
Outka, Paul, 18, 68

"Pantaloon in Black" (Faulkner), 69
Park, Robert, 9
Parker, Dorothy R., 44–45, 49, 53
Parrish, Susan Scott, 29–30
Parry, Tyler, 181n16
Parton, James, 139
pastoralism, 10–14, 112–13, 174n14, 175n15; and the South, 60–61, 62–64, 75, 86, 97
"pastoral city." *See* myths and symbols; urban pastoralism
Patton, Charley, 93–94
Percy, William Alexander: background of, 180n6; and the Great Mississippi Flood of 1927, 67, 81; and nature, 66–67; and race, 69–70; and sharecropping, 62–63, 73, 74; and the South, 15, 60, 65; and the Southern Agrarians, 62–63, 65, 66, 73, 180n6
Phillips, Sarah, 4, 173n2
Pick, Anat, 31
Pinchot, Gifford, 6, 177n13

Pinocchio (Disney), 176n5
Pittsburgh Courier, 157, 158
Pizer, Donald, 13
place, 100, 102–3, 109, 110, 113, 114, 129
plantation myth. *See* myths and symbols
Poe, Edgar Allan, 120
Pohl, Frederick, 144, 186n12
Popular Front, 5–6, 18
postpastoral, 13, 15, 100, 117, 174n13
predator eradication: and the Bureau of Biological Survey, 7, 28, 176n7, 176n8; and the Civilian Conservation Corps, 173n6; and conservation, 24, 25, 29, 36, 39, 97; critiques of, 5, 24, 25, 28, 29, 167, 173n4; and the Fish and Wildlife Service, 176n7
predators and pests: bears, 31–33, 34, 39; boll weevils, 75–76, 89, 92–94, coyotes, 25, 28, 50, 176n8; hawks, 5, 25, 173n4, 177n8; hyenas, 36–39, 176n5, 178n18; rats, 16, 101, 117–18, 120–25, 128–29, 184n16; wolves, 5, 25, 28, 29, 36, 39, 176n8
proletarian literature, 144

Ransom, John Crowe, 60, 62, 64, 73, 180n6
Rasmussen, R. Kent, 159, 160
"Reconstructed but Unregenerate" (Ransom), 62, 64
Reconstruction, 70
Reiger, Christopher, 15, 60, 64, 75–76, 88, 174n13
Reiger, John F., 177n10
"Remarks on the Southern Religion" (Tate), 66
renewable energy, 163–65, 189n23, 189n24
Resources for Freedom (1950), 164
Ricketts, Edward (Ed), 168, 174n8
Rivera, Diego, 169

Robinson, Kim Stanley, 149
Roosevelt, Franklin Delano (FDR), 21, 43, 168, 171, 173n2, 188n20
Roosevelt, Theodore, 6, 178n18
Ruffin, Kimberly, 18, 76, 87, 117, 180n5

Salten, Felix, 24, 27, 175n2
Sand County Almanac, A (Leopold), 168–69, 173n4
Saroyan, William, 169, 175n14
Saxon, Lyle, 177n13
science: and the atom bomb, 151–52, 155; and the Depression, 8–9; and the environment, 133; and the New York World's Fair, 17, 141, 163, 184n1; and race, 157; and the Southern Agrarians, 62, 64, 65
science fiction (sci-fi): and the atom bomb, 152; and ecocriticism, 18, 133, 144, 186n11; and politics, 144–45, 186n12; on technology, 17, 132–33, 143–45
Schoedsack, Ernest B., 120
Schuyler, George: and Afrofuturism, 189n22; *Black Empire*, 157–63, 165; *Black No More*, 161; on colonialism, 17, 132–33, 157–58, 160, 161, 162, 166; on technology, 17, 132–33, 157–58, 160–61, 166, 189n23
Seed, David, 145, 149, 187n13
sf grotesque, 132, 133, 145
Shadow on the Hearth (Merril), 17, 154–56
Shahn, Ben, 169
"Shambleau" (Moore), 187n17
Sharecroppers' Union (SCU), 7
sharecropping, 60, 70, 73–75, 77, 93–94
Silent Spring (Carson), 132, 144, 156, 166, 167, 169, 173n4, 188nn18–19
Sinclair, Upton, 145
slavery, 60, 63, 72
Smith, Henry Nash, 10, 59, 64, 174n9
Smith, Kimberly, 18

Song of the South (Disney), 176n5
Soper, Kate, 34
Souder, William, 188n20
Southern Agrarians, 15, 59, 62, 65–66, 70, 88, 180n6
Stanton, Andrew, 171, 189n1
Stein, Clarence, 8, 138, 142, 185n5, 186n9
Steinbeck, John, 168, 174n8
Steiner, Ralph, 9, 134, 138, 142–43, 179n1, 186n10
Stevens, Wallace, 182n4
Strychacz, Thomas, 38
suburbs, 142, 143, 170
Sullivan, Robert, 124–25, 184n16, 184n20
Sunnyside, Queens, 186n9
Superstorm Sandy, 170
Surrounded, The (McNickle), 14–15, 23, 42, 43–52, 55, 56
Sutter, Paul S., 7

Tate, Allen, 66
Taylor, Graham D., 53–54, 179n24
technology, 8–9, 129, 132, 133, 167; and atom bombs, 17, 129, 132, 150–57, 162, 166; and colonialism, 133, 146, 148, 157–58, 161–62, 166, 187n14; and the New York World's Fair, 16–17, 131–32, 134–36, 139, 141, 143, 165–66; and renewable energy, 161, 163–65, 166
technological sublime. *See* myths and symbols
"That Only a Mother" (Merril), 17, 152–54, 155
Their Eyes Were Watching God (Hurston), 68, 73, 94–96, 181n17
"There Will Come Soft Rains" (Bradbury), 150–51
Thill, Brian, 137
"Thinking Like a Mountain" (Leopold), 29, 31, 32, 34, 39, 173n4
Thomas, Brennan M., 26–27

Tobacco Road (Caldwell), 75–76, 86–87, 180nn9–10
Trachtenberg, Alan, 10
Truman, Harry, 164
Turner, Frederick Jackson, 14, 23, 42, 43–44, 54, 56

Uncle Tom's Children (Wright), 76–77, 86, 119, 181n14
urban pastoralism, 99–100, 101, 103, 107, 108, 110, 117, 128–29, 136, 174n9, 181n1; and dumps, 16, 97, 110, 113–16, 182n7; and parks, 8, 15–16, 97, 101, 102, 103–8, 110, 129; and rats, 16, 101, 117–18, 120–25, 128–29, 184n16; and vacant lots, 108–9, 110, 111–13
Urgo, Joseph R., 177n12
utopia, 133–34, 136, 159, 160

Van Dyke, Willard, 9, 134, 138, 142, 179n1, 186n10

WALL-E (Stanton), 171, 189n1
Wardi, Anissa Janine, 80, 86
Washington, Booker T., 74
Washington Park (Chicago), 103–5, 106
"Watchers, The" (Bradbury), 150
Wayne, John, 42
"Way Up in the Middle of the Air" (Bradbury), 157, 188n21
Wellman, William, 182n7
"What You Don't Know Won't Hurt You" (Wright), 184n18
Whitman, Walt, 181n1
Wilbur, Charles Dana, 149
Wild Boys of the Road (Wellman), 182n7
Wilderness Act of 1964, 21, 168
Wilderness Society, 22, 168
Williams, Raymond, 61, 174n10
Williams, William Carlos, 182n4
Wilson, Alexander, 109

Wind from an Enemy Sky (McNickle), 179n23
Wirth, Louis, 9
Wise, Benjamin, 73–74
Wolfe, Gary K., 145–46
women, 70–72, 132, 142, 143, 152–54, 174n11
Works Progress Administration (WPA), 8, 88, 99, 171
World's Fair (Doctorow), 134, 135
World War II, 21, 132, 143, 168, 176nn2–3
Worster, Donald, 4, 22, 28, 173n2, 189n1
Wright, Henry, 8, 142, 185n5, 186n9
Wright, Richard: and animals, 16, 79–80, 117–18, 120–26, 128, 183n13, 184n19; and the antipastoral, 15, 61, 76, 77, 96; and ecocriticism, 118, 183n13; and flooding, 68, 80–86; and the Great Mississippi Flood of 1927, 80; and Hurston, 95, 183n12; and *Native Son*, 117–29; and place, 102; and race, 68, 117–18, 119–20, 125–26, 180n12, 181n14; and sharecropping, 77; and sociology, 9; *Uncle Tom's Children*, 76–87; and urban pastoralism, 101, 117, 180n13; and violence, 78–80, 82, 85, 180n11
Wyler, William, 60, 71

Yingling, Charlton, 181n16
Yonnondio: From the Thirties (Olsen), 16, 110–16, 182n8, 182n10, 183n10
Young Communist League (YCL), 144, 186n12
Young Lonigan (Farrell), 15–16, 103–5, 106, 141

Zola, Émile, 121

About the Author

Credit: Kim Johnson

Matthew M. Lambert is an assistant professor of English at Northwestern Oklahoma State University, where he teaches courses in American literature. He received his PhD in the Department of English's literary and cultural studies program at Carnegie Mellon University. His work has appeared in the *Journal of Midwest Modern Language Association* and *Journal of Popular Film and Television*. He lives in Alva, Oklahoma, with his wife and two cats.

www.ingramcontent.com/pod-product-compliance
Lightning Source LLC
Chambersburg PA
CBHW030622230426
43661CB00053B/2108